P9-AOA-922

Social Work in Schools

Social Work Practice with Children and Families

Nancy Boyd Webb, *Series Editor*

Social Work in Schools: Principles and Practice
Linda Openshaw

Working with Traumatized Youth in Child Welfare
Nancy Boyd Webb, *Editor*

Group Work with Adolescents: Principles and Practice, Second Edition
Andrew Malekoff

Child Development: A Practitioner's Guide, Second Edition
Douglas Davies

Mass Trauma and Violence: Helping Families and Children Cope
Nancy Boyd Webb, *Editor*

Culturally Competent Practice with Immigrant and Refugee Children and Families
Rowena Fong, *Editor*

Social Work Practice with Children, Second Edition
Nancy Boyd Webb

Complex Adoption and Assisted Reproductive Technology: A Developmental Approach to Clinical Practice
Vivian B. Shapiro, Janet R. Shapiro, and Isabel H. Paret

Social Work in Schools

Principles and Practice

Linda Openshaw

Series Editor's Note by Nancy Boyd Webb

THE GUILFORD PRESS
New York London

A Division of Guilford Publications, Inc.
72 Spring Street, New York, NY 10012
www.guilford.com

Printed in the United States of America

This book is printed on acid-free paper.

Last digit is print number: 9 8 7 6 5 4 3 2 1

Library of Congress Cataloging-in-Publication Data

Openshaw, Linda.
Social work in schools: principles and practice / by Linda Openshaw.
p. cm. — (Social work practice with children and families)
Includes bibliographical references and index.
ISBN-13: 978-1-59385-578-9 (hardcover : alk. paper)
ISBN-10: 1-59385-578-8 (hardcover : alk. paper)
1. School social work—United States. I. Title.
LB3013.4.O64 2007
371.4′6—dc22

2007028549

To my parents for their love and support,
to the students who persevere in spite
of overwhelming situations, and to
the school social workers who help them

About the Author

Linda Openshaw, DSW, LCSW, is Associate Professor of Social Work, Texas A&M University-Commerce. Her interests include school social work, child and adolescent welfare and counseling, clinical practice, and the role of spirituality in social work. Dr. Openshaw practiced as a school social worker for 14 years in Utah and Texas and worked for 3 years in community mental health in Utah and California. She received her MSW and DSW degrees from the University of Utah College of Social Work.

Series Editor's Note

This volume fulfills my longstanding wish to have a book devoted to school social work in the Guilford series Social Work Practice with Children and Families. The scope and depth of coverage in Linda Openshaw's book far exceed my expectations, and I fully expect that it will become a necessary and well-used reference in the office of every school social worker in the country. Solidly grounded in Openshaw's extensive background as a school social worker, this book contains a wealth of information regarding the comprehensive role of the school social worker across the entire span of school years, from preschool through high school.

Children and adolescents spend many hours in the school environment, and, after the family, school is probably the most important influence in their lives. For example, a child's sense of pride in achievement, or feelings of incompetence over academic or other school-based activities, can have a lasting effect on his or her self-image and future life course. In addition, the nature of his or her peer relationships in school can help or hinder the young person's social and emotional development. Because of its enduring positive or negative impact, what happens to a child in school is very serious and demands our best efforts to help create a positive outcome.

The school is a microcosm of the world in which youth experience the same vast array of problems as adults do in modern life. This, unfortunately, includes situations of trauma, violence, and death. Openshaw addresses these topics in separate chapters that discuss how to help children who have been exposed to various upsetting events either at home, in the community, or in the school itself. We know that children bring their problems from home with them to school, and often the school must provide services to help children deal with their anxieties in order to free them to learn. Sometimes the school social worker collaborates with agencies in the community to make connections on behalf of a troubled student. This book emphasizes the importance of working with different systems and professions for the child's benefit. Many case examples demonstrate how to do this within the legal framework of special education and other laws, while also acknowledging the ethical dilemmas related to confidentiality restrictions and other constraints.

As I reviewed the 16 chapters of this wide-ranging account of school social work practice, my admiration for the role increased tremendously. The school social worker must possess a wide knowledge base that includes an understanding of child development; typical disorders that can manifest at different ages; mental illness and other disabilities; legal mandates related to special education; community resources and programs; how to work with noncitizens; and how to form and support partnerships with teachers, other professionals, and children's families. This specialized knowledge base enhances the general practice knowledge of helping children through individual and family interventions and aids in the use of group work. Sometimes the school social worker leads groups that focus on children of alcoholics and drug abusers, or may set up groups to help youth learn to develop their social skills or improve their ability to solve problems or handle conflict. Other times, the school social worker may organize crisis intervention groups to assist the entire school community following a natural disaster or incidents of violence or terrorism.

This is *not* an all-inclusive list of the school social workers' various functions. In truth, such a list might prove to be quite formidable if not somewhat unbelievable! The role is enormous and demands flexibility, the ability to assess a situation from many points of view, and the knowledge and ability to carry out a realistic treatment plan. Lest a reader feel discouraged about being unable to fill these huge shoes, this book comes to the rescue and serves as a detailed guide to performing the multifaceted job with skill and empathy. It will be greatly appreciated both by seasoned practitioners and by students who are new to the field. The strengths-based perspective and detailed and practical guidelines in this book give us hope that it *is* possible to carry out this daunting and all-encompassing work in a manner that will not only help children and youth succeed, but also enhance the image of the school social worker as a master practitioner.

NANCY BOYD WEBB, DSW
University Distinguished Professor of Social Work
James R. Dumpson Chair in Child Welfare Studies
Fordham University Graduate School of Social Service

Acknowledgments

I have deep affection and respect for Nancy Boyd Webb because of her unceasing support and kindness, and thank her for her encouragement and advice during the writing of this book. She is a wonderful mentor and teacher. It was with humility that I accepted her challenge to write about what I learned while practicing as a school social worker. I am grateful to Jim Nageotte, Senior Editor at The Guilford Press, for his encouragement and trust. Every staff member at Guilford has been kind and helpful; I am most fortunate to have been able to work with such a high-caliber publisher.

I am profoundly grateful to the many students with whom I worked in the schools. I always was touched by their trust in me. I grew to admire my students and their families for their perseverance and resilience.

I could not have completed the book without my husband, David, who is my best friend and the best writer and editor I know. He worked diligently with me to complete this book. I am grateful to my five children, Amy, Alison, Lauren, Patrick, and Lindsay, for their support, love, and "technical assistance." Also, thanks to Marty, my dog, who sat at my feet continually during lonely periods of writing.

My parents, Kenneth and Della Leek, lovingly taught me the value of hard work and an education. I love and appreciate them for providing me with a stable and happy childhood and continuous love and encouragement. I am grateful for their teachings and example. I rely on the never-ending support of my siblings, Sandra and Bruce, and their families.

I am grateful to my husband's extended family. His uncle, Marvin L. Pugh, was a pioneer in school social work and pupil services. He led me to my first school social work job. With encouragement from Corinne Hill,

Bill Davies and George Brooks hired me at the Salt Lake City School District. Lois and Weldon Hogan helped open doors for my employment in the Mesquite (Texas) Independent School District. I would not have had the opportunity to work in the schools without these people.

This book reflects what I learned from dedicated school social workers, counselors, teachers, and support staff in both the Salt Lake School District and the Mesquite Independent School District.

Joyce Kelen has been a lifelong friend, and I am grateful to her for sharing her knowledge about social work with immigrant children. Likewise, Rosemarie Hunter and Rocio Paredes-Mora added their knowledge about school–community partnerships.

I am grateful to Texas A&M University–Commerce for a grant to cover the cost of a graduate assistant, Sharla Rocha, who helped with research. Ruth Ann Dorsett also assisted with the initial research. I am grateful to them for their insights and hard work.

Preface

The role of a school social worker is complex and demanding. School social workers face the daily challenge of helping children stay in school when the circumstances in their lives are often overwhelming and in direct conflict with success. Children and adolescents who are not successful in school are often set on a negative course for the rest of their lives. The situations and challenges children now face require that school social workers develop and apply a wide range of skills and knowledge.

I began practicing as a school social worker in 1977, when Public Law 94-142 and the Americans with Disabilities Act were first enacted and enforced in the schools. As a new school social worker, I found that this legislation had a profound effect on my job. I was required to help schedule and place every student with any disability at the high school where I worked. I was unsure about my ability to assure that the correct placement was given to the students, and I wanted desperately to do things right and guarantee the right kind of help for my students. During that time, I sought information from every possible source. After several years in the schools, I took a break to stay home and raise my children. When I returned to the workforce 7 years later, I found that the issues and challenges faced by children and school social workers were more serious than they had been at the time I left the schools.

I discovered that there was a great need for a "how-to" book on school social work. The existing literature on school social work focuses primarily on policies and the role of the school social worker rather than *how* to practice in the schools. School social workers often practice alone without the support of other social workers. Because I often felt overwhelmed and isolated, I wanted to provide a book to serve as a companion to practitioners as well as a teaching tool for social work students. This book reflects my 14 years of experience as a school social worker.

The book gives an overview of the issues that children and adolescents bring to school and provides school social workers and social work students with the tools for understanding the school environment. It offers treatment strategies that will enable social workers to assist children and adolescents with school-related issues and are effective within the constraints of the school environment. The book begins with an introduction to the school system and some of the laws that govern the schools. It covers various techniques for observation, assessment, and intervention and discusses the importance of building relationships.

The book addresses children's issues from preschool through grade 12. The first few chapters cover developmental issues and school problems related to a particular age and grade level. Many of the issues are illustrated by case examples to help bring life and clarity to the situations described. Not all of the case examples provide correct answers, however. Some show how good intentions did not always help the child and family. The identities of those described in the case examples are disguised.

These chapters examine a variety of treatment options, such as group work, play therapy, social skills training, and behavior management. Also covered are some of the more difficult situations faced by children, such as violence, trauma, death, divorce, parental absence, and mental health concerns. Drug and alcohol abuse and poverty are also considered, as these problems continue to have a devastating effect on children and schools. These are issues that must be approached not only on a one-on-one level with students, but also on a community level.

The book includes reproducible forms that I developed or modified to assist in my work in the schools. Each chapter concludes with questions for discussion that are designed for social work students.

I enlisted the help of Joyce Kelen to discuss work with immigrant children, and Rosemarie Hunter and Rocio Paredes-Mora to explore work with communities. These are topics with which I had limited experience, and I wanted to have experts address them in the book.

Schools in the 21st century are really serving as a second home, where youth learn values and social skills in addition to academics. The escalating pressures on families mean that parents may be less available to their children and not able to provide the buffering and help all children need while growing up. School social workers are an integral part of the school system and provide the needed support to help students succeed. School social workers need information and skills in order to provide appropriate and competent assistance to students. I hope that this book will provide social work students and practitioners with a tool to assist in their work with children and adolescents in the schools.

Contents

1

The Role and Function of the School Social Worker

Schools provide a formative experience for children. Schools can be a haven or a horrible and dreaded place, depending on the child's experiences. The images of crayons, brightly painted halls, and bulletin boards can create joy or fear for a child. Peer interactions with other students can be a source of pleasure or alienation. Many children cannot respond effectively to the school environment because of the stress in their home and family lives. The school environment has traditionally required students to conform, and those who could not meet a school's expectations usually dropped out. However, federal and state laws now require school districts to conform to the needs of students and provide a setting in which all children can be educated.

This book focuses on the multifaceted role of the school social worker and the ways school social workers can utilize their knowledge, skills, and values to improve the lives of students. The book attempts to help the reader understand how to incorporate social work skills into the public school system on an individual, group, and community level. It focuses on the basics of being a school social worker, including building relationships, assessment, working with multidisciplinary teams, and helping children and adolescents address the difficulties that keep them from performing well in school. The book addresses issues at each developmental level of a child's public school life from preschool through transitioning out of high school.

Many of the topics in the book are illustrated by case examples, although names and identifying information have been changed to maintain confidentiality. The case examples illustrate actual situations that school social workers address. Some of the examples explain how the social worker was able to help the child. Others reflect the social worker's inability to intervene successfully.

School districts employ social workers to address the needs of at-risk and special needs students. The precise social work role in connection with these students varies from school to school and from school district to school district. Some school districts employ school social workers to serve multiple schools or to work with a single broad population. Other districts assign the social worker to a single school or a narrow population. Many school districts expect social workers to function as members of crisis teams. The school social worker spends most of his or her time helping children with emotional and behavioral disorders. Accordingly, many school districts employ social workers in the special education department, where they are limited to working with special education students. This diversity in the social worker's roles creates a wide variety of functions and responsibilities for school social workers.

BASIC TASKS

In spite of the social worker's many roles and responsibilities, four basic tasks have been identified as common to all school social workers. These are:

- *Consultation* with others in the school system as a member of a team.
- *Assessment* applied to a variety of different roles in direct service, consultation, and program development.
- *Direct intervention* with children and parents in individual, group, and family modalities.
- Assistance with *program development* (Constable, Kuzmickaite, Harrison, & Volkmann, 1999).

The National Association of Social Workers (NASW) has identified important guidelines for the delivery of social work services in schools, including standards for practice, professional preparation and development, and administrative structure and support. These guidelines are set forth in the NASW Standards for School Social Work Services, which were adopted in 1978 and revised in 1992 and again in 2002 (NASW, 2002). School social workers should be aware that they may be held accountable under these standards whether they are members of NASW or not. For example, legal actions may use these standards as a basic measure of competence. School social workers should review and apply these standards, which are set forth in Appendix 1.1.

INTERDISCIPLINARY TEAMS

Social workers often serve as members of interdisciplinary teams to assist in placement, review, and dismissal of students with special needs. As set forth in Standard 9 of the NASW Standards for School Social Work Services, "school social workers shall work collaboratively to mobilize the resources of local education agencies and communities to meet the needs of students and families" (NASW, 2002). Team members may include teachers, counselors, school psychologists, and diagnosticians. School social workers must understand how to work effectively as a member of the interdisciplinary team and how to add to the work of the team. "The unique contribution of the school social worker to the interdisciplinary team is to bring home, school, and community perspectives to the interdisciplinary process" (NASW, 2002, Standard 9). Membership in interdisciplinary teams requires (1) interdependence, (2) the ability to perform newly created professional activities and take on new tasks as necessary, (3) flexibility, (4) collective ownership of goals, and (5) reflection on processes (Bronstein, 2003).

School districts employ an array of professionals who strive to welcome and educate children. The professionals who spend time with children at school are teachers, administrators, counselors, nurses, school social workers, psychologists, diagnosticians, vocational counselors or transition specialists, teachers' aides, speech therapists, and physical therapists.

Teachers have the primary responsibility for educating children. Sometimes students will be placed in special education classes with teachers who have training to assist with both behavioral and educational modifications. Most special education teachers are assisted by a teacher's aide. Teachers must have at least a bachelor's degree and certification from the state in which they teach.

Administrators manage the day-to-day activities in schools and provide leadership by setting goals, establishing policies and procedures, budgeting, determining curriculum, training teachers and other staff, and interacting with the public. They are responsible for the quality of the school district's educational systems. They are ultimately responsible for curriculum and discipline. They hire and fire the teachers and other staff. Most school administrators are former teachers. However, a teacher must obtain additional education and certification to become an administrator. The administrator in an individual school is usually a principal. In some schools, the principal is assisted by one or more assistant principals.

School counselors provide counseling and guidance for students. They assist students with academic and personal problems to help them succeed in school. Many middle and high school counselors also help students plan their schedule of classes. Counselors for students in the higher grades help students plan for careers and higher education.

School nurses provide health care in the school to further children's success in the classroom. The nurse serves as a bridge between health care in the community and the school. Nurses are involved in developing individualized health plans (IHPs) and individualized education plans (IEPs). The variety of nursing tasks in a school ranges from dispensing prescription medications to teaching about the physical changes that take place during puberty. School nurses check children who are ill and injured and determine when a child needs to be sent home because of an illness or injury. Nurses also help report child abuse and neglect. Most school nurses are registered nurses.

School psychologists and diagnosticians help screen children to determine if they have learning or psychological problems. Their reports assure that children are provided with the programs and adjustments that will ensure success at school. These programs range from gifted and talented programs to special education programs. School psychologists must have a master's degree in psychology. School diagnosticians are an emerging profession. Certification for this position usually requires teaching experience and a master's degree.

Speech therapists diagnose and treat speech, voice, and language disorders. Most states require a master's degree in speech–language pathology for licensing.

Physical therapists help children with severe physical problems remain comfortable at school.

Vocational or transition specialists help students plan for effective careers. They frequently provide follow-up services for those students with special needs after they leave the public schools.

School social workers assist children so they can be successful in school. The goal of school social work should be to give all children the opportunity and resources to help them succeed academically and socially in a safe and healthy school environment. Social work in a public school setting plays a vital role in developing students and linking them to the resources and support necessary to maximize their potential in the educational process (O'Donnell, 2000). Most states require a master's degree in social work in order to practice as a school social worker. School social work is one of the most rewarding and interesting areas of social work practice. School social workers can have a life-changing impact on their young clients in a way that those who work with adults rarely experience.

The school social worker and the other professionals described above form an interdisciplinary team that works together on behalf of children and adolescents. This book addresses the experiences of children as they meet with either success and encouragement or failure and discouragement in school.

MULTIFACETED ROLES OF A SCHOOL SOCIAL WORKER

The main goal of school social work is to enable students to function and learn in the school environment. School social workers practice in a secondary setting–the primary purpose of schools is to educate students, not to provide social services. The school social work practitioner will often be the only social worker in a school and sometimes in an entire school district. Therefore, autonomous school social work practice requires skills for all levels of practice–micro, mezzo, and macro. School social workers work primarily with individual students. However, they also develop and facilitate groups for students and parents. Effective school social work practice consists of collaborating, consulting, developing behavior plans, and training others to work with difficult children in the context of a child's daily school experience (Frey & George-Nichols, 2003). School social workers are involved in training and resource-building activities such as staff development, community education, and grant writing.

School social workers assist interdisciplinary teams by providing information from a thorough assessment of students that usually includes information from collateral sources. A treatment team that utilizes experts in testing, diagnosis, and referral is the most comprehensive way to assist needy children and their families. School social workers also provide direct treatment to students, so the social worker reports to team members about the progress students make during counseling.

Some school districts employ social workers as part of crisis intervention teams to assist with severe mental health issues. These school social workers work across all age groups from prekindergarten through 12th grade. Their training and experience in serving a whole system utilizing the ecological systems perspective allows them to add a unique perspective to an intervention team. School social workers are in a position to orchestrate and support a unified and comprehensive intervention plan for children (Frey & George-Nichols, 2003). Members of school crisis teams often include a psychologist, social worker, school nurse, and, sometimes, a school police officer. The goal of these crisis intervention teams is to intervene when there are serious problems such as suicide threats, violence, abuse, severe behavior problems, deaths of students or teachers, and other school crisis situations. Assistance from social workers is often required during a crisis and afterward to provide grief counseling and debriefing or to assist affected families by referral to an outside agency.

SKILLS NECESSARY TO PRACTICE AS A SCHOOL SOCIAL WORKER

School social workers perform on many levels, including work with individual students and their parents, groups of students, teachers, and community agencies. The following provides a brief overview of the many types of skills a school social worker must possess.

Assessment

The ability properly to assess and treat a student is at the core of providing adequate direct services. School social workers must "possess skills in systematic assessment and investigation" (NASW, 2002, Standard 21) and "conduct assessments of student needs that are individualized and provide information that is directly useful for designing interventions that address behaviors of concern" (NASW, 2002, Standard 12). One of the school social worker's most valuable roles is to educate members of the school district and community about the value of early assessment, intervention, and treatment by qualified mental health professionals (Maynard-Moody, 1994).

School social workers contribute an essential dimension to the assessment of students through the use of the ecological perspective, which necessitates consideration of the child's family and neighborhood (Radin, 1992; NASW, 2002, Standard 12). Accordingly, they must "incorporate assessments in developing and implementing intervention and evaluation plans that enhance students' abilities to benefit from educational experiences" (NASW, 2002, Standard 13). The other aspect of assessment that is unique to the social work profession is the use of the strengths perspective (NASW, 2002, Standard 5). As Saleebey (1997) has indicated, practicing from the strengths perspective means that "*Everything* you do as a social worker will be predicated, in some way, on helping to discover and embellish, explore and exploit clients' strengths and resources in the service of assisting them to achieve their goals, realize their dreams, and shed the irons of their own inhibitions and misgivings" (p. 3).

Direct Practice

School social workers should have practice skills for working with individuals, groups, and communities.

Counseling Individuals

Mental health problems are present at all grade levels in the public school system. School social workers can help students with emotional and behavioral problems adjust to the school environment and learn to manage their own behaviors. They also "promote collaboration among community health and mental health services providers and facilitate student access to these services" (NASW, 2002, Standard 26). In addition, school social workers assist parents and teachers in learning to cope with and manage a child's emotional and behavioral problems.

Case Example

Jim, a 10-year-old fourth grader, acted out constantly at school. He tore up books and his assignments. He refused to do schoolwork and would often yell at his teacher. When the school first began to deal with his misbehavior, the teacher or assistant principal would call home and report it. On one occasion, the mother's live-in boyfriend came to the school to pick Jim up in response to such a report. Upon arriving at school, the boyfriend threw Jim against a wall in front of the teacher, social worker, and counselor. It became obvious that calling the home was not a solution. After Jim spent time with the school social worker, it was determined that Jim was being hit, threatened, and locked in his room for several hours at a time by his mother's boyfriend. Jim was frightened and depressed, but these emotions were expressed as anger, which is often the way children deal with depression and frustration. Jim had no control over his environment at home. The school began to assist in solving Jim's problems through the use of behavior management plans and a level system, which helped Jim regulate his misbehavior and rewarded his positive behaviors. With counseling provided by the school social worker, Jim was able to express his anger and learn some healthy outlets for his frustration. The school social worker referred the family to child protective services (CPS), which also worked with the mother and her boyfriend.

Home Visits

School social workers visit the homes of students for various reasons. Some home visits are made to asses the reasons for student misbehavior or absences. When students have prolonged absences, it is the school social worker who visits the home to assess the situation and give information back to the school district. Sometimes the school social worker makes an initial home visit in order to discuss a child's school difficulties when school officials have been unable to contact parents by phone. Social workers also visit student homes to involve the parents in activities that can reinforce programs and behavior management plans that the school has put into place.

Some districts ask school social workers to provide outside intervention in the home, such as teaching parents how to make accommodations for attention-deficit/hyperactivity disorder (ADHD), autism, and special needs. School social workers help implement in-home training for special education students and provide parents with information that will assist them in parenting children with special needs. Program evaluation studies and theoretical and empirical research have indicated that positive intervention outcomes are related to factors other than child-centered activities. Family-centered services are intended to help the family maintain the child in the home and prevent out-of-home placement (Sabatino, 2001). In-home activities and parental involvement can help students succeed in school.

Case Example

Bob, age 15, was in ninth grade at a public high school. His mother would try to bring him to school, usually unsuccessfully. The mother felt desperate because, on many occasions, she could not get him out of bed. On the days that he got ready and went to school, his mother would drop him off at the front door of the building, whereupon he would enter the building, go out the back door, and leave the school grounds as quickly as possible. The school social worker determined that his behavior resulted from a school phobia. To get Bob to school, the school social worker and the assistant principal went to his home one morning, woke him up, and waited for him to get ready. They then took him to school.

The social worker and Bob determined that he could handle school if he didn't have to face people when he first came in the building. He was told that while he was in the building, he was allowed to go to the social worker's office and relax whenever he felt uncomfortable. It was unnecessary for the social worker and assistant principal to bring Bob to school after the initial visit. The school social worker provided counseling and support whenever Bob came to her office. The counseling involved cognitive–behavioral therapy and stress relief, which included teaching him deep breathing and visual imagery with which he could relax when he felt tense, and giving him an escape to the social worker's office. Over time, this intervention was successful, and Bob attended school on a regular basis.

Group Work

Many students receive counseling at school through their membership in groups. Such groups meet the needs of diverse populations and are effective tools in reaching many students at once. Group work in schools includes the three major models of group work: remedial, reciprocal, and social-goals. The remedial model provides group therapy geared toward changing dysfunctional behavior. The reciprocal model focuses on achieving mutual aid or support through group work such as that practiced by Alcoholics Anonymous [Alateen]. The social-goals model addresses social consciousness or responsibility through groups such as social skills and anger management groups (Whitaker, 1980).

Some of the main types of groups with which social workers assist focus on social skills, support for new students, anger management, and grief and/or support related to parental separation. In addition, recreational groups provide field trips and teach new skills. Social workers also train students in group work and counseling skills so they can help their peers.

School social workers assist parents through group work as well. Teaching parenting skills and educating parents on how to accommodate students with specific disabilities are common tasks for school social workers. They also work with transition specialists to help students and their parents prepare to leave public school when the students turn 18 or have completed an equivalency exam for special education students leaving high school. Social workers teach parents about the various community programs and resources and, when necessary, make referrals. Group work in the schools will be discussed more thoroughly in Chapter 9.

COMMUNITY CONNECTIONS

Community Mental Health

Social workers can be the link between community programs and the schools. They should promote student health and mental health and facilitate student access to community health and mental health services (NASW, 2002, Standard 26). "Wraparound programs" involve agencies outside the school system in assisting with delivery of services to needy children and their families. Research indicates that these services should be developed and approved by a community-based interdisciplinary services team that will not deny services to any youngster regardless of the severity of his or her disability. The school social worker must be the link between the school and any outside source of support.

Court Referrals

Most states have mandatory school attendance laws. Many school districts require the school social worker to refer students who have excessive absences to a truancy court. When a student has extended or excessive absences, the school social worker should meet with the student and his or her parents to determine the cause of the absences. Where the circumstances dictate, the social worker must refer the matter to the appropriate court. Once the court referral is made, the social worker usually has the responsibility of attending court hearings and providing the student's attendance and school records to the judge. After a student has been referred to court, the school social worker monitors student attendance through daily teacher sign-in sheets. These sign-in sheets are given to the court to verify that the student attended each class period every day.

Advocacy

An important role for the school social worker is that of advocate. As Standard 8 of the NASW Standards for School Social Work Services recognizes, "School social workers shall advocate for students and their families in a variety of situations" (NASW, 2002, Standard 8). Social workers act as advocates for the parents when they help them understand their rights. Often, social workers must seek out parents who are unwilling to become involved with the school system and help them understand that someone in the school supports them. There is a significant group of parents for whom involvement necessitates outreach and recruitment. Many parents are intimidated by the school system.

The school social worker can reach out to them and assure the successful outcome of their interactions with the school (Banchy, 1977).

Mediation

Mediation is a role in which school social workers can serve both their school districts and clients. Standard 15 of the NASW Standards provides that "School social workers shall be trained in and use mediation and conflict-resolution strategies to promote students' resolution of their nonproductive encounters in the school and community and to promote productive relationships" (NASW, 2002, Standard 15). Mediation involves structured attempts to resolve pupil, parent, and school conflicts without using the formal appeal process, which is very costly (Weiner, 1980). School social workers can be effective neutral mediators to bring about needed change or to find mutually agreeable ways to settle conflicts between parents and schools.

INTERVENTION WITH SPECIAL-NEEDS STUDENTS

School social workers often are required to assist in the implementation and delivery of services to students with special needs. These services may include assessment, early identification, or actual provision of direct services. School social workers in rural communities struggle with the implementation of special programs. Limited resources and cost are two of the major obstacles to the provision of services. Rural school systems face a host of barriers to quality service delivery that urban schools do not. Rural schools usually have less tolerance for diversity, more homogeneous populations, more traditional moral values, and an expectation that the community can take care of its own members (Caudill, 1993). Where areas of need are not being addressed by the local community or education agency, school social workers should work to create services that address these needs. (NASW, 2002, Standard 14).

RESOURCE AND PROGRAM DEVELOPMENT

School social workers interact with outside agencies and provide links to community resources for children and families in need. As set forth in Standard 6 of the NASW Standards, "School social workers shall help empower students and their families to gain access to and effectively use formal and informal community resources" (NASW, 2002, Standard 6).

School social workers refer students and families for outside intervention and testing. When students are on probation, the school social worker is the link between the school and the probation officer, and social workers provide information to juvenile court in truancy cases, as noted earlier. Likewise, outside agencies often contact the school social worker for information. For example, ad litem attorneys may turn to the social worker for information about student progress. Social workers in schools also work cooperatively with the school nurse and teachers to assist in referrals for child abuse and neglect.

Case Example

Ralph, age 12, was in seventh grade in a special education classroom. He was referred to the social worker because he was refusing to do his work at school. Ralph told the social worker he hated school.

Ralph's mother was widowed when Ralph's father was killed in an accident. Ralph was only 6 years old at the time. The mother worked two jobs to support the family. Ralph had an older sister whose friends came over after school and ate a lot of the family food supply. The mother would not ask the sister to stop her friends from eating the family's food because she wanted her children to have friends over to her house rather than going out.

Ralph was upset about the lack of food and his sister's activities, but he also did not want to tattle on her. He became suicidal because he felt the situations at home and school were hopeless. The school social worker contacted the mother to see if she would like assistance, such as food stamps or counseling for Ralph, but she was very independent and refused outside help. Ralph continued to regress, began sleeping all day at school, and was unwilling to do his schoolwork.

The social worker again contacted Ralph's mother, whereupon she received the mother's consent for community mental health intervention. The social worker then arranged for a psychologist from the local community mental health center to perform an intake screening on Ralph at school. After the initial screening, the psychologist arranged for a psychiatrist to evaluate Ralph for medications, and Ralph was placed on antidepressants that lifted his mood. Ralph's teacher assisted by giving him special projects that allowed him to make up the work he had missed. The social worker met with Ralph weekly and helped him focus on his strengths and the areas of his life over which he had control, such as his schoolwork and friends. Ralph's schoolwork improved, he ceased being suicidal, and he remained in school.

HELPING SCHOOL PERSONNEL UNDERSTAND THE ROLE OF SCHOOL SOCIAL WORK

It is sometimes difficult for school social workers to gain visibility and to convince district personnel of the validity of their role and skills. To avoid this problem, the social worker should gain visibility and network with school personnel and parents whenever possible. As stated in Standard 3 of the NASW Standards for School Social Work Services, "School social workers shall provide consultation to local education agency personnel, school board members, and community representatives to promote understanding and effective utilization of school social work services" (NASW, 2002, Standard 3). School social workers should join PTA boards, attend school board meetings, offer classes for teachers, and provide macro work within the system to become visible so that people will gain an understanding of the variety of services offered by social workers.

A school social worker is fortunate if he or she is limited to one or two campuses. The social worker then has the opportunity to become familiar with the administration, counseling staff, and teachers. It is much easier to be successful on a campus when there is a relationship of trust established with the staff. Each school campus has a unique culture that is initially difficult to identify and understand. The social worker must show school administrators and teachers the benefits of having a school social worker on their campus.

TRAINING AND EDUCATION NECESSARY FOR SCHOOL SOCIAL WORK

School social workers must know how to build trust and positive relationships with children and how to practice independently.

The Essential Knowledge Base

The school social worker utilizes a generalist perspective. Generalist practice is the use of the problem-solving process to intervene with systems of various sizes, including individuals, families, groups, organizations, and communities. The problem-solving process is a step-by-step model that includes engaging with the client, assessing problem areas and identifying strengths, creating and carrying out an intervention plan, evaluating the success of that intervention, and terminating the client–practitioner relationship. The generalist operates within a system and person-in-environment framework and recognizes that many problems require intervention with more than one system (Boyle, Hull, Mather, Smith, & Farley, 2006).

Direct practice skills include:

1. Knowing how to develop and maintain professional/helping relationships.
2. Collecting and assessing information about a problem or situation.
3. Recognizing the client's strengths and abilities.
4. Developing a plan to improve the problem or situation.
5. The use of legitimately recognized and researched interventions.
6. Working within the values and ethics of the profession (Boyle et al., 2006).

Autonomous practice skills are required of school social workers because they often work alone or as the only social worker on an interdisciplinary team. School social workers often have to educate other employees in the education system about their skills and capabilities. They also educate students and their parents about the role and function of school social work in order to receive permission from parents to work with their children. School social workers work independently from other social workers and in non-social service settings where each social worker must determine his or her own work routine and job description.

In order to work alone, a social worker should understand the generalist model to intervene on all levels and all situations with individuals, groups, the community, parents, and school teams. He or she must have a clear understanding of the values and ethics of the profession and have the ability to make decisions for clients that are congruent with social work values, without the opportunity to consult with other social workers. School social workers must also understand limits of practice (O'Donnell, 2000).

Getting Ready to Practice

School social workers do not practice in the traditional agencies that employ social workers, such as social service and child welfare agencies. Therefore, many of the employees in school districts are not familiar with the social worker's role and do not understand what a social worker does. For example, school administrators frequently do not understand how to utilize social workers—particularly when a social worker may serve an entire district and visit several schools weekly. Accordingly, school social workers should interpret their tasks for local education agency personnel "so that the primary professional activities and competencies of school social workers are maintained" (NASW, 2002, Standard 3). Social workers should meet school administrators on each campus and discuss the role of social work and how their skills meet the job requirements.

Social workers should also coordinate with administrators to help determine where they can meet with students on their campus, since they are required to "maintain adequate safeguards for the privacy and confidentiality of information" (NASW, 2002, Standard 7). It usually is difficult to find private space to do counseling in school buildings. If the need for space is addressed in advance, most administrators will continue to assist the social worker in reserving a space to work that is private and that will allow for confidential information to be shared.

The school social worker should meet counselors, special education teachers, diagnosticians, psychologists, or personnel who work with special-needs students. Social workers should explain social work skills and the role differences between themselves and counselors. Establishing roles early will help fill in gaps in services, reduce future confusion over respective responsibilities, and eliminate any threats of competition that counselors may perceive from social workers.

Knowledge about Mental Illness and Learning Problems

School social workers benefit from having specific knowledge about learning disorders and mental disorders, as described in the *Diagnostic and Statistical Manual of Mental Disorders* (DSM-IV-TR). Many of the high-risk students whom social workers serve have a learning disability or behavior disorder. Some of the more common disorders seen in the schools are childhood depression, autism, bipolar disorder, conduct disorder, severe behavior problems, eating disorders, and substance abuse. Many children have a dual diagnosis of depression or substance abuse along with another disorder. These children come to school taking five or six different medications. The school day is predictable for children who are on a great deal of medication. They sleep, wake up feeling hostile, refuse to work, act exhausted, try to complete some schoolwork, and usually return to sleep.

Adolescents with learning disabilities are at increased risk to do poorly in school and become potential dropouts. Likewise, a learning disability puts students at risk because they have demonstrated educational achievement below that of their peers. They have twice as great a risk of suffering emotional distress than their peers, and, if female, they are twice as likely to attempt suicide and be involved with peer violence (Constable, McDonald, & Flynn, 2002).

Relationship-Building Skills

Skills in building positive relationships are essential for school social workers, whose ethical principles recognize the central importance of human relationships (NASW, 2002). Children need to build a connection before they will let the social worker help them. Social workers should build strong relationships with children through the use of empathy, genuineness, and positive regard, skills identified by humanistic psychologists as essential for a therapeutic relationship. Once the relationship of trust is developed, the social worker can become the vehicle for change. Social workers need to help children feel valued and accepted and need to be a positive motivator, encouraging children to keep trying in spite of adverse situations.

Knowledge about Child Development and Childhood Risk and Resilience

Social workers should be knowledgeable about developmental and biological factors that affect students' ability to function effectively in school (NASW, 2002, Standard 18). School social workers also need to be aware of childhood developmental risk and resilience factors (Davies, 2004). They should further be aware of the warning signs of suicide and signs of abuse and neglect, grief, and trauma. If these symptoms are not recognized by a knowledgeable practitioner, the child may be misdiagnosed and not treated appropriately.

Knowledge about Specific Needs in Individual School Districts

School social workers assess the needs in the school district and provide inservice training to teachers and school administrators that addresses the goals and mission of the educational institution (NASW, 2002, Standard 10). This training may include instruction on how to deal with mental health issues and students with special needs.

Case Example

A 16-year-old high school junior at a large high school (over 2,000 students) had made a suicide plan. She gave away prized possessions and told each of her seven teachers goodbye at the end of class. She knew her parents and sister would be gone on that particular evening, so when they all left, she wrote a note and went into the garage and hung herself. On Monday when school personnel discovered the suicide, they began to talk about the last time they had seen her. The teachers had been told goodbye but did not think about the significance and impact of that message until they realized that each teacher had been told the same thing. The young woman had given important personal items–a bracelet and a teddy bear–to a couple of her friends. The school social worker was called to help deal with the aftermath of the suicide and to check on other students to see if they had any suicide pacts. When the victim's behavior prior to the suicide was discovered, it surprised the social worker and counseling staff to learn that no one had recognized any of the classic warning signs of suicide. The school social worker and a school psychologist put together a class that described the classic warning signs of suicide and offered it to teachers as part of professional development on an ongoing basis for several years.

THE LEGAL MANDATE FOR SPECIAL EDUCATION AND OTHER LAWS AFFECTING SCHOOL SOCIAL WORKERS

Social Workers and the Laws Governing Services to Disabled Students

School social workers assist students who are receiving special education services. The Individuals with Disabilities Education Act (IDEA, Public Law No. 101-476) is a federal law that has had a strong impact on the role of the school social worker and other educators as they provide special education services. IDEA ensures the rights of students with disabilities to a free public education that meets their unique needs. As with other current and proposed policies and laws, it is necessary for school social workers to understand this law in order to do their jobs effectively (NASW, 2002, Standard 22). The social worker must find ways to assist teachers and administrators to meet their obligations toward students with and without disabilities. The social worker must find ways to translate social work skills and values and social work problem-solving approaches into educational terms (Haddad, 1980).

With an adequate knowledge of the requirements of the law, the school social worker has unlimited possibilities to expand the social work role by assisting other educators, students, and parents to understand their rights and responsibilities under the law. Following are a list of suggestions that can help school social workers who are assigned to work in special education expand and clarify their role.

1. Provide inservice training to educators (regular and special education teachers and administrators) to help them understand social work ideas about individual differences and the philosophy that each situation is unique.
2. Train special educators about how to utilize school social workers.
3. Help regular education teachers learn how to set goals that are matched with students' real abilities. This involves learning about different types of student problems and the goals that would be most beneficial to student growth.
4. Teach small-group skills to teachers.
5. Help teachers develop a peer consultation system.
6. Help acquire money and information for new materials (grant writing).
7. Seek positions on curriculum committees and stress the importance of a curriculum that allows for individual differences.
8. Become a strong advocate for students and parents. Help inform parents about their rights.
9. Teach parents about the IEP and its benefits.
10. Seek leadership positions in schools and unions.
11. Teach educators how to manage the stress that accompanies their jobs.
12. Help mediate differences between special and regular education and serve as a liaison between the two.
13. Provide public relations for the school by informing community agencies about the services that are being provided to students with disabilities.
14. Reinforce the idea of parent–teacher contacts in both regular and special education.
15. Train regular educators about the IEP and how to incorporate school social work services into the plan for problem students.
16. Work within the system to facilitate placement of students with disabilities. Make sure adequate testing is done.

17. Make sure that regular educators who have disabled students in their classrooms understand their conditions and how to deal with them.
18. Work with state vocational rehabilitation programs to be sure disabled students are adequately transitioned after completing public school (Haddad, 1980).

Due Process

The rights of due process guaranteed by federal laws for the disabled present several possibilities for school social workers. If the school social worker is the liaison between the school and home, he or she can assume responsibility for informing parents of their due process rights. Due process has brought changes that are entirely consistent with general social work principles: rejection of labels for children, promotion of self-determination for students and parents, an increase in educational alternatives, and fairer decision-making processes (Banchy, 1977).

Work with Families in Relation to Special Education Law

The school social worker can assist parents through the IEP process by helping them understand how to become effective members of school IEP teams. Often, the social worker can help best in the creation and implementation of the IEP by gathering information on the child in question. The social worker's assessment should have an ecological perspective and should focus on the student, as well as his or her interactions in the school environment, at home, and in the community (NASW, 2002, Standard 12). Much of this information can be obtained from parents, but parents will be much more cooperative when they understand the social worker's purpose for obtaining the information. The school social worker should obtain specific information about the factors that are interfering with the education and adjustment of the pupil. This information is obtained through observation of the pupil and through interviews with various individuals who know him or her. The social worker should always consult teachers regarding the pupil's behavior and academic progress, taking into consideration the classroom rules and the teacher's expectation of the pupil. When interviewing parents, the school social worker must give consideration to their opinions regarding the pupil's behavior in the home, classroom, and community, as well as their attitude toward academic achievement (Parham, 1979).

Social Work Roles in Special Education

Social workers serve many functions when they work in special education. They assist in placing students in special education programs; serve as members of IEP teams; make classroom behavior observations; and interview students, parents, and educators to complete assessments and social histories in order to provide information that will be used in placement of students. Once students are placed, the social worker may help implement any therapeutic or social skills goals prescribed in IEPs.

Meeting IEP goals requires knowledge about special education law and how to work with students with a specific diagnosis. Social workers must be familiar with methods of outcome measurement and evidence-based practice to illustrate how the social work intervention assists students in meeting prescribed goals. "Evidence-based practice is defined as the planned use of empirically supported assessment and intervention methods combined with the judicious use of monitoring and evaluation strategies for the purpose of improving the psychosocial well-being of clients" (O'Hare, 2005, p. 6). School social workers must be able to verify that the intervention they choose and implement meets the student's needs and helps promote positive change.

Federal mandates such as the 1997 amendments to the IDEA have brought special attention to the need to work with disabled students. Rural and poor school districts may not have programs in place but are still required to meet the objectives of these federal laws. The requirements of these laws are:

1. To provide assistance to states in developing early intervention services for infants and toddlers with disabilities and their families. This assures a free appropriate public education to all children and youth with disabilities.
2. To assure that the rights of children and youth with disabilities from birth to age 21, as well as their families, are protected.
3. To help states and localities provide for early intervention services and the education of all children with disabilities.
4. To assess and assure the effectiveness of efforts to provide early intervention services and educate children with disabilities (Atkins-Burnett, 2004).

The family-centered early-intervention practice ideas first introduced in 1986 remain part of the new amendments of IDEA. These require early assessment of both the strengths and needs of the children and their families and the specification of goals for both.

In addition to assessment and intervention with the child, a statement about the family resources, priorities, concerns, and expected outcomes is part of each individualized family service plan (IFSP) (Sabatino, 2001). School social workers often assist in assessments, treatment plans, and linkages to resources (NASW, 2002, Standards 12, 13, and 26). They may screen the child in the home, provide community referrals, and help set up a community network to identify and serve these special-needs children. They can also assist teachers and parents in early identification through inservice training and parent education.

LEGISLATION THAT AFFECTS THE ROLE OF SCHOOL SOCIAL WORKERS

The federal legislation commonly referred to as "No Child Left Behind" authorizes federal funds to be used for prekindergarten programs and additional paraprofessionals in the classroom. No Child Left Behind is based on (1) emphasis on proven teaching methods, (2) stronger accountability focused on results, (3) increased flexibility and local control, and (4) more options for parents. As a result of this law, school districts are adding new prekindergarten programs. School social workers should work with district administrators to be part of the assessment team that identifies at-risk youth for these prekindergarten programs.

All of the foregoing federal mandates require schools to identify and serve children with special needs at birth. States must ensure that all children with disabilities who are in need of special education and related services, regardless of severity of disability, be identified, located, and evaluated. Children who are eligible for services must be offered appropriate educational and related services (Atkins-Burnett, 2004).

ETHICAL DILEMMAS

The school social worker, who must rely on NASW's *Code of Ethics* as a guide to ethical decision making (NASW, 2002, Standard 1), experiences ethical dilemmas in maintaining social work values in a non-social work setting. Sometimes the ethical dilemma may be caused by lack of funding–school social workers are told not to recommend outside services to parents because school districts may have to pay for them. It also is difficult for social workers in the school system to confine their work to helping students achieve in school; often circumstances away from the school environment create the problem, and yet the social worker is restricted to working with the child in the school environment. Ethical dilemmas may also arise when a social worker faces other non-social work professionals who do not understand confidentiality. In such situations, social workers should inform students, families, and other professionals of the confidentiality limitations and requirements when services are initiated.

Since supervision of school social work programs should be provided by credentialed and experienced social workers with masters' degrees in the field (NASW, 2002, Standard 35), some ethical dilemmas arise from supervision by non-social work professionals. School social workers often are supervised by educators, who focus on education and protecting the school district, while social workers focus on the client. The chapters that follow will deal with many of these issues in more detail.

CONCLUSION

The role and function of the school social worker vary among school districts. School social workers are generalist practitioners who must have skills to work with individuals, groups, families, and communities. Each school campus has a unique culture that makes it necessary for school social workers to understand diversity and how to work with unique situations. School social workers must have the ability to work with other professionals in the school district and to connect children and families to community resources. Social workers utilize their professional knowledge and skills to help children who are at risk, who are having difficulties, or who are disabled succeed in school.

Discussion Topics

1. How does the role of the school social worker differ from the roles of any of the other school professionals?
2. Which school social work roles seem most interesting?
3. Can you think of ways to create visibility in schools so that communities and schools will understand the necessity of having a school social worker?
4. Discuss what learning disabilities and DSM-IV-TR disorders may be prevalent among students in schools.

5. Discuss developmental theories and what the school social worker may need to know about them.
6. What laws other than those discussed in the chapter might govern school social work?
7. Do you know of any other laws that have affected the schools?
8. Role play: You are a new school social worker. How would you introduce yourself and your abilities to your principal?

APPENDIX 1.1. NASW Standards for School Social Work Services* Approved by the NASW Board of Directors, June 2002

Definitions

The following terms are defined for purposes of this document.

Case management—Organizing, coordinating, and sustaining activities and services designed to optimize the functioning of students and/or families.

Competence—The synthesis of professional behaviors that integrate knowledge, skills, and activities in the performance of the tasks of school social work. Competence in school social work includes all relevant educational and experiential requirements, demonstrated ability through meeting licensing and certification requirements, and the ability to carry out work assignments and achieve goals while adhering to the values and the code of ethics of the profession.

Certified school social work specialist—A social worker meeting the requirements for a School Social Work Specialist certification issued by the National Association of Social Workers.

Credentialed or licensed school social worker—A social worker meeting the requirements for a school social worker as established by the state board of education or other state entity that licenses or certifies educational personnel, or professional social workers.

Cultural competence—Congruent behaviors, attitudes, and skills enabling an individual to work effectively in cross-cultural situations.

Ecological perspective—The perspective of the interaction of the child and family and their environment. Important concepts include adaptation, transactions, goodness of fit between the students and their educational environments, reciprocity, and mutuality.

Family—The parent(s), guardian, custodian, or other person acting in loco parentis of a child.

Functional behavioral assessment—An approach to assessment that enhances understanding of the purpose and effect of the behavior(s) of concern and provides information that is useful in the development of effective interventions.

Human services—Programs and activities designed to enhance people's development and well-being. Basic human services include personal social services, health, education, housing, income, and justice and public safety.

Local education agency—The local public agency responsible for operating the educational program. In some states, responsibility for provision of special education

---

*The complete text of the *NASW Standards for School Social Work Services* is available on request from NASW or at *www.socialworkers.org*. From National Association of Social Workers (2002).

programs has been assigned to entities called intermediate units, area education agencies, educational service units, and so forth.

Mediation—A collaborative problem-solving process in which a neutral third party guides a discussion intended to help the parties in the dispute define the issues, obtain relevant information, and generate reasonable options for resolution.

Practice modalities—Specific treatment interventions used by the school social worker or other practitioner to help the student, family, or other identified client system reach a desired goal or outcome. Intervention strategies may include casework; group work; individual, group, or family counseling or therapy; community organization; crisis intervention; advocacy; staff training; policy development; and program coordination.

Prevention—Efforts undertaken by school social workers and others to minimize or eliminate the social, psychological, or other conditions known to cause or contribute to physical and emotional illness and some socioeconomic problems. Prevention efforts may include actions taken by school social workers and others that would prevent problems from occurring (primary prevention); limit the extent or severity of the problem (secondary prevention); or assist in recuperating from the effects of the problem and developing sufficient strengths and skills to preclude its return (tertiary prevention).

Professional practice—The ethical principles, provision of services, and responsibilities that school social workers are expected to maintain.

School social work—Social work services provided in the setting of an educational agency by credentialed school social workers. This specialty in social work is oriented toward helping students make satisfactory adjustments and coordinating and influencing the efforts of the school, the family, and the community to achieve this goal.

Student—Any person legally mandated by the state to be enrolled in an educational program or eligible to be enrolled.

Standards for Professional Practice

For the purposes of this document professional practice relates to the ethical principles, provision of services, and responsibilities that school social workers are expected to maintain. The term "local education agency" is used throughout this document to refer to any local or regional public education system and is consistent with the wording of federal legislation.

Standard 1. A school social worker shall demonstrate commitment to the values and ethics of the social work profession and shall use NASW's Code of Ethics as a guide to ethical decision making.

Standard 2. School social workers shall organize their time, energies, and workloads to fulfill their responsibilities and complete assignments of their position, with due consideration of the priorities among their various responsibilities.

Standard 3. School social workers shall provide consultation to local education agency personnel, school board members, and community representatives to promote understanding and effective utilization of school social work services.

Standard 4. School social workers shall ensure that students and their families are provided services within the context of multicultural understanding and competence that enhance families' support of students' learning experiences.

Standard 5. School social work services shall be extended to students in ways that build students' individual strengths and offer students maximum opportunity to participate in the planning and direction of their own learning experience.

Standard 6. School social workers shall help empower students and their families to gain access to and effectively use formal and informal community resources.

Standard 7. School social workers shall maintain adequate safeguards for the privacy and confidentiality of information.

Standard 8. School social workers shall advocate for students and their families in a variety of situations.

Standard 9. As leaders and members of interdisciplinary teams and coalitions, school social workers shall work collaboratively to mobilize the resources of local education agencies and communities to meet the needs of students and families.

Standard 10. School social workers shall develop and provide training and educational programs that address the goals and mission of the educational institution.

Standard 11. School social workers shall maintain accurate data that are relevant to planning, management, and evaluation of school social work services.

Standard 12. School social workers shall conduct assessments of student needs that are individualized and provide information that is directly useful for designing interventions that address behaviors of concern.

Standard 13. School social workers shall incorporate assessments in developing and implementing intervention and evaluation plans that enhance students' abilities to benefit from educational experiences.

Standard 14. School social workers, as systems change agents, shall identify areas of need that are not being addressed by the local education agency and community and shall work to create services that address these needs.

Standard 15. School social workers shall be trained in and use mediation and conflict-resolution strategies to promote students' resolution of their nonproductive encounters in the school and community and to promote productive relationships.

Standards for Professional Preparation and Development

Professional preparation defines the level of training required for school social work practice. Professional development refers to the enhancement of basic knowledge and skills that requires ongoing effort by school social workers.

Standard 16. School social workers shall meet the provisions for practice set by NASW.

Standard 17. School social workers shall possess knowledge and understanding basic to the social work profession.

Standard 18. School social workers shall understand the backgrounds and broad range of experiences that shape students' approaches to learning.

Standard 19. School social workers shall possess knowledge and understanding of the organization and structure of the local education agency.

Standard 20. School social workers shall possess knowledge and understanding of the reciprocal influences of home, school, and community.

Standard 21. School social workers shall possess skills in systematic assessment and investigation.

Standard 22. School social workers shall understand the relationship between practice and policies affecting students.

Standard 23. School social workers shall be able to select and apply empirically validated or promising prevention and intervention methods to enhance students' educational experiences.

Standard 24. School social workers shall be able to evaluate their practice and disseminate the findings to consumers, the local education agency, the community, and the profession.

Standard 25. School social workers shall possess skills in developing coalitions at the local, state, and national levels that promote student success.

Standard 26. School social workers shall be able to promote collaboration among community health and mental health services providers and facilitate student access to these services.

Standard 27. School social workers shall assume responsibility for their own continued professional development in accordance with the NASW Standards for Continuing Professional Education* and state requirements.

Standard 28. School social workers shall contribute to the development of the profession by educating and supervising school social work interns.

Standards for Administrative Structure and Support

An effective school social work program must have adequate administrative structure and support. NASW recommends that the local education agency use the following standards, along with state and federal guidelines, to develop a school social work program.

Standard 29. State departments of education or other state entities that license or certify educational personnel shall regulate school social work practice.

Standard 30. State departments of education or other state entities that license or certify educational personnel shall employ a state school social work consultant who is a credentialed and experienced school social worker.

---

*The complete text of the *NSAW Standards for Cultural Competence in Social Work Practice* and the *NASW Standards for Continuing Professional Education* is available on request from NASW or at *www.socialworkers.org*.

Standard 31. School social work services shall be provided by credentialed school social workers employed by the local education agency.

Standard 32. Local education agencies shall employ school social workers with the highest level of qualifications for entry-level practitioners.

Standard 33. Social workers in schools shall be designated "school social workers."

Standard 34. Salaries and job classifications of school social workers shall be commensurate with their education, experience, and responsibilities and be comparable to similarly qualified professional personnel employed by the local education agency.

Standard 35. The administrative structure established by the local education agency shall provide for appropriate school social work supervision.

Standard 36. The administrative structure of the local education agency shall delineate clear lines of support and accountability for the school social work program.

Standard 37. The local education agency shall provide a professional work setting that allows school social workers to practice effectively.

Standard 38. The local education agency shall provide opportunities for school social workers to engage in professional development activities that support school social work practice.

Standard 39. The goals, objectives, and tasks of a school social work program shall be clearly and directly related to the mission of the local education agency and the educational process.

Standard 40. The local education agency shall involve school social workers in developing and coordinating partnerships with community health, mental health, and social services providers linked with or based at school sites to ensure that these services promote student educational success.

Standard 41. All programs incorporating school social work services shall require ongoing evaluation to determine their contribution to the educational success of all students.

Standard 42. The local education agency shall establish and implement a school social work–student population ratio to ensure reasonable workload expectations.

2

An Ecological–Developmental Framework for Practice in the Schools

SOCIAL WORK ASSESSMENT

The ability to assess and treat students properly is at the core of providing school social work services. School social workers contribute an essential dimension to the assessment of students through the use of an ecological perspective, which considers the child's family and neighborhood (Radin, 1992; NASW, 2002, Standard 12). Complete assessments of children and adolescents in the public schools should include information from collaborative sources, such as parents, teachers, and medical personnel who are involved with the students. Assessment is part of a comprehensive mental health treatment. The assessment process, referred to as a "dynamic diagnosis" by Helen Perlman, "seeks to establish what the trouble is, what psychological, physical, or social factors contribute to (or cause) it, what effect it has on the individual's well-being (and that of others), what solution is sought, and what means exist within the client, his situation, and organized services and resources by which the problem may be affected" (Perlman, 1957).

The use of the strengths perspective (Saleebey, 1997) adds another dimension to the assessment process that is unique to the social work profession. This perspective focuses on the client's capacities and strengths rather than problems and weaknesses. The social worker's presentation of an assessment in any situation should help individuals achieve new, more positive perceptions of themselves and their situations and should focus on their strengths rather than weakness or pathology (Poulin, 2000; NASW, 2002, Standard 5). When a student or parent is able to tell his or her own story with the social worker listening it frees both of them from finding refuge in a defensive stance and allows for the collaboration necessary for decision making (Poulin, 2000).

Relationship Building

A complete assessment and intervention plan is among the ethical responsibilities required of social workers by state licensing boards (NASW, 2002, Standard 12). An assessment should begin with the first interview, which sets the tone for the entire intervention. First interviews with students and their parents often determine if the school social worker will be successful in working with the child. Social workers need to plan ahead to assure that this first meeting is positive.

An effective assessment depends on a positive and productive relationship with the child. Children are very sensitive about rejection and become defensive if they feel someone does not accept them. This is particularly true for those children who have already been rejected at school by peers or teachers. These fragile students will not trust or like someone whom they feel is biased against them.

One of the most damaging things that can happen at the beginning of a therapeutic relationship between a child and a school social worker is for the social worker to rely on unsolicited information (gossip) about a child and his or her misbehavior. Schools are small communities. Consequently, students who are having difficulties or are creating problems in the classroom are infamous among most of the faculty. This is particularly true in elementary schools, where the faculty is small and meets together frequently, such as at lunch in the teachers' lounge. A school social worker's reliance on a student's reputation among faculty may be a barrier to listening to the child and forming independent impressions and can create a bias that may be difficult to overcome.

Ensuring success of the initial contact requires planning. The following guidelines may help build a positive relationship.

- *Begin with small talk to put the student or parent at ease.* Parents and students often feel threatened by the idea of counseling. They may need reassurance from the social worker. Casual conversation helps put both the student and parents at ease. It reveals the social worker's personality and creates a nonthreatening atmosphere, which, in turn, establishes trust. Schools operate with middle-class values and language (Payne, 1995), and parents from lower socioeconomic levels and diverse cultural backgrounds may show a basic distrust of the school system and school personnel. It is the responsibility of the school social worker to remove this distrust (NASW, 2002, Standard 4). Children and parents need to be assured that the school social worker will engage the child appropriately and will be able to help the child feel comfortable.

- *Meet the student or parent in a private, comfortable, nonthreatening environment.* It is difficult to find private unused space in school buildings. Before beginning work on a campus, the school social worker should meet with campus administrators and arrange for a meeting place that will allow for privacy. On large campuses this is very difficult, but essential (NASW, 2002, Standard 7). Stairwells, the school library, and halls are not effective meeting places. Inadequate meeting places cause the student to be distracted and do not allow for the privacy that counseling requires and students deserve. Inadequate meeting places also make the social work intervention seem less than professional. School social workers must advocate for themselves and the integrity of their services by insisting on adequate meeting places.

- *"Start where the student or parent is."* Anticipate their thoughts and feelings and be ready to respond appropriately. Address any preconceived notions about the counseling process and the student's fears. It helps to address these fears initially so they will not disrupt the therapeutic relationship. Where the referral has been made against the child's will, the social worker should address the referral process and ask the child to discuss his or her feelings about having to meet with the social worker. In this way, anger, doubts, and negativity can be dealt with rather than continuing to build throughout the process.

- *Give the student the benefit of the doubt and listen without displaying skepticism or disbelief.* It is essential to learn the student's perspective about the situation for which he or she was referred to the social worker. Don't display doubt about what the student is saying, even if the information is difficult to listen to.

- *Determine the most important treatment objectives and goals.* Help the student and parent prioritize the goals and determine a time frame for treatment and for reaching those goals.

• *Formulate a contract* (Hepworth, Rooney & Larsen, 2002). Children are not used to signing contracts, and they may find it fun. It helps add legitimacy to the treatment process to have the child sign a contract. (See Appendix 2.1 for an example of a student contract form.) Once a contract has been negotiated, children usually feel a sense of relief because they can determine the course of treatment. It also helps to establish the time frame for future meetings. The student can then plan ahead, and there will be less apprehension about how much time will be involved in counseling sessions.

• *Set regular appointment times that will work with the schedules of both student and teacher.* Consult with the teacher to assure that the student is not being pulled out of a class in which he or she is already struggling. Working with the teacher helps ensure that the student will attend counseling sessions and that the teacher will convey critical information about the student to the social worker.

• *Keep appointments and use the contract whenever a meeting takes place with the student.* If appointments need to be changed, give the student advance warning. Students begin to count on the time they spend with the school social worker. When appointments are changed, it can ruin their entire day. Teachers also appreciate knowing if the appointment has been cancelled so they can anticipate the student's reaction.

Assessment Tools

There are numerous assessment tools for use in working with children. Figure 2.1 provides an outline to be used by the social worker during the initial meeting with the student and parent. It is comprehensive and yet brief enough to give the needed information to the school social worker while not overwhelming the student and parent. The outline also provides a basic overview of the student and his or her presenting problem. Assessment includes formulating and prioritizing goals and determining a treatment plan.

Tripartite Assessment

The tripartite assessment is a comprehensive assessment tool that looks at the child in three interacting contexts: (1) individual factors, (2) situational factors, and (3) factors in the support system (Webb, 2003). This assessment method is particularly helpful in looking at students within the school environment and evaluating the problems that may be created by the school itself. Problems may arise because of a bad relationship

Date: ___________

Student name: ______________________________

School: _____________________ Grade: _______________

Date of birth: _________________

Sex: M F

Identifying information:

Referral source:

Presenting problem:

History of current problem:

Symptomatology:

Appearance:
Dress/grooming

Mental status:
Eye contact
Alertness
Orientation
Recent memory

Current school performance:
Grades
Attendance
Discipline problems

Social functioning:

Risk factors:
Suicide risk
Physical violence risk
Alcohol/drug abuse or dependence
Abuse/neglect

Evidence of current learning problems:

Special education services:

Family difficulties:

(cont.)

FIGURE 2.1. Initial meeting assessment outline.

Friends:

Previous treatment:

Health status and substance use:

Developmental history:

Individual background (prenatal, delivery, childhood illnesses, medical history)

School history (preschool, early childhood intervention, Head Start—separation issues when beginning school, grades, peer interactions, teacher interactions, suspensions, removal from school)

Family history (parents' marital status, number of siblings, birth order, stepparents, siblings, history of abuse)

Extracurricular involvement in school or community (sports, the arts, social or service clubs, church affiliation)

Student strengths:

Family strengths:

Community support/deficits:

FIGURE 2.1. *(cont.)*

with a particular teacher or a difficult class whose timing coincides with the child's medication wearing off. Sometimes problems may have a simple solution if the assessment considers all possible contingencies. Likewise, the support system may be the major source of the problem.

Case Example

Jordan, age 15, was the only child of a single parent. He lived with his mother, and his father played no part in his life. When the school social worker met him, Jordan was unkempt and had a history of continual absences from school. His mother was a truck driver who was steadily employed, which meant that she was frequently out of town. The only person she trusted to watch her son was an elderly male neighbor. The neighbor attempted to keep a careful watch–he would call Jordan each morning to make sure he was up and would check on him at night.

Jordan reported to the school social worker that he sometimes did not have food and did not have transportation to look for a job. He rode the school bus but would usually not remain at school for the entire day. He was failing his classes.

When the school social worker called Jordan's mother to discuss his school problems, the mother withdrew him from school and took him on the road with her. His formal education thus ended abruptly. The social worker was trying to get information from his mother in order to help Jordan, but, unfortunately, rather than helping the mother and her son find a solution to his school problems, the social worker's inquiry exacerbated those problems and had a negative impact on the boy.

The social worker could have made better use of the tripartite assessment to understand Jordan's situation. If she had utilized the situational factors as a way of praising the mother for her hard work, the mother may not have become defensive. The social worker also could have been more empathic regarding the factors in the family support system. Literally, the only person in the entire community whom the mother felt was available for help was an elderly neighbor. She and her son had no extended family, friends, religious community, or neighborhood support. The mother was defensive because she was doing the best she could. When her efforts did not appear to be working, she decided to solve the problem in her own way rather than relying on help from the school, which she did not view as a support system.

The tripartite assessment serves as a valuable tool in helping a troubled child like Jordan perform in school. It can be used with children in crisis (as with Jordan) or with bereavement or trauma. Tripartite assessment considers individual and situational factors as they interact with factors in the child's support system (Webb, 2003). This type of assessment could greatly benefit a school social worker who is trying to provide support in the aftermath of a suicide or school or community violence.

Social History

A social history provides a tool for understanding how the child has performed socially throughout his or her life. Social acceptance usually increases self-esteem, while rejection decreases it. The school social worker should observe the student during peer interactions. The school lunchroom is an excellent place to see how a student is accepted by peers. Students who are struggling socially will often sit alone at the lunch table or seem invisible to peers. They will have minimal interaction with other students. When a social worker is observing a student's social interactions, it is best to sit away from the child and not let the child know that he or she is being observed.

Culturagram

Culturagrams (Congress, 1994) are useful tools to help school social workers understand children in their environmental context. Culturagrams help social workers assess the meaning and impact of culture on their clients. They can be used with children who are immigrants, are new to the community, have unique religious/spiritual practices, or are from a minority population. The culturagram assesses 10 important factors concerning culture, including family values regarding education and work, time in the community, reasons for immigration, age at time of immigration, legal or undocumented status, language spoken in the home, health beliefs, holidays and special events, contact with cultural institutions, and impact of crisis events created by the family's uniqueness (Congress, 1994, p. 533).

Culturagrams also assist the school social worker in assuring there is no bias toward the child. If the social worker understands the student's culture, he or she is less likely to misunderstand the student's behaviors and misinterpret them as dysfunctional, thus avoiding the tendency to identify as disordered those whose cultural values and lifestyles differ markedly from those of the social worker (Sue, Sue, & Sue, 1994). (See Appendix 2.2.)

Genogram

A genogram (Hartman, 1978) is a visual method of depicting a particular family. Genograms communicate information about a child and his or her family in a concise and efficient manner. Genograms illustrate familial relationships and show family history, including divorces, deaths, and additional siblings. School social workers should ask children to explain their familial relationships and create a graphic picture of those relationships. This information helps the social worker identify family members by name and understand the child's relationship to family members the child discusses.

Collateral Information

School social workers must obtain prior written permission from the appropriate parent or guardian before working with a child. The initial contact with parents or guardians is a good time to gather information about the presenting problem and the child's history. Because it is often difficult to reach parents, a wise school social worker uses each opportunity to gather information. Accordingly, social workers should keep with them at all times a copy of the forms utilized in this chapter so they can immediately gather necessary collateral information whenever they happen to meet with a parent.

History of Trauma to the Child and Family

It is imperative for the social worker to ask for background information about family and individual trauma. A child who has a history of abuse or neglect or who has experienced the death of a close family member may respond to new situations in an abnormal way merely as a result of previous trauma.

Case Example

Jimmy, age 10, was in the fifth grade. He cried in school every day, especially at the end of the school day. His older brother, who was in high school, had been hit and killed by a car the previous year immediately after he had walked Jimmy home from school. Jimmy had been treated by a psychologist for depression and had been hospitalized in order to stabilize his medications for depression. However, he was continuing to work through his grief. When he met with the school social worker once a week, the meeting was planned to take place at the end of the school day. The social worker gave Jimmy paper and crayons and asked him to express his thoughts on a "thought page." Sometimes he would just speak about his feelings and the social worker would write them down. The social worker let Jimmy express his feelings freely and then discuss his reactions to those feelings. He was allowed to vent his anger and frustration. Jimmy used this time to express his grief and receive support from the social worker. It took several months to ease his distress, but he reached a point where he could face the end of the school day without tears and painful memories of his brother.

Strengths and Resources of the Family

A complete assessment includes an examination of the strengths and resources of the child's family (NASW, 2002, Standard 12). Past family coping patterns produce excellent information about how the child has been taught to deal with difficulties. The social worker should take note of the following factors that have been found to increase family resiliency: middle-class or higher socioeconomic status, access to health care and social services, consistent parental employment, adequate housing, family religious faith and participation, good schools, and supportive adults outside the family who serve as role models or mentors to the child (Davies, 2004). Of course, many students do not come from positive backgrounds, and many poor families provide strong support despite their limited resources.

Collateral Information from Sources Outside the Family

Part of any ecological assessment should include the other professionals with whom the child has interacted. School social workers have access to a variety of other professionals who have had interactions with the child in the school system. Students interact with administrators, teachers, counselors, and diagnosticians. The social worker also has access to school records and tests, which often include testing that has been done by private practitioners.

Some children have had frequent office referrals to school administrators, who can give the social worker information regarding the child's initial behavior and response to any disciplinary actions that have taken place.

Children frequently are taught by more than one teacher during the day. Accordingly, the social worker should talk to each of the child's teachers. If the child is working with an outside agency, as in the case of probation, or is receiving outside counseling, the school social worker should obtain written permission from the student's parent to contact these outside sources of information. If the child has been involved in special programs at school, such as counseling and speech or physical therapy, the school social worker also should contact the professionals who have been serving the child and obtain additional information. When a student is involved in extracurricular activities, the social worker should seek further information from the coach, teacher, or sponsor of the activity.

Behavioral Observations in the Classroom

Behavioral observations measure the types of behaviors exhibited by a student and their frequency. Behavioral observations are most successful when the child is unaware that he or she is being observed. (No matter how circumspect the observation, and regardless of the observer's attempts not to focus on one child, it is uncanny how frequently the child being observed is aware of the observation and watches the observer as intently as the observer watches the child.) Behavioral observations provide school social workers with baseline measures of behavior that can be used to help parents and other school personnel understand the frequency and severity of problem behaviors. The observations also are helpful in determining the effectiveness of interventions because they provide clear data on the behavior prior to the intervention, which provides the social worker with a tool to measure change.

Before making a behavioral assessment, it is helpful for the social worker to meet with the child's teacher to determine what behaviors are causing the child to experience problems at school. The behavior observations should identify behavior problems and monitor them in 5- to 10-minute intervals. The behavior should be measured in the morning and again in the afternoon and on different days, since some children have difficulties only at specific times during the day or during certain activities. A true measurement should be taken more than one time and, if possible, while the student is studying different subjects to see if he or she acts up more during one subject or if the behavior is the same regardless of the subject matter. Behavioral observations should be summarized in writing immediately after they are completed. (See Appendix 2.3 for a sample behavior observation form.)

Functional Assessment of Behavior

A functional assessment of behavior asks what the behavior is, when it occurs, what the activating events are, and what happens as a result of the behavior, both positive and negative (Boys Town, 1989). All behaviors have a purpose. In order to help a child change negative behaviors, it is useful to determine what benefit the child receives from them. Usually a negative behavior can be replaced by a new, positive behavior, which the child can learn and use to meet the same needs as the previous negative behavior. Therefore, functional behavior assessments need to be completed both by observing the child and noting the consequences that follow his or her behavior and by asking the child what beneficial consequences he or she believes result from the behavior. Once the reasons for a child's particular actions are understood, the social worker can help the child learn new ways to behave that are less self-destructive and disturbing to others.

Assessment Challenges

The assessment tools described in this chapter are time consuming. However, school personnel often want a *quick* answer to what is wrong with the child and what can they do about it. The social worker is thus torn between completing a thorough assessment and meeting the demands of his or her employer. These conflicting demands create both professional and ethical challenges to the social worker that must be addressed on a case-by-case basis.

Sometimes it is difficult to obtain needed information from children. Many young students do not know or have access to certain information that the social worker requires, such as medical histories, the family history, or their own developmental history.

While parents are a vital source of information, they often are difficult to reach. In these cases, it is difficult to obtain the necessary permission even to see the child, let alone to see the parent in order to obtain the information necessary to complete the assessment. Children in foster care or in the custody of those other than their natural parents present further problems, since these custodians often have little of the information that the social worker needs to complete a thorough assessment.

Because of the difficulty of obtaining needed information, the school social worker must often work with a student notwithstanding a lack of adequate background information. The social worker may also experience personal and ethical challenges after an assessment has been completed and treatment recommendations have been made, when school personnel, particularly administrators, do not have the resources or time to implement the recommended solutions to the child's problems.

GUIDELINES FOR EFFECTIVE TREATMENT PLANS

Once an assessment has been completed, a treatment plan based on the assessment should be formulated (NASW, 2002, Standard 13). *Effective treatment plans outline who is going to do what, and when and how it will be accomplished.* Treatment plans should contain specific goals.

Student Goal Setting and Charts

School social workers should help the children with whom they work to set and achieve goals that will help them improve their performance in school. Goal setting and goal attainment are part of evidence-based practice, providing both qualitative and quantitative measurements to assist the school social worker in proving that the interventions selected and implemented were effective (O'Hare, 2005). With the help of the social worker, the child should prioritize those goals and determine which one he or she wants to work on first. Student participation in the selection of goals is essential and consistent with social work values of individual responsibility and the related concept of individual participation in one's destiny (Turner, 1974).

The first goal to be identified should address the behavior that is causing the child the most difficulty with teachers and peers. Once the first goal is set, the social worker can help the child decide who among the child, teacher, parents, and social worker will do "what, when, and how" for that goal. The social worker can also assist the child in dividing up the goal so he or she can focus *on the easiest steps first.* This will increase the chance of immediate progress, which, in turn, will lead to feelings of success and commitment to further work on the goal.

After the child has accomplished any of his or her goals, a follow-up plan should be completed to check on the long-term effectiveness of the intervention. The social worker also should implement a measurement plan to see if there has been a real change. Charting behavioral changes can provide a concrete tool for helping students see and measure change. The charts give school social workers the opportunity to monitor, evaluate, and incrementally adjust social work interventions (O'Hare, 2005) if students are not successfully meeting their goals. Baseline data from classroom observations can be used to show student growth and change.

Practice Example

Establish a time frame to work on a goal that coincides with the length of each report card period. Create a chart for the student on which the numbers from 1 to 10 are placed on a *Y*-axis to form a Likert rating scale. Across the *X*-axis write the student's goal and the number of weeks in the report card period. Weekly, the student reports the degree, on a scale from 1 (lowest) to 10 (highest), to which he or she has achieved the targeted goal during the prior week. The student and social worker then mark that assessment on the *Y*-axis of the chart. Children respond to visualizations, and this graphic illustration of their progress encourages them to continue. If the child has trouble and does not make progress, discuss what caused the difficulty and try to encourage the child to make progress for the next week. (See Figure 2.2 for a sample chart.)

Behavior Management Plans

Behavior management plans are tools to help children visualize growth and change. Most behavior management plans include contingency contracts that provide consequences for certain behavior. These plans do not work unless the contract is followed consistently.

Name: ______________________________

Goal: When I don't understand my assignment, I will ask for help instead of tearing up my work.

	Week 1	Week 2	Week 3	Week 4	Week 5	Week 6
10						
9						
8						
7						
6						
5						
4						
3						
2						
1						

FIGURE 2.2. Sample goal sheet for student.

In the example shown in Figure 2.3, Mary wants to improve on remembering to bring her homework to class. A behavior management plan is implemented involving a contract between Mary and her teacher. The goals and rewards of the plan are in writing and are to be signed and dated by the student and the teacher. The chart contains five squares with one day of the week written on each square. The teacher agrees to place a star on a chart each time Mary brings her homework. Mary will receive 15 minutes of free time on Friday to play a game of her choice if she earns four stars in that week.

Level Systems

Level systems are used with students who need a great deal of structure. Most level systems have four levels of student advancement. Students usually begin a level system at the lowest level, which specifies

CONTRACT

Mary will receive a star for each day that she brings her homework to class. If she receives four stars in any week, she can play a game of her choice on Friday afternoon at school for 30 minutes.

Student signature: ______________________ Date: ________

Teacher signature: ______________________ Date: ________

Monday	Tuesday	Wednesday	Thursday	Friday

FIGURE 2.3. Contract for student.

limited privileges. Students on level systems usually spend all day with the same teacher. After they earn a specified number of points, they advance to the next level. Students earn points according to predetermined criteria, such as sitting at their desks quietly, working throughout the class period, bringing books and assignments with them to class, or following teacher directions. After a student has earned enough points on any level, he or she advances to the next level, which has more privileges, such as lunch in the school cafeteria rather than in the classroom with the teacher. School social workers can assist teachers in tailoring their level system to fit the desired behavioral changes for each student. Teachers must keep track of student progress and record points regularly for students so they see the progress they are making.

DEVELOPMENTAL ISSUES AT DIFFERENT GRADE LEVELS

Separation Anxiety

Separation anxiety disorder, as defined in DSM-IV-TR, is excessive anxiety concerning separation from the home or from those to whom the person is attached (American Psychiatric Association, 2000). To be classified as a disorder, the condition must last for at least 4 weeks. Symptoms include recurrent excessive distress on separation from home or major attachment figures. Some children become physically ill or have physical complaints and show preoccupation with returning home.

Social workers should be aware that children who are beginning school often experience separation anxiety. Most children exhibit the symptoms of separation anxiety for a few days after beginning school. However, symptoms also can develop after some life stress, such as the death of a pet or relative, a change of school or move to a new neighborhood, or immigration (American Psychiatric Association, 2000). Children who begin day care or some kind of preschool program deal with separation issues at an early age. Many kindergartners begin school with tears and a sense of fear and foreboding about being away from their home and family. School social workers need to be attuned to the needs of children in these situations and help them adapt to school so that they are not uncomfortable.

Transitions from one school to the next, such as from elementary to middle school or from middle school to high school, also can create anxiety. These transitions are particularly difficult for children who may be developmentally behind. Likewise, children in foster placements and kinship care placements may experience trauma as they advance into new schools and unfamiliar surroundings. The school social worker at the student's present school should notify the social worker or counselor at the new school about the student's transition before it takes place. The social worker at the student's new campus should meet with the new student and help answer questions and alleviate fears. If at all possible, the social workers at both campuses should make arrangements for those students who may have difficulty with a transition to visit the new campus at the end of the school year before the transition is to take place. If a visit is not possible, the school social worker can make arrangements with the school counselor or social worker at the new campus to meet the students and answer questions before they leave their current school. Anticipating transitions and relieving fears is especially helpful for students with emotional problems.

Understanding Developmental Delays

Developmental delays, such as mental retardation and autism, create extreme difficulties with performance in school. Autism is the most severe category of a spectrum of developmental disorders and is associated with deficits in reciprocal social interactions, communication, and behavioral flexibility. Autism, which is diagnosed in 1 out of every 700 children (Miller & McMahon, 2005), is discussed in more detail later in the book.

Effects of Developmental Delays

"All behavior, normal and pathological, emerges through the process of socialization" (Dale, Smith, Norlin, & Chess, 2006, p. 43). School attendance helps to socialize children. Developmental delays and emotional problems limit a child's ability to perform well in social interactions. Social interaction failures set the stage for a lifetime of poor self-concept in social interactions.

Effects of Learning Delays

Cognitive development occurs in stages. Each individual's manner of thinking is qualitatively different at each stage, and each stage is a whole unto itself. Progression through stages does not vary, and no stage is skipped. Each stage builds on and incorporates the next lower stage. The stages are characteristic of all mankind; they do not vary with cultures (Dale et al., 2006, pp. 119–120).

Children with learning delays are often labeled. While society rewards industry, these children are often mistakenly called "slow," "lazy," or "a problem." These labels ultimately affect the child's self concept (Dale et. al., 2006, p. 157).

When learning delays have a cumulative effect, a child may not be able to face the consequences and may try to hide his or her difficulties, particularly if the child is socially accepted and does not appear to have any other deficits. (Appendix 2.4 includes a list of websites that may help school social workers understand many of the learning problems and developmental delays they will see in school.)

Case Example

Matthew, age 15, was a high school sophomore. He was reported to the school administration for continuous truancy and was ultimately referred to the school social worker. He told the school social worker that he did not want his peers to know he could not read well. Therefore, whenever he was in a class where the teacher was asking students to read out loud, he would slip out the door and leave the building. After the social worker spent time with him and learned the real source of his truancy, he was referred to the special education resource program for help with reading. He did not want to attend the resource program at first but eventually attended and received help with his reading.

UNDERSTANDING THE CHILD WITHIN THE OVERLAPPING CONTEXTS OF COMMUNITY, SCHOOL, AND FAMILY

When children begin school, the two principal systems in their lives become the family and the school. Many children also interact with other systems, such as church, after-school day care, and their neighborhood. With an increasing number of social systems, the child must master a greater number of roles (Dale et al., 2006, p. 157). Children who are resilient, with the ability to adapt to change, will find a way to adapt to school. Students who come from poverty, are exposed to racism and discrimination, or attend poor schools will have greater difficulty in adapting (Davies, 2004). The development of emotional resources is crucial to student success. The greatest free resource available to students is the role modeling provided by teachers, administrators, and staff (Payne, 1995).

The Effects of Poverty

The effects of poverty create barriers in communication and socialization for both inner-city and rural youth. Students from low-income families (particularly minority children) do not have access to the formal speech register at home and cannot use it themselves (Montano-Harmon, 1991). These students do not have knowledge of the sentence structure, syntax, and vocabulary needed for the formal register of speech, which establishes barriers very quickly within the school (Payne, 1995). Likewise, patterns of discourse are different for minority children who use a casual form of discourse that meanders around a topic rather than a formal register that gets straight to the point (Payne, 1995). Students who use casual discourse tend to frustrate teachers (Payne, 1995). The effects of this language lag combined with developmental disabilities set a child up for a very difficult time in school.

The Effects of Change

Community violence and concerns about safety at school are factors that increase a child's risk for poor school performance. This is particularly difficult for children who are already victims of violence and trauma at home. These children are hypervigilant and unable to relax because they are always waiting for the next bad event to occur. Family factors, such as recent divorce or remarriage, change in the family culture by blending a family together, custody disputes, and the creation of unique family constellations all put extra stress on children that can affect their school performance.

Case Example

Jared, age 9, misbehaved at school every Friday. He lived with his mother during the week and would stay with his father and stepmother on weekends. He hated to go to his father's house because his stepmother was strict, and he didn't have any of his toys or friends there. He also hated seeing his father being nice to his stepmother's children, who lived with them full time. Once the school social worker and his teacher identified the pattern of his misbehavior and the reason for it, he was given extra privileges at school on Friday afternoons and given a chance to talk out his frustrations. This helped keep him out of trouble at school and prepared him to deal with the weekend.

FEDERAL INITIATIVES AND MANDATES

Federal initiatives, such as No Child Left Behind and the identification of "best practices," have addressed the issue of early assessment and working with the family system. School social workers must become skilled in the use of assessment and intervention plans that can document growth and change in a child. Assessments of children who appear to have special needs begin immediately after birth through early childhood intervention services. Family risk factors are identified early and given support to strengthen the family and support the children. Interventions identified in best practices are "positive behavioral supports" mandated in the federal law known as the Individuals with Disabilities Education Act (IDEA, 1990, Public Law 101-476). These practices include:

1. Functional behavioral assessment
2. Goal setting
3. Contracting
4. Positive reinforcement
5. Group contingencies
6. Cross-age tutoring
7. Peer-mediated tutoring
8. High probability requests: asking the child to do an activity that he or she will likely do
9. Choice making within limits–self-evaluation, self-monitoring, self-recording, and self-management

School social workers are in a position to utilize many of the skills specified through IDEA, as illustrated in this chapter. They can help assess risk factors and create intervention and treatment plans to help children become successful in school.

Most school districts focus on school attendance and achievement. Most states have mandatory attendance policies that, when violated, require that students be referred to juvenile court. The effects of mandatory policies under which students will not be promoted to the next grade level if they do not pass achievement tests, may be devastating to fractured and at-risk families. Juvenile court referrals for truancy may serve to attract the family's attention initially, but often it is not the child's fault for missing school. Family factors are often responsible for a student's truancy. Adding a court referral creates additional stress for the family because parents are required to attend court with the child, and they have to miss work. The normal response from the court is to put the child on "house arrest," which again may not be manageable for single parents who work two jobs. School social workers should help families and communities find positive solutions to truancy and mandatory testing.

School social workers should be aware of community resources to aid families with special needs. Community networking with social workers and practitioners in agencies that may be working with schoolchildren and their families will greatly aid the school social worker in developing a resource and referral list. Along with understanding community agencies, school social workers should assess the availability of public transportation and other services within the community that may help children and their families have access to services.

Planning for a Continuum of Care after Public School

Students who qualify for special education services have access to care after they finish public school. Transition planning helps students with disabilities receive referrals to community agencies that will help them continue to learn and develop their potential after they leave public school. School social workers often work closely with school district transition specialists to help find appropriate agencies and services to help disabled children and their families.

School social workers should also assist other students who do not qualify for special education but are still in need of support from community mental health agencies, work programs, or other community resources. Transition planning is essential for success after high school. Many at-risk students do not plan on attending college or school immediately after high school, but they still need help connecting with support agencies and employment services. School social workers should coordinate work with vocational counselors, transition specialists, and community agencies to assist students and their families in planning the next phase of a student's life after high school.

CONCLUSION

Complete and thorough assessments are the key to effective interventions with children. There are many assessment tools to assist school social workers in understanding children and their environment. Time limitations sometimes do not allow for a complete assessment at school. However, school social workers should become familiar with the various assessment tools and options and choose those that will give them the most thorough information that is relevant to the child and his or her situation. It is essential to have some insight into the child's background and current situation before a school social worker implements a treatment plan.

Discussion Topics

1. What is unique about the tripartite assessment?
2. What do you like about the tripartite assessment?
3. Who are potential collateral sources that could help give assessment information to a school social worker?
4. What do you think creates the biggest challenges in gathering assessment data from children?
5. Write a treatment plan for one of the clients described in the case examples.
6. Identify some potential solutions to school attendance problems in lieu of using the court system.

APPENDIX 2.1. Student Contract

I agree to meet weekly with ____________________________, my school social worker,

during ___________ period for 6 weeks beginning ______________________.

I will honor the following commitments:

1. Set goals that will improve my performance in school.
2. Attend each session on time and work on goals.
3. Show respect for the school social worker.
4. Tell the truth.

____ ______________________
Student signature Date

____ ______________________
School social worker signature Date

APPENDIX 2.2. Culturagram

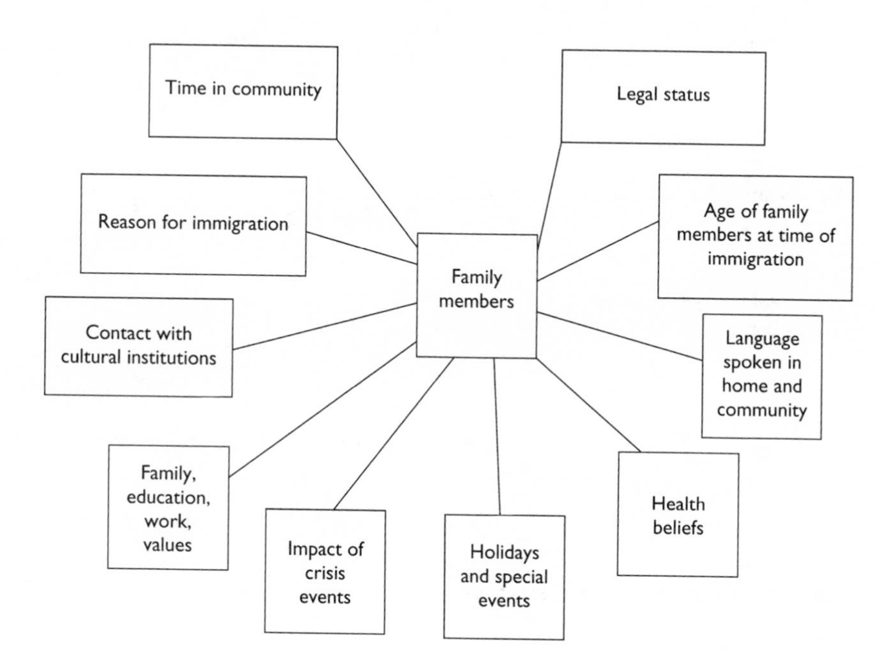

APPENDIX 2.3. Behavior Observation Form

Student Name: ______________________________ Date: ____________

Behavior	Frequency of Behavior					
	8.00 A.M.	8:10 A.M.	8:20 A.M.	8:30 A.M.	8:40 A.M.	8:50 A.M.
Getting out of seat						
Talking out in a disruptive way						
Other						

____

Name of person making the observation

APPENDIX 2.4. Websites for Various Assessments

Learning

The Beery-Buktenica Developmental Test of Visual-Motor Integration, Fifth Edition (Beery VMI), ages 2–18: Includes helpful information about the test as well as developmental learning materials.
www.pearsonassessments.com/tests/vmi.htm

ADHD

Learning Efficiency Test–II (LET-II), ages 5–adult
www.academictherapy.com

Social–emotional

Children's Depression Inventory (CDI), ages 7–17
www.mhs.com/index.htm

Depression

Reynolds Adolescent Depression Scale (RADS-2), ages 11–20: Includes critical items.
www3.parinc.com

Self-concept

Piers–Harris Children's Self-Concept Scale, Second Edition (Piers–Harris 2), ages 7–18
portal.wpspublish.com

Emotional–behavioral screening

Behavior Assessment System for Children, Second Edition (BASC-2); different forms cover ages 2½–18
ags.pearsonassessments.com

Behavioral

Child Behavior Checklist (CBC), different forms cover ages 1½–18
www.aseba.org

3

Uncovering Problems and Working within the System

Thorough assessment is critical in planning an intervention. In conducting assessments, school social workers should rely on diagnosticians and school psychologists, whose role as part of an interdisciplinary team focuses on diagnosing students and assessing their abilities. In contrast, the school social worker's assessment involves the student in the school environment, the home, and the community (NASW, 2002, Standard 12). Chapter 2 discussed the need for assessment and the many types of assessments used by school social workers. Thorough assessment allows the school social worker to discover the root of the student's problem and then to develop effective intervention plans (NASW, 2002, Standard 13).

DIVERGENT ROLES

The most effective assessment is completed within the school system by a variety of professionals. The school psychologist is able to test for many emotional, behavioral, and learning problems. Some districts employ diagnosticians, who are certified professionals with 2 years of teaching experience and training in testing. The school diagnostician can test for learning problems and administer IQ tests to assure that a child is performing at the appropriate level for his or her ability. School counselors also perform testing.

Collaboration between professionals, parents, students, and other family members is essential for proper assessment and treatment. The ability of all members of the professional community to engage with and inform parents and students can positively impact a child's education experience. Combined information from a team of school professionals is much more comprehensive than information obtained from a single source. The typical team consists of the following professionals:

- School social workers
- School counselors
- Psychologists
- Diagnosticians
- Special education or general education teachers
- School administrators
- Speech–language pathologist
- English as a second language teacher or educational interpreter
- School nurses (used only occasionally)

The team must work together and share its assessments with parents, the student, and classroom teachers who would benefit from the information and be able to work more effectively with the student.

A complete assessment must include the following components:

- Vision and hearing screening.
- Cognitive screening, which shows the student's ability to learn
- Achievement tests to measure student's present level of learning in school.
- Tests of social and behavioral functioning to show how well the student gets along with others.
- Developmental history, which gives information about the family background, including developmental delays and illnesses.
- Other areas as needed, such as language difficulties where English is not the student's first language (Friend, 2005).

All assessments used for placement in schools must be completed by professionals who are trained to administer specific tests. Testing must be completed by qualified professionals who use valid assessment instruments. The criteria for determining that testing will be fair and nondiscriminatory is specified in the Individuals with Disabilities Education Act (Friend, 2005).

Once testing is completed, three questions must be answered by the multidisciplinary team:

1. Does the student have a disability?
2. Does the disability adversely affect the student's education?
3. Can the student's needs be addressed through special education (Friend, 2005)?

THE INDIVIDUALIZED EDUCATION PLAN

To qualify for many special education services, students' test results must show a discrepancy between their ability and their performance. If a student qualifies for special education services, an individual education plan (IEP) meeting is scheduled. The meeting must include the parent, the student (if interested), school administrator, special education teacher, regular education teacher, an individual who can interpret the evaluation results, a school district representative, representatives from outside agencies providing transition services, and other individuals with expertise and knowledge about the student. School counselors, psychologists, and social workers often are invited to IEP meetings.

When placement teams determine student needs, special education services provide many options to address these needs. These include resource and content mastery courses designed to work intensively in the areas where students experience skill deficits. Students can be placed in separate classrooms or separate schools that address behavioral problems. Students can be placed in a residential facility, at home, in a psychiatric hospital, or, in some cases, in drug or alcohol rehabilitation programs. School social workers often are utilized to help students who have been placed in separate classes or schools. The IEP committee usually will determine the social work treatment goals. Where the IEP contains such goals, the school social worker must attend annual IEP meetings to report on the completion rate of each goal.

THE INDIVIDUALS WITH DISABILITIES EDUCATION ACT

The Individuals with Disabilities Education Act (IDEA) ensures the rights of students with disabilities to a free public education that meets their unique needs. The act protects the rights of such children and their parents. The principles included in the act "include zero reject, free appropriate public education (FAPE), least restrictive environment (LRE), nondiscriminatory evaluation, parent and family rights, and procedural safeguards" (Friend, 2005, p. 14).

Zero reject means that a school cannot tell parents it will not provide a program for their child. If there is no program for a student with a disability, the school must either create one or arrange for the student to attend one elsewhere. Zero reject includes a system or set of procedures for alerting the public that services are available for students with disabilities and for distributing print materials, conducting screenings, and completing other activities to ensure that students with disabilities are identified.

Free appropriate education means that students with disabilities are entitled to educational programs and services, including evaluations, transportation, and related services, that are free of cost and appropriate to meet their individual needs.

Least restrictive environment means the school must always justify the need to place students out of regular classes and into special classes.

Nondiscriminatory evaluation refers to the rights of students and their parents to unbiased assessments as part of the special education decision-making process.

Parent and family rights to confidentiality are specified by IDEA to assure that information regarding a student's disability is kept highly confidential.

Procedural safeguards are ensured through IDEA so that any decisions concerning students with disabilities are made with parent input and in compliance with clear procedures (Friend, 2005, pp. 15–16).

Students Not Included in IDEA

Students not included in the categories defined in IDEA include the following:

Gifted and Talented

Only 30 states mandate services for students who are gifted and talented. Some students have a disability and are also considered gifted and talented. This means they are considered exceptional twice and need an array of services (Friend, 2005).

Attention-Deficit/Hyperactivity Disorder

Sometimes students with a diagnosis of ADHD receive special education services because their problems meet the criteria described under the "Other Health Impaired" category of IDEA. When students don't qualify for special education services, they may be qualified to receive extra help at school because of Section 504 of the Americans with Disabilities Act, which is discussed below. This support is usually limited to accommodations made in general education classrooms, such as extra time to take tests, shortened assignments, individual help from a teacher, or any other accommodations that will assist the student to perform at his or her maximum potential.

There is a debate over whether mental and learning disorders are a result of genetics or the situation in which the child was raised. ADHD is often found in family genetics. This sometimes creates difficulties in intervention because one of the parents may manifest the same behaviors as the child, and, thus, the child does not appear to be dysfunctional to that parent. Accordingly, school social workers should always consider the family system when they attempt to implement an intervention plan (NASW, 2002, Standard 13).

The most effective treatment for ADHD entails a three-pronged approach. This approach includes counseling with both the parent and child; academic intervention, which includes breaking down work into small pieces; and medication. The school social worker has the flexibility to work with the student at school and to intervene with the parents at home. Consistency in discipline and structured activities at home that are broken into small segments of time can help children with ADHD complete their work and maintain a sense of self-esteem.

SECTION 504 OF THE REHABILITATION ACT OF 1973

The Rehabilitation Act of 1973 (Public Law 93-112) was the first legislation in the United States designed to create civil rights for citizens with disabilities. Section 504, a federal civil rights law that protects individuals with functional disabilities (Friend, 2005), states:

> No qualified handicapped person shall, on the basis of handicap, be excluded from participation in, be denied the benefits of, or otherwise be subjected to discrimination under any program or activity which receives or benefits from Federal financial assistance. (Section 504, 29 U.S.C. Section 794(a))

Disabilities are defined in the act as impairments that significantly limit one or more major life activities, including walking, seeing, hearing, and learning (Friend, 2005). In 1990, the Americans with Disabilities Act (ADA) used the same criteria to describe a disability, but whereas the Rehabilitation Act of 1973 applies only to programs that receive federal assistance, the sanctions of the ADA apply to both the public and private sectors.

STUDENTS AT RISK FOR SCHOOL FAILURE

Among those students most at risk for failure are those who may be homeless, abuse drugs or other substances, live in poverty, or have other problems that can affect their learning (Friend, 2005) and social interactions. Many of these students use anger and aggression at school because they don't have positive outlets for their anger. When a teacher knows a student well enough to see that he or she is becoming angry, the teacher may be able to redirect the student's attention and avert the angry outburst. School social workers should help teachers become aware of the cycle of violence, as described by Colvin, so they can stop such angry student outbursts (Walker, Colvin, & Ramsey, 1995, p. 98). The cycle of violence is discussed more fully in Chapter 6.

School social workers should explain to teachers how to utilize behavior-instruction plans with high-risk students. These plans help clarify what behavior is acceptable and what is not. Behavior instruction plans also reinforce students for behaving in a positive way. They help give responsibility and control to students because they clarify what is expected of them. A behavior instruction plan includes the following five steps:

1. Specify behavior expectation.
2. Explain behavior expectation.
3. Provide structured opportunities to practice behavioral expectations.
4. Provide pre-correction for problem settings and individual students.
5. Provide strong reinforcements for demonstrations of expected behavior (Walker et al., 1995, p. 135).

In other words, tell them what you want, show them what it looks like, practice, and reinforce.

School social workers can stress the importance of creating clear expectations and structure at school so that at-risk students don't encounter frustrating surprises. If there is going to be a change in the school schedule, the social worker can inform at-risk students in advance so they can anticipate and adjust to the change. Providing planners, calendars, and to-do lists and teaching the students how to organize and structure their own time can help eliminate frustration.

UNDERSTANDING PARENTAL BARRIERS AND CULTURAL DIFFERENCES WITHIN THE SCHOOL SYSTEM

Poverty

Poverty and its effects are among the most difficult obstacles for parents and children to overcome. "One-fifth of all children in the United States live below the poverty level" (Lareau, 2003, p. 28). Poverty places individuals in a powerless situation where they don't feel they can make any impact on their own lives, their children's lives, and the institutions they deal with.

Children form beliefs and values based on their experiences within their families and communities. Families who intermittently earn low wages *sometimes* experience vulnerability resulting from their inability to cover their own living expenses, whereas vulnerability has *always* been a concrete experience for those living in generational poverty (DeVol, 2004).

In his mental model for poverty, Philip E. DeVol explains that children from poverty have a hard time just making it through the day. They have constant concerns about health, school, after-school day care, clothing, and safety. DeVol's mental model for poverty provides a frame of reference for understanding the challenges faced by children and parents who are living below the poverty level. These challenges include housing that is either crowded and unsafe or isolated, insufficient transportation, constant worries over money, inadequate food and poor nutrition, health care burdens, more day-to-day problems than can adequately be managed, constant concern over crime and safety, dependence on neighbors for survival, and constant involvement with multiple service agencies (DeVol, 2004, pp. 3–5).

Barriers to Parental Participation

Parental involvement and expectations play a major role in student success. Barriers to parents' participation in their child's education include work, second jobs, or caring for other children or elderly parents. Families who come from foreign countries also face language barriers, a lack of understanding of the customs in the United States, and transportation difficulties (Friend, 2005). Some may be undocumented aliens who are afraid to deal with the system for fear of being discovered.

School social workers can encourage parental participation in the following ways:

1. Use family-centered practice. Use the strengths perspective and provide choices. Support the entire family, not just one child.

2. Respect the uniqueness of families. Ask the family members about their needs, and don't make assumptions about their culture.

3. Recognize that families have different understandings of their child's special needs. Let the family members discuss their specific knowledge and what they think would help their child. Be available to offer whatever assistance the family requests.

4. Match strategies and resources to family needs. Find out the parents' specific concerns and offer specific ideas for help with those issues (Friend, 2005).

5. Encourage school personnel to provide parents with monthly calendars or newsletters containing the school schedule, individual classroom events, and upcoming schoolwide events (Walker et al., 1995).

One of the ways in which social workers and teachers can involve parents in their children's school is with a letter of introduction. A letter introduces the social worker or teacher to the parents and describes the services offered. A sample introduction letter from a social worker is found in Appendix 3.1.

Racial and Cultural Factors

Racial and cultural factors often influence how students succeed and are accepted at school, whether by their peers or school personnel. The way in which a student's racial and ethnic backgrounds are received at school plays a major role in his or her attitudes about school. Likewise, parents' attitudes about school directly affect their children's behavior at school, and those attitudes may vary according to race and ethnicity. When there is trust between children and parents, the child has a sense of obligation to fulfill parents' expectations. If parents feel that the school is a friendly, welcoming place where their race and culture are accepted, they are more likely to help their children succeed. If parents feel that children of their race or ethnicity are unaccepted or mistreated at school, then they will be less likely to encourage their children to succeed.

Asian parents are less likely to talk about school or to help with the child's homework than Caucasian parents, although they have higher educational expectations for their children and stricter rules for maintaining grades (Kao, 1995). Immigrant families also are less likely to join a PTA, volunteer at school, speak to teachers, or attend class events (Kao and Tienda, 1995). Immigrants from Mexico tend to have lower parental involvement in school learning, extracurricular activities, and other learning than immigrant Asians and Caucasian students born in the United States (Hao & Bonstead-Bruns, 1998).

Parenting Style

The term "parenting style" refers to child-rearing practices and parent–child relationships. Parenting styles are not gauged by the *frequency* of the parent–child interaction. Instead, they are gauged on the *strength* and *quality* of the interaction (Pong, Hoa, & Gardner, 2005). Parenting styles vary by racial and ethnic group. Most studies on parenting styles show that non-Hispanic white families are less authoritarian than Asian and Hispanic families (Pong et al., 2005).

The Importance of Understanding Race and Ethnicity

Knowledge about diverse cultures and how parental involvement and attitudes affect children's school performance is essential for school social workers. School social workers should make the effort to understand the various racial and ethnic groups found in each school they serve.

> Different cultures have different beliefs about child behaviors that are acceptable and those that are not. Attitudes about accepting help, such as social or mental health services, vary among cultures and the practitioner must be sensitive to the implications of discussing a child's "problem behaviors" with a parent who may feel that the child's behavior is a reflection on the quality the child's parenting and the family honor. (Webb, 2003, p. 13)

Children and adolescents from immigrant families are often caught between the values and norms at school and those at home (Huang, 1989; Wu, 2001). If the school social worker makes the effort to build relationships with parents and helps the parents stay informed about school activities and problems, there is a great potential for this relationship to influence the child's school performance.

TREATMENT APPROACHES FOR DIVERSE PROBLEMS WITHIN SPECIFIC SCHOOL SETTINGS

Helping Children Deal with Stress at School

This section describes some typical problems presented by students and discusses how social workers can deal with them. Many societal pressures contribute to children's behavior at school. Schools are often large and impersonal. Homework starts at an early age, and many parents are not home for a sufficient period of time to help their children with homework. Many districts have eliminated recess. High divorce rates and the rapid pace of daily life have put pressure on families. In addition, students experience pressure to perform on standardized tests at school in order to be promoted. Some of the consequences of "No Child Left Behind," according to Irwin Hyman, a school psychologist, are that the law puts pressure on school boards, who then put pressure on the superintendent, who puts pressure on the teachers, and the students are the victims (Hardy, 2003, p. 11). These pressures continue through to college. A study of college students at Kansas State University found that the percentage of students being treated for depression doubled between 1989 and 2001 (Hardy, 2003).

Attachment Difficulties

Children who have difficulty leaving home and attending public school can benefit from a number of interventions. Behavioral interventions are common and are usually based on getting the child to stay in school. Cognitive-behavioral interventions, in which the student is rewarded for successful efforts, have had varying degrees of success (Gosschalk, 2004). Students who are not rewarded feel depressed and discouraged. Family involvement can increase the success of behavioral outcomes. The family interventions should be based on behavior management techniques that the social worker teaches the parent. Behavior management also includes parental actions that contribute to the child's success. For example, parents cannot let children stay at home when they cry, act sick, and complain about school. Teacher support for attendance must be included. Also, the school administrators must be part of the intervention plan. Reinforcement should be based on how long the child stays at school, decreasing the frequency of tantrums and crying at school, and working on eliminating anxiety at night and in the mornings before school. The child should not feel forced into compliance but should be coached. The social worker should praise the parent, who then can use positive reinforcement and praise to encourage proper behavior from the child. Teachers also should be involved in encouraging the child to form friendships with other students so that there are positive reasons for the student to attend school.

Anxiety Disorders

Anxiety disorders in children and adolescents include conditions such as posttraumatic stress disorder, panic attacks, obsessive–compulsive disorder, and school phobia (American Psychiatric Association, 2000,

p. 429). Children who experience a specific phobia usually react almost immediately on confronting the phobic stimulus (American Psychiatric Association, 2000, p. 449). Children who live in violent and abusive homes often are hypervigilant at school and show signs of post-traumatic stress disorder. Many anxiety disorders can lead to panic attacks and avoidance behavior. Panic attacks are characterized by intense fear or discomfort in the absence of real danger, accompanied by cognitive or somatic symptoms. Some of the symptoms associated with panic attacks include shortness of breath, dizziness, fear of choking, shaking, sweating, palpitations, chest pain, and nausea (American Psychiatric Association, 2000, p. 430).

A recent study on children with anxiety disorders, which included DSM-IV-TR criteria for separation anxiety disorder, generalized anxiety disorder, and school phobia, found that cognitive-behavioral therapy employed in a group setting along with parent training had significant benefits. The study also found that on a tertiary level it was possible to decrease the amount of anxiety experienced by children at school through behavioral and group therapy (Bernstein, Layne, Egan, & Tennison, 2005).

School social workers can assist children with anxiety disorders by allowing them to visit the social worker whenever they feel an impending attack. Children with separation anxiety and school phobia should be allowed to begin their day in the school social worker's office, as needed, to discuss their fears and to relax. Social workers can teach children how to relieve their own stress through relaxation exercises. These exercises include deep breathing, slow tensing and releasing of muscles, and visual imagery of places that are not stressful.

A tool that works well is to teach children to look at their thumbnail and picture themselves doing something fun while they stare at their nail. They must count to 100 slowly and engage in deep breathing while they stare at their thumbnail and relieve stress. Learning how to do self-relaxation may relieve anxiety merely by giving the child a sense of control over the environment.

Autism Spectrum Disorder/Asperger Syndrome

Autism has three defining features:

1. Qualitative impairment in socialization.
2. Qualitative impairments in verbal and nonverbal communication.
3. Restricted and repetitive patterns of behavior, with typical age of onset being prior to 36 months (American Psychiatric Association, 2000).

Symptoms of autism need to be interpreted based on the child's developmental level, but it is difficult to meet the DSM criteria before at least the age of 3 (Gomez & Baird, 2005). Early childhood intervention programs are often involved in assessing children with autism. Once a child is identified, school social workers can be of assistance to families beginning at the age of 3. Many families are relieved by the diagnostic process itself and the development of a treatment plan that results from a new understanding of their children (Barton & Robins, 2000).

Some school districts employ autism experts to work with families at home. The school social worker can assist the autism specialist by accompanying him or her on home visits to help establish therapeutic rapport. Social workers can help the parents understand the diagnosis of autism and be of assistance in helping the parents make adaptations in the home and with behavior management.

School social workers also can be of assistance in working with other school professionals to assure appropriate classroom placement for autistic children. As autistic students begin to make plans for graduation and for transitioning into different types of learning environments after leaving public school, the school social worker can provide information on community agencies and programs that will help the students make the transition into new programs and services.

Case Example

Tim, age 18, had been receiving special education services throughout his attendance in public school, having been diagnosed as autistic with borderline mental retardation. He was in a transition program that was assisting with employment skills and had been removed from several work placements because of an array of problems, including not following instructions and poor social interactions. The parents were deeply concerned about his ability to hold down a job and continue in some kind of training program. It was supposed to be Tim's last year in public school. Because of his age and his status as the youngest in the family, the parents wanted him to make an effective transition from high school.

Both parents worked during the day, so the school district autism specialist and the school social worker scheduled 1-hour weekly visits to the home in the evenings to assist Tim and his parents in learning and applying social skills to help him hold down a job. The treatment lasted for 1 full school year. The school social worker taught social skills and had Tim role-play behaviors in specific situations. The social worker also addressed issues such as hygiene, appropriate dress, language, and behavior that could be applied on a job. The autism specialist followed through on applying some of the principles addressed by the school social worker. For example, she took Tim on the city buses the first time and then, to create independence, assigned him a route to follow the next week on his own. He improved over the course of the year-long treatment. The intervention served as a support to the parents and made it possible for Tim to enter the work force after completing high school.

Skill Deficits

When teaching social skills to students, the school social worker must distinguish between skill deficits, performance deficits, fluency deficits, and competing problem behaviors (Gresham & Elliott, 1990; Gresham, 2002). A student with *skill deficits* does not know the proper way to behave and needs to be taught specific skills just like academic skills. Teaching social skills involves giving explicit instructions that include modeling, coaching, and behavioral rehearsal. *Performance deficits* are corrected by focusing on motivation or reinforcement to increase the frequency with which a particular skill is demonstrated. This can be done by manipulating antecedents (e.g., cues, prompts) or by manipulating consequences. *Fluency deficits* are evident when the student attempts to perform a specific skill but does it in an awkward, stilted manner. Practice and corrective feedback with reinforcement are the best ways to teach these skills (Gresham & Elliott, 1990; Gresham, 2002).

Mental Disorders

School social workers have the clinical ability to help children deal with special DSM-IV-TR diagnoses by helping them understand their particular disorder and learn to cope with it. In doing so, the social worker will need to exercise skills involved in forming relationships and building trust and rapport. Children who are failing, not attending, and misbehaving at school are often acting out fears and frustrations that originate in bigger issues in their lives. The school social worker often has to get to the root of the problem. He or she should never take any problem at face value but must look deeply into the issue to find the source of the problem. Likewise, the social worker must let self-determination guide the treatment approach for the student, even when it may seem counterproductive (NASW, 2002, Standard 5). Students will do much better if they have a choice in determining their own treatment goals.

Use of the Strengths Perspective

School social workers must utilize the strengths perspective to assist students in seeing the problem as one that they can solve. Six principles have been identified as critical for strengths-based practice:

1. Every individual, group, family, and community has strengths.
2. Trauma, abuse, illness, and struggle may be injurious, but they also may be sources of challenge and opportunity.
3. Assume that you do not know the upper limits of the capacity to grow and change, and take individual, group, and community aspirations seriously.
4. We best serve clients by collaborating with them.
5. Every environment is full of resources.
6. Caring, caretaking, and context are important (Saleebey, 1997, pp. 12–15).

The following guidelines can assist social workers in completing a strengths-based assessment:

1. Give preeminence to the client's understanding of the facts.
2. Believe the client.
3. Discover what the client wants.
4. Move the assessment toward personal and environmental strengths.
5. Make the assessment of strengths multidimensional.
6. Use the assessment to discover uniqueness.
7. Use language the client can understand.
8. Make the assessment a joint activity between worker and client.
9. Reach a mutual agreement on the assessment.
10. Avoid blame and blaming.
11. Assess, do not diagnose (Cowger, 1997, pp. 63–66).

School social workers have access to an entire school community full of knowledgeable professionals to assist in interventions and to help implement treatment. The school system can provide a wonderful source of support for the student and family when the proper resources are mobilized by a social worker. School social workers have the opportunity to build positive relationships with students. When students feel a sense of trust in one of the adults in the school, they have a sense of empowerment and control that may help them improve their academic performance and social interactions.

Advocating for Students

School social workers are often the only advocate for students in a large school (NASW, 2002, Standard 8). If students have difficulties with teachers or administrators, they are often too shy to speak for themselves. The school social worker can empower students, and with the social worker's support, they can act together to solve problems.

Case Example

The assistant principal for discipline and attendance problems in a large urban high school had a very quick temper. He would usually respond with a loud voice and a red, angry face whenever a student was out of line. The school social worker knew that the assistant principal really cared for the students and had their best interests at heart but had a hard time keeping his temper under control.

Whenever any of the students on the social worker's caseload had trouble with the administration, the school social worker would coach them on how to behave. She would tell them to approach the assistant principal in an apologetic and sincere way. She would encourage them to take responsibility for their misbehavior and to stay calm and not become angry if the assistant principal lost his temper. The social worker tried to help the students understand that the assistant principal's behavior was not really directed toward them personally. The social worker told the students that if they would remain calm, the assistant principal would help them come up with a positive solution to their problems once he had calmed down. The information and support from the social worker helped students have more positive interactions with the assistant principal than they might have had without the social worker's help. Those students who were not coached by the social worker would often lose their own tempers and get into deeper trouble than those who would remain calm and apologetic.

Making Referrals

School social workers coordinate the efforts of educators, families, and outside agency personnel to ensure that students receive all the support they need. The school social worker needs to become familiar with the array of services outside the schools so that he or she can assist in linking families with specific needs to agencies that can offer help (NASW, 2002, Standard 6). Social workers can link families with needs to charitable organizations that can provide clothing and food and arrange for counseling when necessary (Friend, 2005).

In large urban areas, it can be difficult to learn about all of the agencies available to provide services. Most cities publish a social service directory that every social worker should obtain. Likewise, social workers should become familiar with agencies in the specific community in which they work and make visits to the agencies to assess the quality of services.

Social workers should remember that referrals are not complete until the person being referred has made contact and has determined that the new agency can meet his or her needs. Social workers are accountable for the referrals they make, so they should make sure that the agencies to which they make referrals are legitimate and provide the services they claim to provide. If a client is harmed as a result of an inappropriate referral, the social worker who made the original referral may share in the liability.

In small rural communities, it is often easier to gain direct information about available services. However, the difficulty in most small communities is a lack of services and lack of public transportation to help clients access the services. A school social worker may have to take on a broader role in small communities because he or she may be the only social worker in the community. Generalist practice skills are helpful for all school social workers as they work across all levels of practice.

CONCLUSION

School social workers are essential to coordinate assessment information, involve the professionals at the school, and include the family in developing effective treatment plans. They work within the system to understand barriers that affect parental involvement, such as poverty. Social workers provide links to community agencies and act as advocates for students. They are advocates both within the school system and with outside agencies and family members. The support of a school social worker is invaluable in retaining high-risk students and helping them find success in school.

Discussion Topics

1. Research the history of IDEA and special education laws.
2. How does poverty affect a child's school performance?
3. Discuss how parental interactions with the school affect children.
4. How does the use of the strengths perspective improve school social work services?

APPENDIX 3.1. Sample Letter from a School Social Worker

Dear Parents:

Welcome to [Name of School]. I am [Name], the school social worker. I am available to help you with any school-related problems that either you or your child may have. I can be reached at [phone number] or [e-mail address]. Please contact me anytime you have a question or whenever you or your child would like to talk with me. I look forward to meeting you.

Sincerely,
[Name]

4

School Social Work with Children in Preschool to Grade 3

Beginning public school is a milestone in a child's life. It is an exciting time for children and parents. Children with special needs can and should be identified prior to beginning kindergarten, and placed in classrooms that are appropriate to their individual needs. Government programs, such as Child Find and Best Practices, help provide families with support before their special needs children start school. Many government programs, such as Head Start, help smooth the transition into kindergarten for children and parents.

School social workers are often part of the diagnostic team that helps identify special developmental, learning, and emotional needs. They are in a strategic position to assist families in coping with the difficulties encountered when a child is diagnosed with a disability or a special need. Because social workers are part of the school system, they have specialized knowledge that can help prepare the family and child to enter school.

An estimated 29% of children with disabilities drop out of school (U.S. Department of Education, 2002). Some childhood disorders become diagnosable once the child enters school. Intervention at a primary level with a disabled child and family can be critical to ensure future success in school.

EARLY DIAGNOSIS OF DEVELOPMENTAL DELAYS

Early diagnosis of developmental disorders helps the family understand, accept, and deal with the child's problems. A child with a disability and his or her family are given educational options and support through the Individuals with Disabilities Education Act (IDEA). IDEA applies to preschool children, as well as children in grade school and beyond, until the child is 21 years old. If the child is found to have one of the categories of disabilities outlined in the act and it involves a significant problem, such as mental retardation, physical and sensory disabilities, or autism, then he or she can receive help through the school. Children with less significant disabilities related to language development or motor skills will be labeled developmentally delayed but can still be served through IDEA (Friend, 2005).

Early assessment and diagnosis provide professionals with the opportunity to help children learn to adjust to a disability. Parents of children with disabilities need to learn how to help them, and the family needs to adjust to and cope with the disability. Child Find is the public awareness, screening, and evaluation mechanism set up to help school districts locate and identify children with special needs. If the family has a pediatrician, the doctor will usually make a referral for assessment and tell the parents about help through the local school district. However, immigrant children and those from lower socioeconomic levels who do not have access to adequate health care may not hear about the services available through IDEA unless school districts reach out to them.

Case Example

Max was lying on the floor of his kindergarten classroom screaming and crying when the school social worker walked in. His special education teacher had called the social worker to see if she could help calm him down. Max had been crying and screaming for the previous hour. It was the second week of school and Max had exhibited the same behavior every day.

The social worker sat on the floor with Max while the teacher removed the other students from the classroom. She started speaking slowly and softly, telling Max that he would be okay and that he was safe. The social worker was able to calm him down by giving him individual attention and speaking in a soothing, nonthreatening voice that constantly reassured him. Once Max was calm, the social worker was able to find out that he was frightened and that he did not want to be at school because he didn't know the teacher or his classmates.

For the next week, the social worker met Max at the door when he came to school and talked to him about what would happen during the day. Max was able to begin meeting his classmates and forming relationships with them. The constant reassurance and intervention helped him relax at school. Max was developmentally delayed and afraid, and did not want to be in school.

The social worker worked closely with Max's teacher to find out what was planned for the next week at school. The social worker wrote down the lesson plans and called Max's mother weekly to inform her what would be covered in school each day. Max's mother was able to prepare Max for school activities and eliminate the element of surprise. It helped him begin to look forward to school. The social worker also referred Max to the community mental health center so that he could be evaluated for medications. The mental health center determined that he needed medication and provided it. The combination of daily intervention at school to help him feel at ease, meetings with the mother, and intervention from an outside agency helped Max adjust to school.

THE DIAGNOSTIC PROCESS

Children with delays are sometimes misdiagnosed. A child who develops slowly may be slow because of abuse or neglect rather than a lack of innate abilities. School social workers assist in the diagnostic process by obtaining information from a variety of sources, such as teachers, parents, siblings, outside agencies, the child's medical doctor, and any other professional who is involved with the family. In some cases, a child's developmental delays, such as problems with toilet training, language lag, fear of separation, and attachment difficulties, can be tied to difficulties in the home. Language lags may occur because the child is learning English as a second language and may have no English spoken in the home. School social workers need to obtain as much information as possible to assist in making a thorough and complete diagnosis of a child.

Multilevel Perspective

School social workers should be instrumental in helping identify families in the school district who have special needs. School districts currently send out letters and announce preschool screenings and testing. The school social worker should be listed in the announcements as the contact person in connection with these screenings so that families have one specific individual with whom they can interact. Likewise, school social workers should work with community agencies, such as those offering early childhood intervention (ECI), to let them know about the services provided by the school district. If a referral is made to the school district through an outside agency, the social worker should be the contact person in the school district for the referring agency and the family who is being referred. Families benefit from a positive relationship with one staff member at a school, such as a social worker, who can also help manage the services provided to their children.

When someone such as a school social worker understands the background of a child's disorder, he or she can help the child. School social workers also provide the added dimension of the strengths perspective (NASW, 2002, Standard 5), which can help the child and family to focus on their positive abilities and assets. When a child focuses on strengths and the social work relationship is based on collaboration and empowerment, the child will develop the self-esteem and positive attitude necessary to overcome the obstacles associated with his or her disability.

Family members need help in understanding their child's disability. Social workers have communication skills that can assist the families in getting answers to their questions. They also can serve as the family's advocate with the school district (NASW, 2002, Standard 8). The school social worker is also the person in a school district with knowledge of outside agencies who can help families with appropriate referrals, either for services or information from community agencies (NASW, 2002, Standard 6).

Sometimes behaviors that are totally appropriate for the child's native culture may seem inappropriate at school. For example "a male who has been taught that 'macho' means 'stand up for yourself' cannot be criticized for initiating a fist fight with a bully who called him a 'wimp' " (Webb, 2003, p. 13). Knowledge about unique features of the child's culture may help prevent a misdiagnosis. The social worker needs to find the best approach to assist the school community in becoming aware of the different cultures of students attending the school. The questions addressed in a culturagram are discussed in Chapter 2. Some of the cultural issues school social workers should identify are the language spoken in the home, the parental legal status, and the reasons for immigration. Social workers can reach teachers and administrators through staff development and communication about the diversity issues on each campus. Social workers should assist teachers in trying to meet the individual needs of new students and help the teacher make the child and parent feel comfortable.

Children with language skills impairment may be misdiagnosed initially. Many parents do not speak English, and their children may be speaking English as a second language at school. It is necessary to know the difference between a child who has a language lag because he or she is trying to speak a second language and a child with true impairment in language skills. Providing school districts with information about family background is an important contribution that school social workers can make.

Because of increased immigration to the United States, school districts are dealing with diverse populations (Boothe, 2000), and school social workers should assure that the school setting meets their needs. As school social workers become aware that children from different cultures will be entering the school, the social worker should help the teachers and administration become aware of any unique cultural differences or behaviors that might be encountered. This information will assist school professionals as they diagnose a child.

GOAL SETTING

Parents' wishes and aspirations for their children begin to form during the preschool years. Sometimes these wishes are manifest as goals or wished-for outcomes (Lysyuk, 1998). When parents learn that their child has a disability, they need help restructuring their goals and expressing grief over the loss of their previous expectations about the child. Parents need a complete and accurate picture of the child's capabilities in order to restructure these goals.

School social workers should understand the types of activities and goals that are appropriate for children at different developmental stages so they can convey this information to the parents. Parental expectations and goal setting should be linked to the child's abilities but should also stretch the child. Parental expectations that communicate belief in a child's abilities help build resiliency and self-esteem, particularly when the child successfully masters the goals. When parents have realistic expectations and the child is able to meet those expectations, it builds confidence that can become a protective factor to assist the child when other obstacles are encountered. The child is then able to transfer the successful strategies that were employed in mastering one goal to mastering another.

It is difficult to learn what is important to very young children. However, beginning at about age 2, children can express their needs and wishes. Productive goal development emerges at about this age and is accomplished by learning from the child what he or she would like to achieve. Productive goals come about as a result of learning how the child would transform the environment either concretely or in an imaginary way (Lysyuk, 1998). The school social worker can learn what the child considers important and wants to achieve through behavior observation and through play and art therapies that allow the social worker to uncover feelings that the child is unable to express in other ways.

Positive adult–child relationships help provide the encouragement children need to express their wishes and achieve their goals (Lysyuk, 1998). School social workers should assist parents in gaining an understanding of what the child wants to achieve. The social worker also should communicate the child's wishes and goals to other school personnel.

When the school social worker understands the needs of the child and family, it is possible to write a treatment plan that provides a method for working toward all of their goals. A treatment plan helps clarify what work needs to be done by setting goals and objectives and clarifying how they will be accomplished. A good treatment or action plan indicates who will do what, when, and how. (See Appendix 4.1 for a sample treatment plan format.)

ECOLOGICAL PERSPECTIVE/ HOME–SCHOOL NETWORKS

The ecological perspective emphasizes observing the child within the context of the family home to understand the influence of the social environment on the child's development (Allen & Tracy, 2004). Observing a child's self-directed abilities is part of a complete assessment. The social worker can gain useful information on family interactions and patterns by observing the child at home. School social workers are skilled in making behavioral observations and can be of assistance to the parents while the child is being tested and observed. They are in the perfect position to provide the link between the school, home, and community.

A home–school collaboration model that seeks to support families and the long-term development of the child is critical for the child's success (Meyer, 2000). Using the strengths perspective, a school social worker should assist the parents in building a positive vision about their child's future, one that includes the services and support that will enable the child to live, work, and recreate in the community (Meyer, 2000).

Parent Support Groups

School social workers can assist in setting up a support group for parents of children with developmental delays and disabilities. The group can provide mutual support and information so that parents are not totally dependent on school personnel for information and services for their children. The group will fare better if it has a "nonprofessional atmosphere" and the parents feel free to take the lead on issues. Parent-to-parent sharing should be encouraged (Meyer, 2000). The group may become an informal source of support to other parents with disabled children.

Parental Involvement

School social workers are in a position to build rapport with the family. When a child with difficulties begins school, the social worker should serve as the contact person for the family. The most important aspect of professional intervention is genuine care about the families and children served (Fox, Vaughn, Wyatte, & Dunlap, 2002). School social workers are a key link between the school and the home, promoting the family's involvement in the child's education and helping school staff understand and relate to the diversity of family forms, lifestyles, and backgrounds (Allen & Tracy, 2004).

Children do much better in school when their parents are involved and interact frequently with the child's teacher or other school personnel. According to researchers, the best way to achieve positive outcomes for the child, the family, and the school is for families to be involved in their child's education (Allen & Tracy, 2004). If the link with school personnel is established early for the family, the transition to school will be smoother, and there is an increased likelihood that the family will continue to interact with the school. Family involvement in education is a strong predictor of student achievement across all economic groups and grade levels (Booth & Dunn, 1996; U.S. Department of Education, 1994).

Home–school partnerships have received increasing support since the 1970s. Epstein and Lee (1995) noted that home–school communication signals to children the value of education and provides support and continuity between these two primary spheres of influence in a child's life (Epstein & Lee, 1995; Broussard, 2003).

Germain (2002) observed that school social worker "stand at the interface not only of child and school, but of family and school, and community and school. Thus, they are in a position to help child, parents, and community develop social competence and, at the same time, to help increase the school's responsiveness to the needs and aspirations of children, parents, and community" (Germain, 2002, p. 27). School social workers must work to ensure that parents stay involved in their child's education (Underwood & Kopels, 2004).

Program Example

Frederick County, Maryland, has created a program for at-risk families and their children from infancy through age 18. The program, which is known as Community Agency School Services (CASS), includes a network of 10 licensed, master's-level social workers. Each social worker is assigned to a high school and a feeder school.

The program began with identifying a need and community networking. It was initially funded by private and state grants. The program provides affordable, accessible resources and support. The emphasis of the program is on prevention and early intervention. CASS has formed partnerships over the past twelve years with local and state governments, health departments, juvenile justice agencies, mental health providers, the department of social services, churches, community charities, businesses, and citizens (Klein, 2004, p. 40). This program can serve as a model for school social workers to emulate within their own school districts and communities.

CHILDREN EXPOSED TO VIOLENT OR NEGLECTFUL HOME ENVIRONMENTS

Young children who are living in violent or neglectful situations are at risk for developing emotional disturbances and behavioral problems. Before beginning school, most children do not have outside sources to which they can reveal the trauma with which they may be living. Children also do not have enough perspective and experience to realize that the violent or neglectful situation in which they are living is not normal. School social workers who routinely make home visits to at-risk families may be able to detect child abuse and neglect at an early stage and make a referral to child welfare agencies that can help the child and parents.

Exposure to violence can be direct, such as experiencing actual physical injury, or indirect, such as witnessing parental violence. The types of behavioral problems resulting from exposure to violence include aggression, cruelty to animals, tantrums, "acting out," immaturity, truancy, and delinquent acts. Emotional problems resulting from exposure to violence include anxiety, anger, depression, withdrawal, low self-esteem, posttraumatic stress disorder (PTSD), and attachment disorder. However, sometimes the link between these problems and violence in the home is not detected.

Intimate partner violence has a profound effect on a child, even if the child is not the direct target of the violence. Indirect effects of intimate partner violence include:

1. Inconsistent or harsh disciplinary practices.
2. Disagreements about child rearing between the parents.
3. Parental stress, which may cause an inability to maintain close and positive parent–child relationships, ineffective and inconsistent discipline, and lack of attachment.

Often children are afraid to discuss abuse and neglect because they feel they are the cause of the problem. Families with a history of violence are often socially isolated. If there is no extended family nearby to notice the effects of the violence, the violence may go undetected until the child starts school. A professional social worker may be able to intervene early and help provide services for the child before he or she has been exposed to long-term violence. The longer a child is exposed to violence, the more severe the consequences are for the child (Groves, 2002; Osofsky, 1997).

Preschool children and those in the first few years of elementary school are the most vulnerable members of a household in which there is domestic violence. The child has no means of escape and no information to help him or her understand that the behavior is not normal and does not have to be endured. Children spend the majority of their time at home and school and have no other sources from which to gather information about appropriate behavior. This is particularly true for families who live in isolated rural communities or away from their extended family, or who are otherwise isolated. School social workers should pay particularly close attention to children in these vulnerable situations.

If treatment begins at a preventative level, the child's problem may not escalate to the tertiary level, in which the extreme consequences of abuse and neglect must be treated. School social workers frequently are in the position of being the one to whom abuse or neglect is reported. However, teachers sometimes hear about abuse or neglect from the child and ask the social worker to refer the case to child protective services for them. Surprisingly, the social worker's answer must usually be no. Most states require that the "outcry" witness (or person to whom the abuse or neglect was reported) must be the one to file the report with child protective services. The best way for a school social worker to handle these situations is to suggest that he or she accompany the teacher while the report is made and talk the teacher through the report. This will give the teacher the sense of security that is necessary when dealing with a new situation and will assure that the case is reported.

CLINICAL DISORDERS MANIFESTED IN EARLY CHILDHOOD

Attention-Deficit/Hyperactivity Disorder

"The essential feature of Attention-Deficit/Hyperactivity Disorder [ADHD] is a persistent pattern of inattention and/or hyperactivity-impulsivity that is more frequently displayed and more severe than is typically observed in individuals at a comparable level of development" (American Psychiatric Association, 2000, p. 85). ADHD is characterized by decreased attention and impulse control and increased activity levels. There are three types of ADHD: inattentive, hyperactive, and combined hyperactive and inattentive. ADHD must be diagnosed in more than one setting. Many of its characteristics do not become evident until a child is required to stay in a seat and concentrate on schoolwork for an extended period of time. The disorder can greatly affect the child's ability to take advantage of his or her educational opportunities, keep behavior under control, and interact with others in a positive way.

Boys are diagnosed with ADHD at a ratio of 3 to 1 over girls (Barkley, n.d.). This may be because boys with ADHD tend to be more mobile and physical than girls. Girls will often sit and daydream or withdraw when they have the inattentive type of ADHD rather than disrupt a class. As a consequence, girls with ADHD are not as readily noticeable.

Because ADHD must be diagnosed in more than one setting, school social workers, who are experienced at making behavioral observations, should observe the child at least twice at school. These observations should take place at different times during the day in order to see if some of the behaviors are related to factors such as being hungry, tired, or bored. The social worker should ask what specific behaviors the child is exhibiting before beginning the observation. Then the behavior observation should track the frequency of those behaviors during the observation period. A behavior observation form is included in Appendix 2.4 of Chapter 2.

A medical doctor (usually a neurologist) who is trying to make an accurate diagnosis will have more to work with if the school can provide specific data tracking the frequency and types of behaviors manifested at school. School social workers also should assist parents in observation of problem behaviors at home for a specific time period.

Once a child is diagnosed with ADHD, a school social worker should assist parents and teachers in breaking down student tasks into small, manageable pieces. School social workers should assist in teaching children with ADHD organizational and problem-solving skills to help them keep track of their schoolwork. Time management is also a necessary skill that must be taught to children with ADHD because ADHD is a temporal disorder. School social workers should help the child and parents realize that ADHD is not something that will go away but that it can be managed effectively if the tasks are small and the child receives support and positive reinforcement for incremental progress.

Children diagnosed with ADHD may qualify for special education under the "other health impairments" category (often referred to as OHI) of IDEA (Underwood & Kopels, 2004). The school social worker should work with school district special education departments to provide parents with a copy of the procedural safeguards and placement procedures for special education. The school social worker should try to help prepare the parents for the placement meeting, at which an individualized education plan (IEP) is created, so that the parents will understand the process and feel comfortable requesting what they feel is necessary as part of their child's IEP.

The most negative aspect of ADHD is that it rarely exists alone. It may be dually diagnosed with depression. ADHD also can lead to oppositional defiant disorder or conduct disorder if it is not managed. Children develop depression with ADHD because they often feel they have minimal control over their own behaviors. Teaching how to break down tasks and solve problems in incremental steps, along with helping the child to become organized, is the best gift a school social worker can give a child with ADHD.

The three-pronged approach that is most commonly recommended for ADHD includes behavior management for the child, counseling for the child and parents, and medications when necessary. This approach should be set up by the school social worker. Intervention with parents is essential to assure that the positive work done at school is consistently reinforced in the home. Helping parents and children learn to manage ADHD gives them a sense of control over the condition rather than a feeling of desperation. Once a positive approach has been effective, this helps encourage other positive actions from both the child and parents.

Case Example

Jimmy was continuously on the move in his kindergarten class. He would constantly get out of his seat and move around the room. The teacher could not get him to focus for more than 5 minutes at a time on a project, and he would not leave the other children near him alone. The teacher had reported his behavior to his mother, but the mother said she did not see any of the same behaviors at home and thought that the teacher needed to try some new techniques. The school social worker observed Jimmy's behavior at two different times during the school day and wrote how frequently Jimmy disrupted class activities by leaving his seat, talking out, and bothering other children. The school social worker gave this information to the mother. She also asked the mother if the school could arrange for a psychologist from the community mental health center to complete an assessment of Jimmy. The mother consented. She was invited to the school and given specific information from the psychologist, social worker, and teacher that convinced her that Jimmy's problems were real. The mother took Jimmy to his pediatrician. The doctor was able to use the information provided by the school to diagnose Jimmy with ADHD and prescribe medication.

The social worker and psychologist worked with the mother to teach her how to break tasks down for Jimmy and use positive reinforcement when he was successful. Both the mother and teacher were able to incorporate some of these strategies. Jimmy's behavior improved, and he had a successful second half of the school year. The early intervention and treatment helped put Jimmy on a path leading to positive outcomes at school rather than negative interactions and failure.

Autism Spectrum Disorder/Asperger Syndrome

Researchers continue to debate whether the social impairments in autism come from a social or cognitive deficit (Ruble, 2001). In DSM-IV-TR (American Psychiatric Association, 2000), autism is characterized by impairment in social interactions and communication and restricted, repetitive, and stereotyped patterns of behavior, interests, and activities (Friend, 2005). The DSM-IV-TR definition of autism encompasses pervasive developmental disorder, Asperger syndrome, and pervasive developmental disorder not otherwise specified (American Psychiatric Association, 2000). Quality of care by family members and professionals is critical in the development of children with autism (Simpson & Zionts, 2000).

Asperger syndrome is difficult to diagnose. Many of the symptoms also fit other diagnoses. In DSM-IV-TR, Asperger syndrome (called "Asperger's disorder" in DSM-IV-TR) is characterized by impaired social interaction and restricted, repetitive, stereotyped patterns of behavior, interests, and activities (American Psychiatric Association, 2000). Unlike autism, there are no significant early language delays.

Sometimes parents are afraid of having their child labeled at school, even if the parent already knows the child has a problem. School social workers should assist parents in understanding the programs and options available to a child with special needs. Parents need information about the steps involved in assessment, testing, and placement. They also need to know about placement options. Once parents understand the services available to their child, they no longer fear placing the child in special education.

The school social worker can assist children with autism spectrum disorder and Asperger syndrome by developing a positive relationship with these children. Once a relationship is developed, the social worker should be able to teach social skills that can help develop more positive peer and teacher relationships. Some of the teaching of social skills may have to be simplistic and done through short stories or while doing some other activity, such as puzzles or games. Many children with autism are particularly bright and like stories and games. Short stories that teach social skills are a great help.

Reading stories, especially fairy tales, can help teach social skills. Whenever the characters behave in an inappropriate manner, the school social worker should stop and ask why the behavior is wrong and what the character should do instead. Then the social worker can practice the appropriate skill with the child. School social workers can also cowrite stories with the child and have the characters act in a socially appropriate manner. The social worker and child can then practice the skill. Children respond to stories and games and do not even realize they are learning new skills.

The school social worker also can assist teachers and other school personnel to assure that there is structure and consistency in the daily routine at school for these children. The students' schedules should have the same activities each day at the same time. As much as possible, there should be little change, and if change is anticipated the children should be told in advance. Once a routine and schedule are stabilized, these children will begin to look forward to things they can count on. There should be little alteration or surprise in the daily routine. For these children there is comfort in an environment that is predictable and the same each day.

Case Example

Isaac was in kindergarten when the social worker first met him. He had a history of both sleeping and throwing tantrums at school. The teacher could not get him to do any work. He would enter the classroom each day, lay his head on his desk, and try to go to sleep. When the teacher would make demands on him to stand up and stay awake, he would throw tantrums. He bit the student next to him and tipped over his own chair and desk. He would scream and carry on until the teacher referred him to the office. In the office he would continue his tantrum. The school staff would try to calm him down, but eventually he would just stop and go to sleep. The school social worker spoke with Isaac's mother and learned that Isaac's pediatrician had told the mother he thought Isaac had Asperger syndrome and had put him on several different medications, including an antidepressant. The medications were making

Isaac so tired that he did not want to do anything but sleep. The school district requested the doctor's records, had Isaac tested, and had him placed in special education.

The mother felt that the school was not trying hard enough to make him work—even though the mother had not initially given the school any information about his diagnosis or medications. She had been afraid that if the school labeled him and put him in special education he would never have a chance to be in regular education classes. The social worker talked with the mother and learned that Isaac's parents were separated and that he was very depressed. He did not want to be at school because he was afraid his mother would leave him as his father had done. He was unable to verbalize his fears, so he acted out or slept.

The school social worker and special education teacher wrote a behavior management plan for Isaac that gave him 5-minute breaks each time he worked for 5 minutes. He was also allowed to call his mother in the morning for the first month of the program. His mother reinforced him with a reward at home each time he had a positive note from his teacher. The social worker visited with him daily for the first few weeks after he was placed in special education to help him feel comfortable in the classroom. The school social worker also assisted the teacher in providing a tightly structured schedule and daily routine for Isaac. He slowly became comfortable with his school schedule and teacher.

Over the next 3 months, the time limits for work and reinforcement were further apart, allowing less time to rest. The social worker suggested that the mother discuss Isaac's progress at school with his pediatrician so that his levels of medication could be adjusted. The school social worker helped Isaac through play therapy in which he could draw pictures of his fears and express some of the feelings he had about his parents' separation. The social worker read him stories, and he helped make up stories about losses involving pets, moving, and going to a new school. He sometimes showed concern for the characters in the stories. Isaac made slow but steady progress. Eventually the school social worker saw him only once a week, and he no longer found it necessary to make phone calls to his home while at school.

Attachment Disorder/Separation Anxiety

Kindergarten is the first time that many children leave home for an extended period of time. Most children will adjust to the school environment in a few days and thrive at school. At the beginning of school, children with attachment problems, such as those who have suffered abuse and neglect, may feel completely confused and may cry and throw tantrums for an extended period of time. Students with separation anxiety may need the constant reassurance that their parents are okay. School social workers can look for themes of separation anxiety in the child's play or in their interactions with others (Webb, 2003). These children may do better if they have the chance to talk to one of their parents on the phone at least once during the school day for the first few weeks of school.

Students with attachment problems need the intervention of a school social worker. Social workers need to work with these children in a manner that reassures them. They may need to help a child anticipate what is coming each class period and talk the child though the day. Social workers should meet the students as they come to school for the first week or two to help them form a positive attachment with one person in the school. They should spend time with the children and teachers to help children begin to rely on the teacher and develop a sense of trust and safety in the classroom. Social workers may need to keep the children in an intimate setting and let the teacher work with them individually for a while until they become comfortable. Early intervention to minimize risk factors may eliminate the possibility of more severe reactions to school and will help to offset negative outcomes for the child (Davies, 2004).

Often, large class sizes are intimidating to a young child. School social workers can work with the school counselor and other adults in the school who can help the child receive a great deal of individual attention at first. This individual attention should be gradually reduced over the first 6 weeks of school until it is no longer necessary. Most children will begin to lose the sense of uneasiness once they have become familiar with the teacher and classmates.

HELPING STUDENTS LEARN SOCIAL SKILLS AND SOCIAL COMPETENCE

Contextual factors, the child's innate abilities, and the environment in which the child was raised all influence a child's behavior. School social workers need to assess a child's inappropriate social behavior in more than one setting to assure that it is not the result of a particular classroom teacher's style or the behavior of other students within the class. If it is determined that the child lacks social skills, there are many solutions. The best way to teach social skills is to help the child interact with other students and teachers who model and use appropriate social skills. Students are likely to work toward achieving goals and objectives inherent in the demands of the classroom, and most students will try to achieve what is expected of them (Wentzel, 2003).

Students improve in their social skills and have positive peer and teacher interactions when they are provided with resources that promote the development of their competencies. These resources may come in the form of modeling appropriate behavior or creating positive experiences that facilitate learning. Sometimes other students may model or explain teacher instructions or provide mutual support when a student makes a positive attempt at a new social skill. Social interactions also can lead to the development of personal psychological attributes related to the development of social skills (Wentzel, 2003). One of the keys to developing positive social skills is a positive teacher–student relationship. When asked about ways to be a "caring teacher," teachers mention the establishment of a positive relationship with the student (Wentzel, 2003).

The school social worker can also intervene and teach appropriate social skills to students. The best programs break skills down into minute parts. School social workers should review social skills curricula and teach the one that meets the need of the individual student. The curriculum established at Father Flanagan's Boys' Home (Dowd & Tierney, 2005) is an excellent example of a program that teaches social skills in specific steps. Each skill is broken down into teachable parts. For example, the skill of learning how to greet others is broken down into the following parts: (1) Look at the person, (2) Use a pleasant voice, (3) Say "Hi" or "Hello" (Dowd & Tierney, 2005).

ETHICAL CONSIDERATIONS

Social workers must obtain parental consent for any type of intervention with students. Because obtaining parental consent is necessary to provide services to a child, school social workers face an ethical dilemma when a child is in need of help and the parents refuse to give consent for social work services. When requesting information from collateral sources, such as doctors and mental health professionals, the school social worker must obtain a written consent from the parents in order to make the contact. The social worker must then safeguard the records or information obtained so that they are not put in school files or given to other school personnel who do not have the right of access to the information. School social workers must keep school information confidential from outside agencies and other school personnel and be aware of the privacy and confidentiality requirements of the Health Insurance Portability and Accountability Act (HIPAA; Public Law 104-191).

It is sometimes awkward for a school social worker to have diagnostic information about a child because the social worker cannot discuss details of the case with those who do not have the right to know except in vague terms. Often school personnel, such as office staff and lunch room helpers, want to know what is wrong with the child. Because they do not have the right to the child's medical information, the social worker cannot discuss the child's problems. It helps the child if others who interact with him or her in the school understand that the child has difficulties, but most school personnel do not need extensive details about the child's background. School social workers should answer all questions about the child in a way that gives useful information, but does not violate confidential information or the child's trust.

CONCLUSION

The first years of elementary school set the tone for the rest of a student's public education. When a student has a learning, emotional, or developmental problem, early assessment is imperative. If a student is assessed appropriately and placed in programs that can help correct or work with deficits, it will help the child make a positive start. Many problems may not go away initially, but they can be managed and supported if the problem is diagnosed and treated correctly. School social workers serve as a resource to parents and children. The school social worker should offer comfort and support to children who are experiencing fear or anxiety at school. The social worker is also a source of support to parents who have children with special needs and who do not know how to find helpful resources. A positive relationship between the home and school is vital as a child begins school, and school social workers have the skills and abilities to provide this vital resource to parents and children.

Discussion Topics

1. List ways in which school social workers assist in the assessment process.
2. How can school social workers develop positive connections between the home and school?
3. Discuss the effects on children of exposure to intimate partner violence.
4. How would you help a child with ADHD and his or her parents learn how to break down work and tasks so they are not overwhelmed?

APPENDIX 4.1. Treatment Plan

Goal: ____

1. Objective: ____

____

2. ***Who*** will do the work for this objective? ______________________

____

3. ***What*** work needs to be done? ______________________

____

4. ***When*** should the work be started? ______________________

____

5. ***When*** should the work be finished? ______________________

____

6. ***How*** will the work be accomplished? ______________________

____

7. Report accomplished work to whom? ______________________

____

8. Evaluate solution: ____

____

9. Reward positive accomplishments in the following: ______________________

____

10. Consider other options: ____

____

5

School Social Work with Children in Grades 4 to 6

A national study in the early 1990s found that approximately one-half of school social workers were practicing with elementary school students (Jonson-Reid, Kontak, Citerman, Essma, & Fezzi, 2004). School social workers serve as a source of support and help prevent future problems by intervening with at-risk children during elementary school.

Service models for grades 4–6 vary from district to district. Some school districts place grades 5–7 in separate schools, while others move grade 6 into middle school. A school district's particular combination of grades usually depends on the district's finances.

Children in grades 4–6 are at the age when they are beginning to be more dependent on peer opinions than on the opinions of their parents and teachers. In addition, the gaps between children with developmental delays and other children are becoming more evident and more difficult for teachers to deal with. Students who have undiagnosed or untreated learning difficulties are beginning to fall behind and are becoming at risk for not being promoted to a higher grade. This possibility has greatly increased in states with mandatory testing requirements. Many states now require students to pass competency exams in order to be promoted. When a child does not show proficiency at the required level on standardized state examinations, many states require that the child be retained in school until he or she can pass the tests. The children who have been retained in a grade for another year frequently experience emotional harm from being held back and removed from their peers. They also may face ridicule from peers.

School social workers should be aware of students who may be failing and who are in need of help. This requires that the social worker frequently review student progress. When a teacher begins to notice school failure and sends a failure notice to parents, the social worker should also arrange to be notified. The social worker is then in a position to meet with the child and determine the cause of the problem. The child may be failing because there are family problems that interfere with his or her concentration, or the failure may be the result of skill deficits. The social worker can determine the most appropriate referral for the child.

WORKING WITH DIVERSE POPULATIONS IN ELEMENTARY SCHOOL

Children who are dealing with cultural issues often feel out of sync with the other students at school. This becomes more pronounced for children as they enter the last years of elementary school and become increasingly concerned about peer acceptance. "As increasing numbers of culturally diverse children enter schools, they will encounter students and professionals who are not of their cultural background." In some cases these children will "experience problems deriving from fragmented and destabilizing service delivery systems, insensitive staff, and in some cases a school environment that is nonsympathetic and rejecting" (Caple, Salcido, & di Cecco, 1995, p. 160).

School social workers should address diversity issues by developing inservice training programs for teachers and staff to make them aware of the different cultures in the school. School social workers should work jointly with the parent–teacher association (PTA or PTSA) to help provide programs that will increase parental awareness. For example, the program may include a performance featuring music, dances, or costumes from a specific culture or it may simply consist of handouts that explain some of the customs and traditions of different cultures.

Building understanding of diverse cultures is part of cross-cultural social work practice. Sometimes it may be difficult to obtain specific information on each culture present in a particular school. However, school social workers are trained to be aware of cultural differences and to work toward increasing their own personal awareness of cross cultural practice (NASW, 2002, Standard 4). "Social workers should understand their own cultural biases and learn about the culturally based beliefs of their clients regarding role expectations, typical ways of expressing feelings, and patterns of social exchange" (Webb, 2003, p. 12). School social workers should assist students from different cultures by linking them with others in the school from their own culture and educating students and professionals in the school about those cultures. Raising cultural sensitivity and awareness is easier when others in the school realize that (1) there is no single American culture, (2) members of each cultural group are diverse, (3) acculturation is a dynamic process, and (4) diversity should be acknowledged and valued (Caple et al., 1995).

Case Example

Raymond, a fourth grader, was in special education classes because he exhibited behavior problems. He hated riding the special education bus each day because it told the children in his neighborhood that he was in special education classes. He was African American and lived with his grandmother some of the time because his father was an alcoholic. When the father went on a drinking binge, Raymond's mother would send her children to stay with their grandmother. Raymond often expressed feelings of inferiority and isolation. He attended a school with very few African American students.

The school social worker was asked to lead a social skills group with Raymond and his classmates. The social worker had all of the students complete notebooks that told all about themselves. The students were given work sheets each session and asked to elaborate about things such as their favorite foods, clothes, music, stories, famous people, or relatives. Each student also had to tell about their favorite role model or hero. Raymond took great pride in telling about his mother, grandmother, and family. He shared stories about his grandmother's great home cooking and some of the ethnic dishes she made. It helped the other students gain an appreciation for Raymond and his family. It was a way of connecting him to the other students and using his diversity as a strength. The school social worker was able to help the group members and Raymond open up and become more friendly and accepting of each other.

RESILIENCE

Students who are not resilient are less likely to succeed at school. School social workers should be able to assess whether or not a child possesses the skills and attributes that characterize resilience. Krovetz (1999) has observed that every person has the ability to overcome adversity if important protective factors are present in that person's life. Resilient children have been found to have four common attributes:

1. Social competence (the ability to elicit positive responses from others, thus establishing positive relationships with both adults and peers).
2. Problem-solving skills (planning and resourcefulness in seeking help from others).
3. Autonomy (a sense of one's own identity and an ability to act independently and exert some control over one's environment).
4. A sense of purpose and future (goals, educational aspirations, persistence, hopefulness, and a sense of a bright future) (Benard, 1993, p. 44).

The following protective factors help a person with the attributes listed above bounce back from adversity. These factors are needed within the family, school, and community.

1. A caring environment–at least one adult who knows the child well and cares deeply about the well-being of that child.
2. Positive expectations–high, clearly articulated expectations for each child and the purposeful support necessary to meet those expectations.
3. Participation–meaningful involvement and responsibility (Krovetz, 1999).

Children who are already at risk will benefit and develop a better self-image if these protective factors are part of their family life. Their presence may balance and offset risk factors (Davis, 1999, p. 43). Social work intervention should include educating teachers and parents about how to increase their skills in creating a positive environment and positive expectations for children.

CHILD ABUSE AND NEGLECT: WHAT TO LOOK FOR, HOW TO FILE REPORTS

Where school social workers have a reasonable, good-faith suspicion that a child is being abused or neglected, they are required to report it. "Failure to report can lead to civil penalties, criminal misdemeanor charges, disciplinary actions or all three" (Ryan, 2003, p. 73).

The definitions of abuse and neglect vary from state to state, but "many states classify any harm or threatened harm to a child, including physical abuse, sexual abuse or exploitation, emotional maltreatment, and abandonment, as child abuse" (Ryan, 2003, p. 73). Some of the common warning signs of abuse or neglect include physical markers: bruises, welts (particularly those shaped like belt buckles), teeth marks, or burns from cigars and cigarettes. Other signs include physical injuries such as fractures, abdominal bruises, and genital lacerations and abrasions. If the child has marks or bruises and his or her explanation about the injury is not consistent with the injury or seems suspicious, it should be explored in more detail.

Child sexual abuse is a prevalent and debilitating event (Walrath et al., 2003). A survey completed by the Department of Health and Human Services in 1999 revealed that 1.3 out of every 1,000 children 18 years or younger had experienced sexual abuse. The same survey found that females are two times more likely to have reported sexual abuse than males (U.S. Department of Health and Human Services, 1999). Often, the experience of childhood sexual abuse is associated with higher rates of mental health problems and behavioral problems (Walrath et al., 2003). Likewise, though not all sexually abused children experience mental health problems, those who do have a propensity toward mental and behavioral problems often experience these problems throughout their lives.

As school social workers gain information from a child about the possibility of sexual abuse, there are several areas about which they should show extra concern, such as the need for sensitivity and confidentiality and the child's willingness to disclose. It is also important to consider other people (i.e., caregiver, child, and clinician) who may become collateral sources of information and who are able to contribute to the overall assessment of the child (Walrath et al., 2003).

The school social worker should ask about the abuse or neglect with open-ended, nonleading questions. If the child exhibits marks from abuse, the school social worker should take the child to the school nurse, who will verify the marks on the child. Most school nurses will take photographs of the marks as a form of documentation. If it is not possible to document the abuse with a photograph, the social worker should document in detail what the marks look like, their size, and the affected area of the body. The social worker should fill out any forms required by the school district to document the abuse or neglect, then either call or file a report online with child protective services. Each referral should be given a case identification number, and the social worker should file this number with the other documentation on the case to assure that the report can be verified. The social worker should document the time and date of the report and referral. Reports must be filed immediately. Most states require reports to be filed within 24 to 48 hours of discovery. The school social worker should make this a high priority.

When a report is filed, the social worker must know the child's date of birth and address and the parents' names, address, and home and work phone numbers. Often, a child welfare staff member will visit the child at school. If possible, the social worker should try to meet with the caseworker. However, child welfare workers do not usually contact the social worker when they visit a school, so it is not always possible to have an in-person meeting. If the social worker has not heard back from child welfare within 2 weeks, he or she should check on the status of the case by calling child welfare. Reported cases are given a priority rating by child welfare. This rating determines how quickly the visit must take place, usually within 3 to 10 days. When the child does not appear to be in a life-threatening situation, the caseworker may not make the visit to the school or home for as many as 10 days. These delays are frustrating for school social workers, who continue to have contact with children who have reported abuse or neglect and who are hoping for further assessment. The social worker should explain the reason for the delays to the child. Direct and truthful explanations often put a child at ease by helping him or her understand that the social worker is still trying to help but that situations are not always in the social worker's control. It may help the child if he or she understands that child welfare services handle many cases and that there are delays as a result.

Sometimes teachers and classroom aides are the "outcry witnesses," the person to whom the abuse is reported. If the teacher or aide has never filed a report, the school social worker should help in filling out the required forms and telephoning the report or making the report online. Making reports to child welfare may seem intimidating to someone who has never done it, and school social workers can be a great asset in helping others through the reporting process.

The child welfare staff will usually keep the child in the custody of his or her own parents. This can be frustrating for the social worker, who is concerned about the possibility of ongoing abuse when the child remains with the family.

Case Example

Shawn, age 9, was in third grade and was living with his mother and her boyfriend. The boyfriend would often hit Shawn and throw him against the wall. Shawn had red marks and welts on his back at least once per school year over a 3-year time frame in which he worked with the school social worker. The social worker referred the case to the state child welfare agency. The caseworker visited the family, and they entered family therapy. However, Shawn would continue to be hit and thrown by the live-in boyfriend as soon as child protective service staff released the case.

The school social worker would file another report when she saw welts on Shawn's back, resulting in a cyclical situation of abuse, reporting, intervention, and recurring abuse after the intervention. This situation continued for over 3 years.

The school social worker asked child protective services (CPS) why they could not intervene on a deeper level and why the continuous reports needed to be filed since the intervention did not seem to solve the problem. CPS said that they were building a case and that the school social worker must continue to report the abuse. The school social worker and teacher tried to help the mother realize the harm that was coming to her child as a result of her boyfriend, but, unfortunately, she chose to stay with him.

Sometimes it is discouraging and even overwhelming to try to help a child when the parents are not willing to make the necessary changes in their own lives to improve the situation for their child. Whatever the outcome, school social workers must comply with the law and report the abuse or neglect. The social worker should try to intervene with the family at the appropriate level to help the child. Unfortunately, it is not always possible to make permanent changes in bad situations. It also is very difficult for the social worker to continue seeing the child when child welfare has finished and nothing has changed. The social worker can only explain to the child that he or she has the support of the social worker and the school district, and that if the child will report abuse or neglect when or if it occurs again, the school social worker will report it to the agency again.

School social workers can assist parents who are under stress by linking them to community services that provide counseling, financial support, or other support systems that help alleviate stress in the family. They can take the lead in setting up a collaborative network with agencies near the school district to provide additional support to families. Often, just having an appointment at an agency or the name of someone to contact will help overcome the obstacles that seem to be preventing the family from taking advantage of services. School social workers can establish a resource list of contacts in community agencies, both governmental and private, that will expedite the process of gaining access to services at those agencies.

USE OF LEVEL SYSTEMS

Students with behavioral problems are sometimes placed in alternative education or special education classes that utilize a "level system." Level systems are a behavior management program used for students who exhibit challenging behavior. "They are designed to be an organizational framework for managing student behavior where students access greater independences and more privileges as they demonstrate increased behavioral control" (Heward, 2003, p. 306). A level system is a program that describes clear behavioral expectations. Level systems are used in many hospital and juvenile justice programs. In the school, a level system helps provide structure and reinforcement at each level as students meet predetermined behavioral expectations. Students progress through the level system by continually improving their behavior. Movement within a level system is contingent on earning enough points in each level to move to the next higher level and eventually out of the level system. Most level systems are designed so that they can be individualized for each person. A teacher will list the areas in which the student must improve. During each class period, students can earn a certain number of points in each identified area. At the end of a specified time period, the students can earn enough points in each level by improving individual behavior in order to move up to the next level. By the time a student completes the level system (the shortest time period is usually 1 month), he or she has presumably improved the behaviors that have been targeted.

Each level within the level system has increased privileges. For example, a student on Level 1 may have to sit in his or her seat facing the wall, eat lunch in the classroom, and have supervised bathroom breaks. Level 2 may allow the student to each lunch in the school cafeteria and go to the bathroom without supervision. Level 4, which is often the highest level, will allow the student to have the same privileges as other students at the school, such as attending regular education classes, no supervision during class breaks, and the ability to each lunch in the school cafeteria.

The benefit of using a level system is that it gives students a clear picture of what is expected and grants rewards frequently. Likewise, loss of points is determined by the student's behavior, which helps students take personal responsibility for their actions rather than blaming someone else for their problems.

Case Example

Wallace, age 11, was in the fifth grade in special education when the school social worker first met him. He had been in a behavior adjustment special education classroom since first grade because he had frequent outbursts and tantrums at school. He lived with his mother, who was usually not home when Wallace returned home from school. He usually had cold cereal for dinner because of his mother's absence during dinner. The mother's normal reaction to phone calls from the teacher regarding Wallace's misbehavior was to blame the teacher and claim he did not understand how to work with Wallace. On occasion, Wallace would attack his teacher, hitting and kicking him.

The school social worker and special education coordinator helped write a level system for the children in the behavior adjustment classes. When Wallace was first placed on the level system, he would yell and tell the teacher or aide to stop taking off points every time he misbehaved. However, over a period of time, the tight structure of the level system and the accountability it placed on Wallace for his own actions started to make a difference in his behavior. He began to see that when he stayed in his seat, did his schoolwork, did not harass his classmates, and followed teacher instructions, he had increased privileges and free time at the end of each class period. He seemed to respond to this sense of power by controlling his behavior and earning increased privileges. The intervention of the level system helped him understand specifically what was expected of him, and the constant positive reinforcement (or in some cases loss of points) helped him understand very clearly what behaviors were and were not acceptable. This helped him become accountable for his own actions. He stopped yelling at the teacher every time he lost a point and began to see that he was in control of his own actions. It took him a full school year of earning his way into one regular education class at a time, but eventually he was spending the day out of special education, and finally was removed from the behavior adjustment classroom completely.

Bullying

Bullying is common in the school environment. National and international surveys report that close to 75% of all students report having been the victim of a bully. Bullying has been found to be a consistent factor in the school shootings of the last 10 years. However, the shooters were not bullies; they had been the victims of bullies (Green & Nelson, 1999).

Bullying is the repeated harming of a student through words or physical attacks at school or on the way to or from school, which is unfair because the bully is either physically stronger or more skilled verbally or socially than the victim. Bullying is differentiated from play, teasing, or fighting, in that harm is done, the bullying is repeated, and there is an unfair match of participants (Hazler, Miller, Carney, & Green, 2001).

As noted, bullying can be physical, which includes pushing, kicking, hitting, pinching, or any form of violence. Bullying also can involve threats of several types: (1) verbal, which includes name calling, sarcasm, the spreading of rumors, or persistent teasing, (2) emotional, which involves tormenting, threatened ridicule, humiliation, or exclusion from groups or activities, (3) racist, which includes racial taunts, graffiti, or gestures, and (4) sexual, which is unwanted physical contact or abusive comments (Green & Nelson, 1999). Four elements make up a bullying event: the victim, the bully, the school, and the parents (Green & Nelson, 1999).

Bullying occurs in many places. The most common sites of bullying are the school playground, school hallways during transition times (especially when few adults are present or when adults who are present do not appear to have authority), on the school bus, and in the school restrooms (Green & Nelson, 1999). Students report that telling parents and school administrators or teachers is an effective way of solving the problem of bullying.

Boys bully almost three times more than girls. Males are physically and verbally aggressive, while girls try to socially isolate and verbally harass their victims, relying heavily on manipulation and gossip. Girls also may be physically aggressive if that is a norm in their peer group (Blessing, n.d.).

Bullying by girls can start as early as preschool. Girls use relational victimization, in contrast to the physical victimization used by boys (Crick & Nelson, 2002). Relational victimization was defined in the early 1990s by Dr. Nicki Crick as "emotional violence and bullying behaviors focused on damaging an individual's social connections within the peer group" (Crick & Nelson, 2002).

Some of the common characteristics displayed by victims of bullies are that they avoid control, have a poor self-image, are kind and considerate to peers and teachers, are insecure, are vulnerable and isolated, are not physically strong, put others' feelings before their own, are disabled, or are perceived as different socially or racially. Victims usually display a combination of two or more of the foregoing characteristics (Green & Nelson, 1999).

According to Green and Nelson (1999), there are three levels of bullying:

- Level 1: "I'm being bullied, I don't want help."
- Level 2: "I'm being bullied, I do want your help, but will not share the bully's name."
- Level 3: "I'm being bullied; I do want your help and will share the bully's name."

Sometimes students will show signs of being bullied before they actually report it. These signs include an "unwillingness to come to school; withdrawn, isolated behavior; refusal to discuss the cause of that behavior; complaining about missing possessions; being easily distressed; damaged or incomplete work" (Green & Nelson, 1999, p. 10).

Prevention is the best way to avoid bullying. Schools can help avoid bullying by providing a supportive environment and creating a feeling of belonging for the students. School policies should state clearly that bullying will not be tolerated. An atmosphere that is conducive to bullying is one in which secrecy is condoned. Students support bullying through the myth that it is not okay to report another student. Schools must combat this through publicity that states it is better to tell than remain a victim. Children should be taught that it is okay to tell teachers about bullying and seek solutions from adults rather than seek them from peers (Green & Nelson, 1999). A confidential reporting system should be established in each school where students feel it is okay to report bullying incidents to teachers and administrators.

School social workers and counselors should work together to teach inservice classes to teachers and staff to help them recognize the signs of bullying and characteristics of those who bully. Likewise, teachers and other school personnel need to teach and implement a plan to deal with bullying. There should be advisory programs during homeroom in which teachers, counselors, and social workers teach students how to avoid being the victim of a bully. Teachers should be present in the halls before and after school and whenever students are making transitions between classes. If the culture among students can be changed, the problem can be alleviated.

Teasing

Teasing is a step away from bullying but can create the same kinds of reactions to bullying in the child who is being teased. Some children are teased regularly and spend time worrying about being teased. Feeling vulnerable and worrying about being teased send a message of weakness to those who are looking for someone to tease. Those who tease have two motives: "I can show others that I am superior to that kid," and "That kid's weak, and I better show him that he needs to toughen up" (Fay, 2006, p. 1). The only person who can truly keep a child from being teased is the child him/herself (Fay, 2006, p. 1).

The solution to teasing is to help the child who is being teased develop skills that will help him or her handle teasing. A child must be taught by his or her parents, teachers, counselors, or school social workers how to appear in charge and tough rather than cowering. The child must also be taught to ignore teasing or respond as if he or she could care less about the teasing. This nonchalant attitude can be incorporated as part of social skills training for children who seem vulnerable. Children who have been bullied should also be taught to recognize the times and places when they are most frequently bullied and to avoid those places, if possible. They also should be taught not to retaliate either physically or verbally.

School social workers should assist children who may be teasing or bullying others. Collaboration between the school social worker and the bully's parents may help curtail the problem. Bullies thrive on control and power, usually have a poor self-image, do not respect peers or teachers, feel insecure, try to seek attention, are often bullied at home, envy others and their things, and often focus on things rather than others (Green & Nelson, 1999). Many of these characteristics are similar to those found in victims. Many bullies have been victims of bullying themselves. "A strong correlation appears to exist between bullying other students during the school years and experiencing legal or criminal troubles as adult" (Blessing, n.d.). Bullies often have no concern for the feelings of others, and they disregard rules.

Students who are prone to bully will avoid others who act confident or assertive. Because many children who bully or tease are also victimized themselves, they should be taught how to deal with their own anger and lack of power in a positive way. These children need an opportunity to talk about bullying and teasing and come to an understanding about why they do it. The children who bully are similar to an involuntary client who does not welcome or want services. It will be up to a skilled social worker to build rapport and trust with bullies to help them understand that their behavior is dysfunctional and destructive both to themselves and others. They must be taught alternative ways to feel good about themselves, such as involvement in school activities, sports teams, or other extra curricular activities, where they may experience success on their own and not at the expense of others. If there is no intervention, the chances of the child becoming a "chronic bully" and carrying the negative behaviors into adulthood are very high, which means that they will not be able to maintain positive relationships as adults (Oliver, Hoover, and Hazler, 1994).

Appendix 5.1 lists several websites that may assist school social workers in obtaining additional information on bullying and how to work effectively with this population.

PHYSICAL AND HORMONAL CHANGES

Children in grades 4–6 experience many changes in their bodies and appearance. Girls are beginning to wear jewelry, makeup, and heels. They want to be noticed. At this point, the maturation differences between boys and girls seem most obvious. Research involving brain scans shows that the prefrontal cortex of the brain, where scientists believe humans organize complex thoughts and control impulses and behavior, reaches its maximum thickness in girls by age 11. With boys, this process is delayed by 18 months (Tyre, 2006). Girls are becoming interested in boys and dressing to impress them, whereas boys are often still unaware and unconcerned about girls at this time. Many schools do an excellent job of providing movies and information about maturation and the physical changes in the body. Students become sexualized at different ages, but it is not uncommon for children at about age 11 to become sexually aware and active. Children who have been victims of sexual abuse may be sexually active long before puberty. Some preteen girls like to flaunt the fact that they are menstruating.

Case Example

Jane, age 11, was in fifth grade when she began working with the school social worker. She was misbehaving in class and being disruptive by talking out of turn and getting out of her seat. Whenever Jane met with the school social worker, she would clean out her own purse. This involved dumping everything on the desk and slowly putting it away. The contents of her purse were mostly makeup and tampons. She would hesitate and wait to put away her tampons. She would make sure that the school social worker noticed them and commented on them. Jane wanted to be recognized for her maturing and changing body but did not have the emotional maturity to deal with it in a normal way. The school social worker discussed the changes with her and helped her become more comfortable with her "new body."

Some early teen pregnancy programs report serving girls who are pregnant as early as age 11, when the girls are in fifth or sixth grade. School social workers should be involved in working with children who are pregnant. Because of the young age of the mother, the intervention needs to involve the mother's family. Decisions must be made about who will raise the baby or if the baby is going to be adopted. The proper intervention during this time is essential to assist in helping to make the right decision both for the mother and baby.

"Students who receive support from their families, attend schools with greater resources, and are engaged in school have a reduced risk of teen motherhood" (Manlove, 2004). School engagement seems to be a critical factor in keeping young girls from becoming pregnant and dropping out of school. The school social worker can be instrumental in helping students become involved and engaged in school. Strong school performance with high levels of school involvement are associated with reduced risk of pregnancy for black, white, and Hispanic girls. Students living in an intact family with two biological parents have a reduced risk of teenage pregnancy (Manlove, 2004). School social workers can assist students who are at risk because of declining grades and absenteeism. If the problem is addressed during elementary school, there is less likelihood for it to continue into high school.

WORKING WITH BOYS

"Boys are biologically, developmentally, and psychologically different from girls–and teachers need to learn how to bring out the best in every one" (Tyre, 2006, p. 47). Throughout elementary school, girls seem to have the edge over boys both in physical and mental development. Boys' different behaviors have been shown by scientists to be the result of male brain chemistry. "In elementary school classrooms, where teachers increasingly put an emphasis on language and a premium on sitting quietly and speaking in turn, the mismatch between boys and school can become painfully obvious" (Tyre, 2006, p. 48). Likewise, the increasing pressure on schools to have students prepared to pass standardized achievement tests leaves little time for boys to have a physical release from the pressures that build as they try to sit quietly and learn.

Rather than individualizing education to meet the needs of students, schools are put in the position of trying to educate more students to meet specific standards in a predetermined amount of time. School social workers can assist in helping teachers work with boys whose behaviors are creating problems in the classroom but who are behaving normally for their age. Social workers can intervene with the boys in these situations to help them learn that their behavior is normal and that they are not stupid, which is how many children label themselves when they continue to fail in school. They can teach social skills and self-management skills to help the students adapt more effectively to classroom expectations, work on the self-esteem of students who are continually being disciplined, and help the teachers become more accepting of little disruptions in classroom routines.

Many of the problems between elementary boys and teachers result in power struggles in which the teacher feels he or she must win. The school social worker can intervene in these situations and help the teacher and student build a more positive relationship. The way to detect these situations is to keep in close communication with teachers, eat lunch with them, and listen to their complaints. When they discuss a problem student, ask if it would be okay to observe the student's behavior. Once the negative communication patterns become clear, it will be possible to work with both the teacher and student. If the school social worker is viewed as a friend and ally to the teachers, recommendations on how to improve relationships with students will be taken in a positive manner rather than as criticism. School social workers should work very hard to develop positive relationships with all of the teachers in their schools (NASW, 2002, Standard 3).

CONCLUSION

Many of the problems that first appear in elementary school have solutions. Students need an advocate like a school social worker to help them solve problems early in their educational experience. If the problems are left unresolved, they will lead to a pattern of failure and eventually lead to more serious school-related and societal problems. School social workers are most needed in the early years of a child's education. They should be aware which students are having difficulty and intervene as soon as possible to help them avoid developing feelings of failure and a bad attitude toward school. The most positive way to intervene is to listen to teachers and ask questions about students who are misbehaving. Visit the classrooms and make recommendations to the teachers, then seek parental permission to work with the child. Most parents welcome having help with school-related problems rather than continually hearing about how poorly their child is doing. School social workers are truly the light at the end of the tunnel for children who are struggling in elementary school, and many of the problems that begin in elementary school can end there with the appropriate intervention.

Discussion Topics

1. Discuss the difficulties that families encounter when their child is diagnosed with a disability. How may social workers assist?
2. Krovetz listed characteristics to help overcome adversity. How can school social workers help develop these characteristics in young children?
3. Discuss how school social workers can help students deal with the emotional aspects of puberty.
4. Discuss how school social workers can help boys learn to stop disruptive habits before their self-esteem is affected.
5. How can school social workers help students who are victims of bullies?

APPENDIX 5.1. Websites on Bullying

www.teachingtolerance.org (free resources)

www.ipacademy.org (International Peace Academy)

www.bullybeware.com

www.nobully.com

www.education-world.com

www.drphil.com (antibullying pledge)

www.nwrel.org (antibullying worksheet)

www.goodcharacter.org (lesson plans and activities)

www.schoolsafety.us (National School Safety Center)

www.algra.com (educational and inspirational posters)

Websites courtesy of Region 10 Service Center, Dallas, Texas.

6

School Social Work with Children in Grades 7 and 8

School social workers perform a wide range of tasks, including crisis intervention, case management, and counseling. There is an immense need for school social work intervention in the middle schools. Many problems that were present only in high schools a generation ago are now prevalent in middle school, including teenage pregnancy, drug abuse, gang membership, violence, criminal activity, and dropping out. This chapter addresses some of the difficulties encountered by students in the seventh and eighth grades, particularly those that require interventions from school social workers. These include issues such as anger, risk taking, eating disorders, delinquent acts, and gangs. Middle school students experience hormonal and physical changes that often alter their self-concept. These changes create havoc on the child's emotions and behaviors.

ANGER AND AGGRESSION

Middle schools are often the scene of altercations, student violence, and other manifestations of anger. Eggert (1994) has identified 12 motives or reasons why students choose anger rather than resolving problems in a productive manner:

1. To manipulate those who are afraid of you—typically younger and smaller students.
2. A handy excuse ("I couldn't help it").
3. To get one's own way (others would rather give in than put up with anger).
4. To avoid intimacy.
5. To break down communication when feeling threatened by someone else's competence.
6. To avoid hard, straight thinking.
7. To get attention.
8. To excuse poor performance or losing.
9. To direct responsibility to someone else instead of taking personal responsibility.
10. To feel sorry for oneself (self-pity).
11. To manipulate others with guilt.
12. To take the heat off oneself and avoid working on self-improvement.

When school social workers can help a student understand the issues behind his or her anger, it becomes possible to deal with the root causes. When students understand how they use anger to deal with other issues, they can be taught alternative behaviors to deal with their feelings.

The social worker can help students deal with anger by understanding that the expression of anger has more than one stage. Colvin (1992) has described the cycle of violence and aggression as involving seven steps. During phase I, the child is calm, goal oriented, and following rules. The trigger or antecedent, which is either a denial of something the child needs or a negative infliction on the child, takes place during phase II. This causes a series of unresolved problems, particularly in children who have poor problem solving skills. During phase III the child becomes agitated and unfocused and begins to withdraw from the surrounding group. In phase IV, the acceleration phase, the child tries to engage and provoke others, particularly the individual who upset him or her. The child is noncompliant, verbally abusive, whining, and intimidating during this phase. Phase V is the peak stage, during which the child is out of control and displays physical abuse, assault, self-abuse, screaming, running, and violence. Phase VI is the deescalation stage. During deescalation the child withdraws, becomes confused, sleeps, blames others, and avoids discussing the problem unless there is the possibility of blaming someone else. The final, or seventh, phase is the recovery stage. During this phase, the child will show independence and eagerness for work but will avoid discussion of the problem or debriefing. The child also may be subdued or defensive (Colvin, 1992).

Familiarity with the cycle of violence can help teachers avoid untimely confrontations with students. School social workers can help teachers become familiar with the stages of anger in order to disrupt the cycle before it gets out of control. Some students use aggression and anger to control the behavior of others. When a teacher recognizes that the student is using anger for control, the school social worker can confront and deal with it. Sometimes, students with a history of coercive behavior problems or those who have been diagnosed with oppositional defiant disorder or conduct disorder may respond to punishment by trying to "outpunish" the person who initiates the punishment (Patterson, 1982). Awareness by the teacher and school social worker of individual student patterns and uses of aggression can help break the cycle. The student can then be taught how to deal with his or her feelings in a more productive way.

School social workers need to help teachers become aware of the situations that create stress for students in order to limit the number of negative situations in the classroom. The following behaviors have been identified as creating stressful classroom situations for students: personal rejection, personal attack, being blamed for something they didn't do, not being called on or being chosen last, commands or demands by teachers, public criticism by peers or teachers, not understanding a teacher's directions, not understanding the content of an assignment, failing an exam, not having appropriate classroom materials such as books or pens, expectations beyond ability, and personal put-downs or teasing by peers (Couvillon, 2000).

The Functional Analysis Interview Form developed by O'Neill et al. (1997) can be used by teachers and social workers to gain insights into a student's abilities and triggers. The form focuses on student strengths, negative triggers, circumstances that create triggers, and problem-solving abilities (see Appendix 6.1). Social workers can assist teachers in dealing with anger problems by analyzing the purpose of anger-related behavior. A functional assessment asks the following questions:

1. When/where/with whom does the behavior occur?
2. What is the targeted behavior?
3. What is the reinforcement after the behavior occurs?
4. What is the purpose of the behavior?
5. What new skills/behavior need to be learned?
6. What reinforcement will be given for new skills/behavior (Couvillon, 2000)?

Peer Mediation

Peer mediation is an effective and cost-saving process that leaves students with a feeling of satisfaction and self-respect while resolving conflicts (Angaran & Beckwith, 1999). Peer mediation is useful for dealing with anger issues because it teaches students to listen to others and consider others' opinions. It teaches students to find solutions rather than just exploding when angry. Mediating restitution with those they have offended is a positive learning experience for youth and helps them learn to appreciate others' points of view. Mediation allows students to meet in a safe, supportive environment where it is safe to be honest rather than hostile. Mediation allows for students to show how much something is hurting them, rather than pretending to be tough (Angaran & Beckwith, 1999). The ability to manage conflicts in a positive manner provides students with one of the most important competences that young adults need to master (Stevahn, Johnson, Johnson, & Schultz, 2002).

Students are often more comfortable sharing their feelings and concerns with a peer than with an adult. Peer mediation is valuable because students can share their feelings with other students whom they respect and whose opinions they will listen to more readily than an adult. Peer mediators from the same culture as the student who is experiencing difficulties can help resolve cultural and ethnic issues more readily than adults whose backgrounds differ from that of the student.

In many middle schools, conflict resolution skills are taught in conjunction with peer mediation programs. The need for preventative approaches to school violence, disruption, and aggression is becoming more evident, in contrast to the traditional ways in which schools have dealt with these issues, which usually involves teacher and administrative punishment.

Peer mediation and conflict resolution programs are based on the sociological theory that students at the middle school level value peer relationships highly and are heavily influenced by them (Daunic, Smith, Robinson, Miller, & Landry, 2000). Conflict resolution taught in conjunction with peer mediation can help students resolve conflict, learn problem-solving skills, increase their self-esteem, and foster independence. It allows students the chance to have a say in how conflicts are resolved. As students learn to resolve their own disputes and understand another's perspective, they are less likely to engage in aggressive or destructive behaviors (Daunic et al., 2000).

School social workers often act as the school sponsor for peer mediation programs. Social workers also work frequently with school counselors to teach the curriculum of conflict resolution and to train the peer mediators. Peer mediation programs need a good selection process to find appropriate students to serve as peer mediators. Once selected, the peer mediators need to be properly trained and encouraged. School social workers have the knowledge and skills to select and train peer mediators and can act as an effective backup to the peer mediation program if difficulties arise.

In spite of the overwhelming success that school administrators, teachers, and social workers report for peer mediation programs in the schools, there has been very little empirical research to prove the effectiveness of these programs. However, one study reported that approximately 85% to 95% of the mediated student conflicts resulted in lasting agreements and that referrals to administrative personnel for inappropriate student behavior decreased (Smith, Daunic, Miller, & Robinson, 2002).

The factors that inhibit the use of peer mediation in schools include:

1. Students' attitudes, feelings, and behaviors regarding mediation.
2. Students' methods of dealing with conflict.
3. Students' attitudes, feelings, and behavior in school.
4. School climate.
5. Structure of the mediation program.
6. Societal issues (Theberge & Karan, 2004).

Another factor contributing to the success or failure of a peer mediation program is the program's physical location. Students want mediation to be based in the guidance office rather than an administrator's or dean's office (Theberge & Karan, 2004).

Peer mediation depends on participation of students, both as mediators and disputants (Theberge & Karan, 2004). Some students may shy away from utilizing peers for problem resolution because of their concern with what Elkind (1967) refers to as an "imaginary audience," the false belief by adolescents that others are as concerned about their behavior and appearance as they are. The "imaginary audience" creates extreme self-consciousness, sensitivity to criticism, and an inflated sense of self-importance and uniqueness. Many students are afraid that the peer mediators will laugh at them or not keep the information confidential. Some also feel that they should be able to solve their own problems.

There is a range of approaches people use to deal with conflict, from passive avoidance of conflict to taking action and using aggression or assault. Theberge and Karan (2004) found that as many as 79% of students reported that they resolve conflict by avoiding it, while 55% of students reported that they resolve conflict by ignoring it. Some of the main issues that cause conflict for students are name calling and spreading rumors. For the most part, students try to ignore these. Schools that are overcrowded, with tight schedules–particularly urban schools–contribute to the possibility of student stress and conflict.

Case Example

A middle school in a rapidly growing suburban community was faced with extreme overcrowding and student outbursts. The school administration took a proactive stance and spent money on a second set of textbooks for each student. The students kept the second set of textbooks at home and could not bring backpacks to school. The first set of textbooks remained in the classrooms. The students could go to their lockers only before school, after school, and at lunchtime. The purpose of this restriction was to cut down on the congestion in overcrowded halls during the class breaks and to help eliminate student conflict. The school administrators and teachers watched the halls closely as students moved to new classes during class breaks, kept the students moving, and did not allow for much conversation. If a dispute did break out, any student who hung around and watched was in as much trouble as the ones who were fighting. This also eliminated the number of altercations because many students will continue to fight just to please their audience.

RISK-TAKING BEHAVIOR

During the teen years, many youths are prone to risk-taking behaviors. One of the latest crazes to affect teens is to videotape themselves doing risky things, such as "car surfing" (standing on top of moving cars) and "skitching" (hanging on to a car while riding a skateboard or rollerblades) ("Teens Court Danger," 2005). Some children are prone to become thrill seekers ("T" types). They can be identified as early as age 2 because they are the children who do not cling and who wander off by themselves ("Teens Court Danger," 2005). The best way for school social workers to intervene with these students is to get parents involved and make them aware of what is going on with their children.

Temple University's Frank Farley, who has been researching risk-taking behaviors for several years, recommends parental involvement and helping the teens to become involved in extreme sports or activities that can safely satisfy the need for danger through participation in an organized sport ("Teens Court Danger," 2005).

SELF-INJURY

Another self-destructive behavior that becomes evident during middle school is self-injury. There are many different names for this behavior, including self-harm behavior, nonfatal suicide, focal suicide, self-abuse, self-mutilation, self-inflicted violence, self-attack, self-wounding, parasuicidal behavior, antisuicide, wrist-cutting syndrome, wrist slashing, carving, delicate cutting, and indirect self-destructive behavior (Czarnopys, 2002).

Many who are involved in these destructive behaviors never receive medical help because they usually engage in the behavior in private to relieve personal anxiety. The level of self-injury usually seen in the schools is classified as superficial/moderate self-injury, which has three subtypes: compulsive, episodic, and repetitive. The compulsive subtype, which is associated with obsessive–compulsive disorder, includes hair pulling, nail biting, skin picking, and scratching. Episodic and repetitive self-harm are impulsive acts, the difference between them being primarily a matter of degree. Episodic self-harm is usually a symptom of some other psychological disorder. The episodic subtype is characterized by frequent skin cutting and burning. The transition from episodic to repetitive can occur after as few as 5 episodes or as many as 10 (Favazza, 1996). Episodic self-harm becomes repetitive when what was formerly a symptom becomes a disease in itself. Self-harm is impulsive in nature and often becomes a reflex response to any sort of stress, positive or negative. Repetitive self-harm is marked by a shift toward ruminating about self-injury even when not actually inflicting it, and self-identification as a self-injurer (Favazza, 1996). Girls have a higher reported incidence of self-injurious behavior than boys.

Self-harm usually begins in early adolescence and sometimes continues into adulthood. There is often a connection between the beginning of self-injury and a recent experience with either a significant trauma or disruption in the individual's childhood. There is a strong link between self-injury and trauma—particularly for adolescents who are unable or afraid to ask for help. Types of trauma that have been described as links to self-injurious behavior include witnessing or experiencing acts of physical or sexual abuse, domestic violence, loss of a significant person through death, incarceration, abandonment, verbal abuse, physical or emotional neglect, parental alcohol or substance abuse, and divorce (van der Kolk, Perry, & Herman, 1991).

Depression is often the consequence of childhood trauma (Favazza, 1996). School social workers are often asked to assist in helping students who suffer from depression as a result of self-injury. Skills training and cognitive-behavioral therapy have become standard methods for treating self-injury. Skills training includes teaching positive coping skills, problem solving, anger management, stress management, and communication skills. All of the skills mentioned above provide a student with a sense of control and an ability to solve his or her own problems, which will help increase self-esteem. The increase in self-esteem should help eliminate some of the depression. However, sometimes it is necessary to address the traumatic experience and help the child process it before improvement can occur.

School social workers can help students identify the times when negative thoughts and behaviors occur most frequently. Through journaling and monitoring their own thoughts, students can become aware of the times when they feel the urge to commit the self-injurious behavior. Social workers can incorporate the use of cognitive therapy, which can help change the way one thinks about events in one's life and help a person learn to turn negative thoughts into positive ones. A functional behavioral assessment may be a useful tool (see Appendix 6.1). Students need to be taught alternative ways to relieve the anxiety that builds and leads to self-injury. It is a slow process, but it can lead to positive results. Once the function of the behavior has been determined, a more positive behavior can be put in the place of the self-injurious behavior to assist in stopping it.

Case Example

Brandon was in seventh grade when he was referred to the school social worker because he was pulling out his hair on a regular basis. He had many bald spots on his head. This particular self-injurious behavior is called trichotillomania (American Psychiatric Association, 2000, p. 677). Brandon did not like the way his peers made fun of him for the bald spots on his head. He could not identify when or why the hair pulling behavior started, but he knew he did it at school, particularly when he was called on to speak out in class or to take tests.

The school social worker helped Brandon complete a functional behavioral analysis and learned that he was most likely to pull out his hair if he became the center of attention or had to complete schoolwork that he did not know very well. The hair pulling served the purpose of relieving anxiety.

The school social worker helped Brandon find alternative behaviors through experimenting with different types of ways to keep his hands busy. Brandon put soft rubber balls in his pockets and would squeeze those. Eventually he began to use a pencil with a slide-on eraser on each end. He would play with the pencil and keep his hands busy. He also started taking medication and worked on deep-breathing techniques to learn how to self-relax and de-stress at school. He eventually decreased his hair pulling and became more comfortable speaking out in class.

EATING DISORDERS

Part of personal and social development in middle school is the development and continued evolution of one's body image (Akos & Levitt, 2002). The physical changes that take place are accompanied by a growing emphasis on peer relationships, and finding a new identity that matches one's changing body image is an important part of early adolescent development. School social workers need to be aware of both risk and protective factors for eating disorders in adolescents. Risk factors include gender, low self-esteem, timing of maturation, and poverty. Protective factors include healthy self-esteem, positive feelings about maturation and the physical changes taking place, accurate information about puberty, and healthy eating and exercise patterns (Akos & Levitt, 2002; Davies, 2004). The onset of eating disorders usually comes during early to middle adolescence and is often tied to both biological and social changes. Body dissatisfaction is the strongest single predictor for eating disorders (Archibald, Graber, & Brooks-Gunn, 1999).

Creating a positive body image and increasing protective factors are interventions that can be promoted by school counselors and social workers. One's body image is an extension of the physiological, psychological, and sociological self (Stout & Frame, 2004). School counselors and social workers have the training and sensitivity to understand how developmental issues affect middle school students (Akos & Levitt, 2002). This knowledge must be shared with students, teachers, and parents in order to create an understanding of the complex difficulties middle school students face.

Types of Eating Disorders

Anorexia Nervosa

Anorexia nervosa "is a disorder characterized by the pursuit of thinness through voluntary starvation. It includes a refusal to maintain body weight at or above a minimal normal weight for age and height, intense fear of gaining weight or becoming fat, distorted body image, and amenorrhea (cessation of menses) in females" (Zastrow, 2001, p. 434). There also is a propensity for those with anorexia nervosa to have depression.

Anorexia nervosa is a very serious disorder. An estimated 20% of those with anorexia nervosa who go untreated die from complications such as heart attack, kidney damage, liver impairment, and suicide following severe depression (Zastrow, 2001).

Bulimia Nervosa

Bulimia nervosa is an eating disorder that affects a slightly older population than anorexia nervosa. About 50% of those diagnosed with anorexia nervosa also develop bulimia if they begin to gain weight. Bulimia usually involves episodes of binge eating followed by purging (Pope, Hudson, Yurgelun-Todd, & Hudson, 1984).

Binge-Eating Disorder

Binge-eating disorder, "referred to as compulsive overeating, is characterized by an uncontrollable impulse to consume food usually within short periods of time and often in secret" (Zastrow, 2001, p. 435).

Obesity

Obesity is "an excessive accumulation of body fat that results in a condition of being overweight" (Zastrow, 2001, p. 435). About 55% of the U.S. population is overweight. There has been a great deal of focus during the last decade on the problem of childhood obesity. There is debate about whether obesity should be regarded as a psychiatric or a behavioral disorder, and there is not an easy solution for treating the complex relationship between obesity and mental health (Fitzgibbon, 2004). Obesity is associated with high levels of anxiety and depression, and other eating disorders.

The school social worker needs to approach an obese child or adolescent by understanding how the obesity is affecting the child's self-image and peer relationships. "Often children who have been the subject of ridicule from classmates and family members may react positively when the clinician appears more accepting of their obesity and shows an understanding of the barriers and challenges that face those trying to lose weight" (Fitzgibbon, 2004, p. 152). School social workers should assess whether the obesity is related to physical or sexual abuse or is associated with stress in the home. Likewise, the school social worker should determine whether or not to focus primarily on possible psychological problems, such as depression and low self-esteem, before introducing an exercise and diet plan.

Both boys and girls struggle with body image as they enter puberty. Because American society places emphasis on being thin and fit, the mind-set of middle school students often revolves around feeling fat when, in fact, the feelings experienced may have little to do with actual body image (Akos & Levitt, 2002). School social workers and counselors can help promote a climate of acceptance for all body types.

Akos and Levitt (2002) propose integrating treatment strategies with individual students to help them focus on the social and developmental changes that may trigger an eating disorder. Getting students to visualize themselves as strong and encouraging them to become involved in physical activities, and to change hairstyles and clothing styles to work with their current body image, could all be included in counseling to help students accept themselves as they are.

Group counseling can also serve as a support system for students, but it must be carefully monitored by a school social worker or counselor in order to provide the proper structure and agenda for the group. Activities that build self-esteem and teach healthy eating and exercise habits may help students gain a sense of control over their body image. Many treatments for eating disorders are built around giving individuals the understanding that they have control over their body. Students also can be taught positive ways to stay healthy and feel good about their body.

Akos and Levitt (2002) suggest that schools should monitor verbal harassment that is focused on students' body image. Schools should focus on keeping body image a positive conversation topic and develop a zero-tolerance attitude toward making fun of students because of how they look. School social workers can assist school counselors in this educational process through classroom discussions during advisory periods.

SELF-CARE AND CRIME

Adolescent self-care occurs when children ages 12–18 have no direct adult supervision (Stewart, 2001). At age 13, most children are not allowed in private day care centers, and there are few school-based programs for them. As a result, many early adolescents are forced into self-care.

When left to themselves for extended periods after school, many adolescents get into trouble. The age group that most frequently commits crimes is between 8 and 15, and most crimes are committed between the hours of 3:00 P.M. and 6:00 P.M. These are the hours between school and when parents return home from work. This time frame, when students are home without adult supervision, becomes an increased risk factor if there are weapons in the adolescent's home or access to alcohol, drugs, and tobacco. Teenage sexual activity also occurs during these hours because teens are looking for someone with whom to connect to end their isolation.

Because early adolescence is a time of physical and mental change, as well as a time of transition from elementary school to middle school, it becomes a time in a child's life when he or she is highly vulnerable. As adolescents mature physically and emotionally, they need guidance, nurturing, and protection. Ironically, it is at this stage of life that adolescents are given unprecedented levels of independence and autonomy (Carnegie Council on Adolescent Development, 1995, cited in Stewart, 2001). As a result, many experience a sense of isolation. Students who feel isolated often seek out any group that will accept them, with the result that they are likely to be exposed to and accepted by peers who are equally confused. Because they are influenced by peers who are equally immature, they make many poor decisions, which often have harmful or lethal consequences (Stewart, 2001). These risks become greatest for adolescents living in poverty.

GANGS

Students who join gangs often started out as the victim of a bully. (Bullying is discussed in more detail in Chapter 5.) "Most bullies learned their craft as a victim" (Green & Nelson, 1999, p. 6). Gangs offer protection and safety to students who are vulnerable or victims of bullies. Identification with gangs does not begin overnight. Pregang behavior often begins in elementary school. Students may not dress or act like gang members initially but may try to mimic some gang language or gestures in private.

In order to be classified as a gang, a group must have the following elements:

- Three or more individuals
- Common identifying sign or symbol
- Leadership or council
- Participation in one or more criminal activities

Police officers view gangs as organized crime. Gangs are usually led by older youths who seek to expand their power and wealth through illegal activities, intimidation, and recruitment (Pesce & Wilczynski, 2005). Research suggests that many youths join gangs to feel accepted or to attain status, which may increase their self-esteem. Students who are particularly vulnerable to the lure of gangs may feel disenfranchised or threatened, have a poor school connection, have troubled family relationships, have siblings or friends who are in gangs, or be looking for fun and excitement (Pesce & Wilczynski, 2005).

In 1995 a report by the U.S. Department of Education 37% of students surveyed indicated that there was a gang presence in their school (Chandler, Chapman, Rand, & Taylor, 1998). Students involved in gangs are more likely to be involved in criminal activities, have academic problems, drop out, be suspended, expelled, or arrested, and become victims of violence.

Gang Prevention

Gang prevention in schools should be implemented on three levels. First, schools should have a primary prevention program that creates a positive school environment where all students are included and all students can have a voice. A positive school environment can reduce the feeling of being isolated that often leads a student to seek gang membership as a way of feeling connected and involved with others. A school program can begin with banning gang colors and not allowing students to dress in gang paraphernalia.

Many middle schools divide classes into teams or learning communities, keeping students in the same team throughout their middle school years. The teams have their classes and lunch periods together, and the teachers work very hard to know the students on each team individually. School social workers can help facilitate homeroom "ice-breaking" activities where the students learn things about each other and develop rapport. Under the guidance of the social worker, who makes sure that every student is included and interactions are positive, such ice-breaking activities can help create a positive atmosphere and eliminate isolation.

The secondary level of gang prevention involves intervening with students who are already identified as at risk for violence (Osher, Sandler, & Nelson, 2001). The school social worker should make home visits and try to involve the parents in realizing the nature of the risk their child is experiencing. At-risk students should have weekly meetings with the school social worker to keep them feeling that there is an adult in the school who cares about them.

Tertiary interventions for gangs include working closely with probation officers and parents to help the students stay involved in school rather than dropping out. Tertiary interventions are intended for students who have engaged in some type of violent behavior. Strategies for tertiary intervention include behavioral and skills-building activities, a strong family therapy component, and wraparound services that address multiple needs (U.S. Department of Health and Human Services, 2001). School social workers are the main school district employees who have access to parents and community resources and who employ a systems approach to treatment. They should work to assure that administrators do not suspend students when they misbehave but have in-school suspension so that they are not left at home without parental supervision, where older gang members will have access to them.

Case Example

Brett was in seventh grade and had joined a gang while he was spending the summer with his mother during his annual stay with her. His mother lived in an apartment surrounded by drug dealers. Brett had joined the gang to be included with the guys in the neighborhood and had been tattooed, shaved his head, and wore gang colors. When he returned to his father's home, the father was alarmed at his changed appearance and attitude. Even though many schools do not permit gang colors or headbands, Brett wore the same color to school every day and said it was his gang's blue. The father called the school and asked for help to make sure Brett was not in classes with any members of the gang. The school administration, teachers, and the school social worker worked closely with Brett to help him meet new friends and feel accepted during his first year in middle school.

Unfortunately, Brett had begun selling drugs and was arrested at school for possession of marijuana. He was sent to a school district alternative placement program for the rest of his seventh-grade year. The school social worker continued to visit Brett weekly and listened to his concerns about staying in school and wanting to make his father proud of him. He did not go to stay with his mother the next summer, and during eighth grade, the school social worker continued to interact with Brett's probation officer and teachers to help him stay motivated and away from the gang. He was able to break his gang contacts. The court ordered him to have the tattoos on his hands removed as a condition of his probation. His grades and school attendance continued to improve, and he was able to make some positive friendships at his new school.

INVOLVEMENT WITH THE LEGAL SYSTEM

If students become involved with the legal system, they will probably be assigned a probation officer, who will maintain contact with the school to monitor the students' grades and attendance. Working with the legal system can provide support for school social workers because it often provides incentives to students to attend school and complete their work. School social workers should closely monitor student attendance and academic reports for students on probation so that whenever they receive a call from the probation officer, they will be able to inform the officer whether the students are attending school and passing their classes.

CONCLUSION

School social workers can help address most of the problems experienced in middle school by helping early adolescents form positive bonds with the school and other students. Schools should provide after-school programs for students and work to establish activities that reach all students, not just athletics, but clubs and intramural activities where students can feel they are part of the school. School social workers should assist in advisory activities and get to know the students in the schools. When a student is failing or missing school, the social worker should intervene immediately and determine the cause of the problem. If possible, the social worker should help parents and school administrations work together in finding positive school activities to keep the students involved and interested in school.

DISCUSSION TOPICS

1. Discuss the cycle of violence described by Colvin. Does it match your experience?
2. Complete a functional behavioral assessment on one of your own behaviors and discuss what you have learned.
3. What are the benefits of peer mediation?
4. How can school social workers help create a positive atmosphere on a campus to reduce the isolation that causes some students to want to join gangs?

APPENDIX 6.1. Functional Analysis Interview Form

Student Name ______________________________ Date: ______________________

Interviewer: ______________________________

1. What are the student's strengths?
2. What are the student's challenges?
3. What does the student like to do?
4. What does the student like least?
5. What are the major behavior problems?
6. When do the problems occur?
7. What triggers the behavior?
8. Is there a specific time frame in which the behavior occurs?
9. When do the problems not occur?
10. Are there medical or physical problems that exacerbate the behavior?
11. What are the student's abilities to control the behavior?
12. What are the student's skill deficits in controlling the behavior?
13. How does the student express his/her needs?
14. When the student expresses his/her needs—who meets them and how?

7

School Social Work with Children in Grades 9 and 10

Entering high school as a ninth grader presents many potential difficulties, including drugs, alcohol, dating, sex, driving and the freedom associated with it, entering the work force with part-time jobs, school pressure with more difficult classes than in any previous years, and the opportunity to become involved in extracurricular activities. High school opens up a whole new world for ninth and tenth graders. It allows for adult decision making and adult consequences.

Most ninth graders are 14 or 15 years old, but they are mixing with older students and are not prepared for the typical everyday activities and experiences of the older youths. Many schools keep ninth graders in classes together, but there are some language, music, and elective classes in which ninth graders may be interacting with older students. For well-adjusted, emotionally mature students, this does not usually cause many difficulties. However, for students who have academic or learning problems, there is additional pressure to perform and pass their classes. Each credit earned is now applied toward graduation, and students who may have failed previously have the additional pressure of needing to pass each class in order to graduate and plan for college or vocational training.

ALTERNATIVE PROGRAMS

Sizing down can be a wonderful option within a school to keep students from feeling too overwhelmed. The creation of school teams can help. For example, the Sarasota, Florida, school district has piloted a program in which the ninth grade class is broken down into "Cornerstone Teams" consisting of 90 students each. The students spend 4 years with their team. Each incoming ninth-grade class is organized the same way. Students have a group of peers with whom to interact, and they all have the same teachers, counselors, and administrators so they build a rapport with them. "Each ninth-grade team has become for its students 'their neighborhood and their home' " (Hardy, 2003, p. 17).

Some school districts have alternative programs to help students who are not adjusting to school. These programs often become very useful for ninth and tenth graders who have difficulty in regular public schools. The pressure to conform to higher academic standards and accept personal responsibility for one's actions may be too difficult for students who are not emotionally mature or up to grade level with their academic skills. Alternative programs allow students the chance to succeed in a tightly structured environment that is not as large as a normal high school. Class changes are monitored, and usually the students stay with only one or two teachers. Some school districts house the alternative programs on regular high school campuses, whereas other districts have separate facilities for the students.

Because of the additional pressure of knowing that each class counts toward graduation, students who fail a class sometimes become discouraged and drop out. The dropout rates are staggering: 11.2% of the U.S. population drops out of high school. Of those dropouts, 10.5% are white, 11.3% are black, and 29.5% are Hispanic (Ginsberg, 1999). The rates vary according to age. Students who are in grades 9–10 (ages 14–16) drop out at the following rates: 5.9% of whites, 7.4% of blacks, and 15.8% of Hispanics (Ginsberg, 1999, p. 145). The school social worker should help target students who are at risk of dropping out and offer ongoing support to help these students remain in school.

SUPPORT FOR AT-RISK STUDENTS

One possible solution to the dropout problem is for social workers to work closely with middle schools to help identify those students who appear to be at risk when they enter high school. These students may be in special education or in alternative programs or may have failed classes or received counseling from the school counselor to help them cope with school-related problems. Once the school social worker has identified a group of students, they may be placed in support groups for the first few weeks of high school. These students also could be required to obtain weekly progress reports from all of their teachers to assure they are attending classes and completing work. These reports can serve to prevent problems before they occur in high school.

The school social work role will initially be one of support and problem solving. Treatment approaches and interventions should be completed with students individually, in groups, and with parents and the school system to assure that all levels of help are in place. Parents often do not realize the kinds of stress that students encounter when they begin high school. School social workers can create parent information groups or provide a chat room online to answer parent questions and concerns, providing parents with information on school rules, the school schedule, and how to contact teachers. Likewise, it is helpful to alert teachers to parental and student concerns and help the teachers deal with issues before they escalate.

The school social worker can be instrumental in helping students establish a peer support group by linking students with those who can serve as mentors. Many 11th and 12th graders love the opportunity to assist new students, and the opportunity to meet weekly with these students and answer questions may prove invaluable to a new freshman. Simple things like having someone to sit with in the school cafeteria can help a student get through the school day without feeling like a failure.

School social workers can also assist with students' schedules. It is important to place students who may have difficulty in a class with a teacher who has a track record of responsiveness and concern for students.

School social workers can meet the needs of incoming ninth graders by assisting with a special orientation group that offers information on school services. Groups should meet with the school counselors, special education teachers, school librarian, assistant principals, and any other important people who could help clarify school policies and procedures for the new students. Regular school orientations usually include a brief introduction of all of the people mentioned above, but this can be overwhelming. A group that would meet for the first few weeks of school can reintroduce these people and allow them to give information to the students about programs that could be of assistance to them. The students involved in the group can also become a peer support group to each other. The group could meet during lunchtime to allow the students a chance to interact with each other weekly for the first few weeks of school.

Group Intervention

Students who experience anger and cause discipline problems at school are often lacking in self-esteem. One school social worker has had success in improving students' self-esteem through group intervention. Bonnie Dockery, a school social worker in Terrell Independent School District in Terrell, Texas, uses what she calls "history groups." The format for the group includes having students discuss what parts of their lives they can change and what they cannot. Once they look at their history and current situation, it becomes liberating to them to realize that they don't have to follow any certain path just because they have a tragic home situation, no money, a learning problem, a background of abuse, or other problems. Then they can begin to dream and create their own future by realizing that they are in control of their own destiny. They dream and plan about the future and write their own stories about it. Dreaming about possibilities instead of being stuck in the past is an empowering concept and can be accomplished through group activities involving writing and drawing. The final focus of the group is planning for the future and setting goals.

Extracurricular Activities

Many extracurricular activities take place after school hours and require students who participate in the activities to stay after school. This excludes students who lack transportation and who have two working parents who are unable to leave work. There is frequently a fee to pay for joining clubs and organizations or uniform costs for cheerleading, drill team, or band. This cost becomes prohibitive for some students, and yet research shows that involvement in extracurricular activities keeps students in school.

A school social worker can be involved in fund-raising with community and private organizations or through a grant for funding to help low-income students take part in extracurricular activities. Students who have a connection to the school are much less likely to drop out or to become involved in drugs, alcohol, and gangs. School social workers also can work with the coaches and sponsors of organizations to help them recruit students who might have no other chance for activities.

Participation in extracurricular activities usually requires a minimum grade point average and passing grades in all classes, as well as maintaining good citizenship grades. Many students make themselves ineligible just by acting up in class, missing too much school, or failing a class. The school social worker should make sure that parents are aware of eligibility requirements for participation in activities.

Students could discuss their interests with the school social worker and take vocational interest tests to see what kinds of extracurricular activities they would be suited for. The school social worker and counselors could then help direct them to the sponsors or coaches of the various activities.

Case Example

Monty, age 15, in ninth grade, was from a home with financial problems because of his father's alcoholism. His mother worked hard, but the family did not have much money. Monty was the oldest child and would often have to protect his mother and siblings from his father when the father would come home drunk. There was a great deal of family violence. Monty had no outlet for his frustrations and would often lose his temper at school. He was placed in special education to help him learn to deal with his violent behavior. However, Monty wanted desperately to be involved in school activities such as football and did not want other students to know he was in special education.

The school social worker took him to meet with the coach and trainer to see if he might be involved with the team as a trainer. They both were welcoming to Monty, but after a short time Monty could not keep his anger under control and would cuss at the football players. He did not want to be a trainer, he wanted to play. He was eventually removed from the position of trainer, and he was devastated.

The school social worker and Monty's special education teacher then worked with the drama teacher to help Monty become involved in school plays. Monty took a drama class and was able to perform in several plays before he graduated. Once the drama teacher knew his financial and emotional difficulties, she was able to use his strengths to help him achieve success. He graduated from his high school with a sense of self-worth and personal pride because of his involvement in drama.

DRIVING

Most ninth graders are 14 or 15 years old. They are too young to have a driver's license, yet they are interacting with older teens who can drive and are invited to school activities that occur after school hours. This inability to transport themselves to activities and dependence on parents or friends is difficult for students, especially because many feel that they have reached a level of maturity by being in high school and yet are still unable to act completely as an adult.

STATE-REQUIRED TESTS

The focus of No Child Left Behind is to ensure that schools are making adequate yearly progress as reflected in annual tests. Many states are using statewide competency exams as a criterion to determine whether or not a student will be promoted. This puts additional pressure on students to pass the examinations. If students do not pass the test, they will be held back. Between 1980 and 1992, grade retention rose from 20% to 35%, in spite of compelling evidence that retention does not help improve students' academic success and may increase dropout rates (Hardy, 2003).

The pressure from advancement tests sometimes creates actual physical illness. One school counselor stated that during a 3-day testing period she had between 15 to 20 cases where students got sick during the test (Hardy, 2003). Many teachers spend their time teaching to the test in order to help their students pass the examination and not reflect negatively on the teacher or the school. Many schools provide incentives, such as a day at an amusement park, a movie, or a party for students who have passed the test. This puts even more pressure on students to pass and creates a negative stigma for students who do not pass, not only when they learn of their failure but also when the special activity takes place and friends want to know why they are not attending.

Teaching Relaxation and Stress Reduction Techniques

School social workers can set up a study support group for students who are at risk of failing standardized examinations. Whether working with students in a group or individually, the school social worker can also teach relaxation techniques to help students manage stress and relieve anxiety, since many students experience profound anxiety when taking tests. The group could begin with an explanation that stress is a physiological and emotional reaction to stressors such as tests, peer pressure, and difficult circumstances. The typical reactions to stress include:

1. Alarm, which creates physiological signs such as increased heart rate, breathing, and blood pressure, contracting muscles, and problems with the digestive and gastrointestinal tract.
2. Resistance when the body tries to repair any damage created.
3. Exhaustion when the body remains in a high state of stress for a prolonged period of time and cannot repair itself.

The school social worker can teach students how to use relaxation techniques, such as deep breathing; progressive muscle tensing and then relaxing; imagery relaxation in which the student pictures himself or herself in a pleasant environment; exercise; and meditation. (See Appendix 7.1 for a narrative on progressive muscle relaxation.) Likewise, the social worker can teach students how to use the principles from cognitive behavioral therapy that include self-talk to learn to relax and interpret stressors in a more positive way.

Students who are not doing well in school experience continual stress and anxiety, which can lead to depression and feelings of worthlessness. Cognitive-behavioral therapy is a way of helping students understand that it is not always the event that creates problems but the way the event is interpreted. Students can be taught to replace negative thoughts and feelings with more realistic positive thoughts. Because cognitive-behavioral therapy is a collaborative effort between the therapist and the client, it is helpful for the school social worker to begin the session by helping students to identify problem areas and set treatment goals. Students will be given assignments to help them identify areas in which they have the most difficulty and develop strategies and positive self-talk to remedy the problems. This technique is very useful in helping students overcome the feelings of helplessness that are associated with depression and anxiety.

SEXUAL IDENTITY ISSUES

Sexual identification and awareness often emerge during adolescence and constitute "rites of passage" for young people. Most individuals pass from awareness to positive self-identity between ages 13 and 20, and a positive lesbian, gay, or bisexual identity is being established earlier today than in the past (Owens, 2003).

The questions asked along the way are similar:

"Am I really lesbian (or gay)?"
"Why me?"
"What will my parents think?"
"Am I the only one?"
"Should I tell my best friend?" (Owens, 2003, p. 520)

Youths in the process of discovering same-sex attraction report going through similar stages, and their experience includes feeling different. Seventy percent of gay and lesbian adults report that they felt different as early as age 4 (Owens, 2003). Many gay and lesbian adults report that they often felt like an outsider within their peer group and family. The mean age for awareness of same-sex attraction is between 10.9 and 13.2–most gay and lesbian adults report that they knew their own sexual orientation by high school (Owens, 2003).

Sexual self-identification is part of adolescent development. Adolescent development is usually a confusing, and sometimes contradictory, process, and when sexuality is not clearly delineated, many teens become confused. Adolescents may partially understand their feelings but not be able to clarify them. To add to this confusion, they experience the need to conform while they fight for independence. For some, the struggle to determine "Who am I?" is intertwined with a second question: "What does it mean to be lesbian, gay, or bisexual?" (DeMontflores & Schultz, 1978).

Coping strategies for understanding sexuality include:

1. Repression of desire, with rationalization, relegation to insignificance, and compartmentalization.
2. Suppression of homosexual impulses–withdrawal to celibacy and asexuality, denial of heterosexual dating and sex, or heterosexual boyfriends or girlfriends used as a screen.
3. Redirection of energies into other areas (compensation).
4. Self-acceptance and disclosure to others (Owens, 2003).

Case Example

Lana was in 10th grade. She had started dating in 9th grade and found she was unhappy with the boys she dated. Lana had always realized that she was more comfortable with women and had lesbian tendencies. She developed a close relationship with another female student and wanted to let her parents know about her sexual orientation before she made any formal announcements to friends. She came to the school social worker and asked if the social worker would help her tell her mother that she was a lesbian. The social worker was already acquainted with the student and her mother and was willing to help the student.

Lana's mother was invited to come to the social worker's office at school. Lana waited in the social worker's office until her mother came. When her mother arrived Lana and the social worker helped her understand Lana's feelings. The mother cried but was loving and accepting, and the social worker helped her express her feelings to Lana. Lana was very open with her mother. After the discussion, she was able to move ahead and help her friends understand. The school social worker was able to help Lana through a difficult situation and helped her feel comfortable with herself.

GANGS

Students are interested in gangs for many reasons. They usually want to gain a sense of support and acceptance. Many students who are interested in gangs spend a great deal of their time alone and unsupervised. Gangs provide structure and a sense of belonging. Ninth-grade students often feel like they want to be in a gang. These students do not have a clear understanding of the criminal aspect of gangs and the difficulty of leaving once one is a member. The students merely want to belong and feel accepted by someone.

Children raised in poverty learn that power is about respect for the individual and that showing disrespect is an affront that must be challenged (DeVol, 2004). If someone is disrespected, they must fight or have someone fight for them to show their strength. These children may be powerful on an individual level but powerless against institutions and against change in their lives. Gang membership provides members with a sense of empowerment and the semblance of protection from others on the street (Miller, 2001).

The school social worker can assist students by introducing them to a former gang member and letting them get information directly from someone who knows the pitfalls of gang life. The social worker should be present when the students are talking to the former gang member to assure that the information reported is accurate and that it is not glamorized.

Case Example

Bruce had been in a gang since he was in sixth grade. During ninth grade he was arrested for drugs at school and put on probation. One of the requirements of his probation was that he had to drop out of his gang and have the tattoos on his fingers removed. He was moved to a different campus by his parents to help him find new associates. The school social worker became involved in the case. Bruce went through the tattoo removal procedures. He worked with the social worker to help teach other ninth-grade students about the pitfalls of gang involvement. He was an excellent source of firsthand information and a big help to other students.

CONFLICT AT SCHOOL

School administrators must help maintain the safety and security of all the students and staff. Ninth graders are particularly vulnerable to violence from older students because it is easy to distinguish younger students, and they are often intimidated.

Many school districts have tried to cut down on school violence by punishing onlookers as well as those in a conflict. Most conflicts flourish when there is an audience.

School social workers can assist in working toward social justice within a school and community by getting to know the agencies outside the school that may have culture-specific information. An information fair could be held to help students, parents, and teachers develop an understanding of the diverse groups in the community.

Case Example

A large urban high school had many Tongan students who were not integrated into the school community. The students kept to themselves and had few friends in their classes even though some of them were on the football and basketball teams. Each class in the school held its own assemblies. The school's assistant principal was the previous school social worker. He reached out to the Tongan population and invited them to perform in the ninth-grade assembly. The students performed a native dance in costume with drums, and it was very favorably received. They also performed a dance number to current pop music in which they did some sensational and innovative break dancing. It was an instant sensation and the students were immediately brought into the mainstream social groups of the school.

This school district employed some of the strategies that can help build relationships within a school. These include:

1. Having a school vision to promote justice and respect.
2. Diverse staffing.
3. Professional development with staff members.
4. Special events to celebrate the diverse cultures and promote awareness.
5. Programs that include conflict resolution, mentoring, tutoring, and after school cocurricular programs.
6. Development of consistent standards of behavior across all groups.
7. Parental involvement.
8. School–community links with local and national communities (Henze, 2000).

PEER PRESSURE

Peer pressure exists at all levels of society. High school seems to be the place where students are most vulnerable to the pressure to conform.

Children from lower socioeconomic levels cannot compete with students who have their own cars, cell phones, and spendable cash. They may resort to other means to get money, such as selling drugs, selling their own medicine, or stealing and then bartering away the stolen objects. School social workers can assist in creating after-school programs with community centers in which there is peer support for students and legitimate activities that do not cost money. Community agencies can be enticed to work with schools through grant funds to offer job-training skills, youth intramural sport activities, and school support, such as tutoring. Many communities have city-sponsored leagues for soccer, basketball, baseball, and football. Students can participate in these activities without much cost, particularly if the community centers are located close to schools.

DATING

A large number of students begin dating during ninth grade. School social workers can be helpful to students as they begin to consider dating. Peer support groups can help students begin to deal with some of the issues involved in dating. Many students have not begun to date, and yet there are school dances, sporting events, and various activities that require dating in order to attend. Dating creates a whole realm of decisions, including those involving drugs, alcohol, and sexual activity.

Many youths do not have clear ideas about dating etiquette, values, and behavior. School social workers can be helpful in running dating groups. These groups would have teens discuss what they consider to be proper behavior and etiquette on dates. Discussions should include issues such as how much time couples should spend together, how couples who are dating should behave at school, standards concerning sexual activity, how couples break up, how much to give up to be with a boyfriend or girlfriend, and whether steady dating is okay. Membership in this group could be made up of students who are interested in having the dialogue or those who have been referred by the school counselor.

Using a PTA meeting to present information to parents about dating trends and problems, and student attitudes toward dating is very helpful because parents are often not informed about what youths are doing. It would be especially beneficial for parents of ninth grade students to be told about proms, school dances, and activities and what the school norms are for these activities. When students tell each other about norms and standards, they often become inflated, too expensive, and elaborate. Students can create unrealistic standards for prom limousines, expensive dresses and tuxedos, flowers, pictures, where to eat before the dance, and what is being done afterward. Some students feel it is necessary to rent hotel rooms for a group and have an all-night activity. The school social worker could work with the school administration to assure that this information is disseminated to parents at the beginning of high school both as a public presentation and in a written format such as a newsletter.

TEENAGE PREGNANCY

Female students are most likely to drop out because of pregnancy (Zachary, 2005). Many school districts have special programs or alternative programs in place for teenage mothers. These programs focus on retaining the mother in school and giving her needed information on child care. If the teenage mother decides to keep the baby, many of the school programs offer day care services so the mother is able to complete her education. Some of the programs include keeping the baby at school and leaving class to feed or change the baby whenever necessary.

School social workers can assist in various capacities, including helping teen mothers make plans for the baby's birth or possible adoption. Social workers can assist families in dealing with the changes in their lives. Once the baby is born, social workers can be instrumental in teaching young mothers about attachment, prevention of child abuse and neglect, and how to meet the emotional and financial needs of a new baby. The school social worker can network with community agencies and family members to assure that the new mother and baby have a secure place to live, with family support whenever possible.

EATING DISORDERS

Eating disorders are particularly difficult to deal with for a school social worker because students with these problems are often in denial or just at the beginning stages of developing the disorder. The best prevention is to make students aware of the types of eating disorders and the problems associated with them. School social workers can work cooperatively with school nurses, health teachers, and counselors to help disseminate the needed information to students. Social workers should also teach an inservice class to teachers giving them details of the major types of eating disorders and their symptoms and danger signals. If a teacher then recognizes the signs in a student in the classroom, the teacher can make a referral to the school social worker, who can begin intervention at a primary level of treatment rather than when the disorder has become a serious problem.

IMMATURITY

The biggest difficulty experienced by ninth graders who enter high school is their lack of maturity and an inability to comprehend long-term consequences for their decisions. This is particularly true for boys because they are both physically and emotionally behind girls.

Ninth graders often fall behind academically. They are involved in extracurricular activities but are unaware of all that is required to keep up their grades. Even good students are caught by surprise by the extra amount of schoolwork and testing required. As mentioned previously, most school districts have participation rules and eligibility standards for extracurricular activities. Students must be passing all classes and maintain good citizenship grades to participate. Ninth-grade students do not always grasp what is required in their classes, and, as a result, sometimes they fail to stay eligible for extracurricular activities. When students become ineligible, it is devastating and affects them socially. They are embarrassed by their own failure and have a difficult time explaining the situation to their friends.

Case Example

Leslie was a ninth-grade student who was in the school band. She had always been an A–B student and had always been eligible for her school band and choir activities in middle school. Her high school band was planning a 4-day trip to a city out of state. The cost was $500 per student. Leslie saved her birthday and Christmas money, and her parents paid for the rest of the trip. Two days before the trip, the band teacher held a meeting with parents to give last-minute details. The teacher said that some ninth-grade students had become ineligible to go on the trip because they had failed a class. The term had ended the previous Friday and all the grades were turned in, but students did not know their grades. That evening after the meeting the band teacher called Leslie's home and said he had seen her grades and she was ineligible for the trip. Leslie learned that she had failed math and would not only be ineligible for the trip but would not get her money back. Leslie had failed to turn in some extra credit points she had earned to her math teacher. The parents went to school the next day and met with the band teacher. When she saw the extra points Leslie had earned, the math teacher was willing to accept the work, which would have changed Leslie's grade to a passing grade. However, the school administration and the band teacher said that if a grade were changed, it might make the band ineligible for competition and therefore they would not allow the teacher to change the grade. Leslie could not go on the trip, and the money was not refunded. The teacher had failed to notify the parents that Leslie was close to failure and that a poor grade on the final would harm her. The grade was a surprise to the parents and Leslie. Because Leslie had always been an A–B student and had never failed a class, she did not comprehend the seriousness of her situation in math until it was too late. A school social work intervention at an earlier date could have helped the student turn in the work on time, eliminating the entire problem.

School social workers can work with teachers and receive reports on students who are failing. The school social worker can send out weekly or daily progress reports. The student can then become aware of his or her grades in each class and can work with the teacher if necessary to improve the grade.

High school teachers often express the feeling that students need to take responsibility for themselves, but during the ninth-grade year they are in transition and do not fully understand the seriousness of school rules. There are few advocates for students and parents in a large high school. A school social worker can bridge the gap between home and school to help families understand school policies and help keep parents informed about student progress. School social workers can be instrumental in working with students who are having academic difficulties through progress reports and constant monitoring and sharing information between the student and the teacher. Teachers in large high schools often teach 40 students in each class and cannot spend individual time with each student who is failing. However, a school social worker, when informed of a student problem, can serve as a link to help monitor grades and advise students on how to improve their situations.

CONCLUSION

Because ninth grade becomes a pivotal year for success in high school, students need to get a good start. School social workers are instrumental in helping create positive experiences for at-risk students and their families. School social workers can assist with peer relationships, orientation to school programs, and links to extracurricular activities. They also can offer help to prevent academic and social problems.

Discussion Topics

1. What difficulties do you remember facing as you entered high school? How could a school social worker have helped?
2. What can be done to alleviate the pressures created by competency tests? How can school social workers address these pressures?
3. How can school social workers address issues related to immaturity?
4. How can school social workers help students want to stay in school and do well when their families do not put an emphasis on education?

APPENDIX 7.1. Narrative for Progressive Muscle Relaxation

This can be done sitting, which is most appropriate in the school setting.

- Close your eyes
- Tighten your toes (hold for 10 seconds—narrator counts)
- Relax
- Tighten your calf muscles (hold for 10 seconds)
- Relax
- Tighten thigh muscles (hold for 10 seconds)
- Relax
- Tighten stomach muscles (hold for 10 seconds)
- Relax
- Tighten buttocks (hold for 10 seconds)
- Relax
- Tighten hands into fists (hold for 10 seconds)
- Relax
- Tighten arm muscles by bending arms (hold for 10 seconds)
- Relax
- Tighten shoulders (hold for 10 seconds)
- Relax
- Squeeze eyes tight and grit teeth (hold for 10 seconds)
- Relax
- Rotate head in circular motion at least three rotations
- Shake hands and rotate arms
- Shake feet and rotate them
- Take three long, deep breaths and exhale slowly
- Relax

8

School Social Work with Children in Grades 11 and 12

The final years of high school present new challenges to students and their families. During this time, students begin to deal with adult issues and consequences. They are given greater responsibility and freedom as they begin to drive, which gives them the ability to leave school on their own. Some students become emancipated minors at this time. Even though schools are required to educate students with disabilities until they are 21, parental rights for these students may transfer to the student at the age of majority, which is usually 18 years old. School social workers can be helpful to students and their parents as they begin to make plans to leave high school.

This chapter deals with issues related to leaving high school. These include preparing for graduation, alternative programs, and meeting state and federal testing requirements for graduation. Drug and alcohol problems often surface during the final years of high school as students are given freedom through driving and have more expendable income through employment. Students who have been in the foster care system are placed in preparatory programs that are designed to prepare them for independent living. Special education students begin working with transition specialists to assist in proper placement in a job or job preparatory services. The last 2 years of high school can become a time of decision making and looking ahead to the future or a time of desperation for those students who have not met the requirements necessary for graduation.

Some students choose to drop out or are permanently suspended before they complete high school. When a student reaches the age of 16, no matter what his or her grade in school, he or she may choose to leave school with very few repercussions from the school system. Even agencies like child protective services place lower priority on referrals made for students who are over the age of 16. Many schools do not pursue court referrals for truancy after this age. Therefore, students who are at risk for dropping out become a special concern for school social workers during the final years of high school because of the lack of court support to keep students in school. School social workers should use their creative abilities to keep at-risk students in school.

Basic tasks like monitoring daily and weekly progress in class and consulting with teachers can often be the foundation for student success. (See Appendices 8.1 and 8.2 for student progress report forms.) Likewise, having students check in with the school social worker at the beginning of each day and giving the student access to the social worker's office as a place of refuge when things become difficult can often be enough support to get the student through each day.

School social workers need to allow themselves time to learn the names of students who have failed previous classes, who are repeating grades, and who may need individualized attention. This is particularly beneficial at the beginning of the school year before the student already has failed and it is too late to change his or her class schedule. If the school social worker has the option of assisting with student scheduling, he or she can often prevent difficulties by scheduling students into the classrooms of exceptional teachers who have a history of success with difficult students. (This means that the social worker also must know the teachers and their strengths and weaknesses.) Students may have difficulty with just one subject, and being scheduled into the classroom of a teacher who can teach that subject to struggling students often can make a big difference in whether or not the student succeeds.

GRADUATION/TRANSITION PLANNING

Graduation is identified as a major stressor for teenagers. Even students who have done well in school may begin to experience difficulty associated with leaving school and their friends. School social workers can coordinate services between educators, families, and outside agency personnel to ensure that students receive all the support they need (Friend, 2005). This coordination of services includes assisting in transition planning for special education students and assisting other students in making plans to help them continue in school or receive skills training for jobs.

When a student with a disability is 14 years old, the individualized education plan placement team (IEP team) must address transition. By age 16, the student's team must specify what services the student needs in order to successfully transition from school to a postschool option (DeFur, 2000). These services could include career exploration; a vocational preparation program; training in skills such as keeping a budget and writing checks; experience in a work setting; or any other service or activity related to the student's postschool plans (Friend, 2005).

Special education students receive assistance through a transition specialist as they make the transition from high school to work or community support. The transition specialist often works closely with school social workers. One of the key roles served by transition specialists is to refer families and students to community agencies that can serve as an ongoing source of support to the student and family. School social workers can assist in this process if they have knowledge about community resources. The social worker should become familiar with all of the sheltered workshops, mental health agencies, group homes, and other community services that may help in this transition. School social workers also should become familiar with transportation options in their communities to help students travel on their own. Some school social workers arrange for students to ride public transportation to and from school or work to help them make this transition.

Students and their families often lack the knowledge or skills necessary to avail themselves of resources they need. In addition, individuals with severe and persistent mental illness, those with developmental or physical disabilities, and foster children need a case manager, who may also be a social worker (Hepworth et al., 2002). These individuals and their families put their situation in the hands of the school social worker and expect competence. The school social worker should know the case manager and assist the student and his or her family. Referrals must be based on personal knowledge, not hearsay. If the social worker does not make the effort to become personally familiar with community agencies and transportation sources, he or she may encounter legal difficulties. A student or family member could bring a legal action against the social worker if the services are not what they have been led to believe or if they are inappropriate. School social workers should always be familiar with the agencies and services to which they are referring students and their parents.

When dealing with students who are disabled, the school social worker should help family members and adolescents understand the laws in their state. Many states give individuals with disabilities the right to be responsible for decisions about their own future at the age of majority. Students need to be informed of their rights and responsibilities at least one year before those rights are transferred to them.

FEDERALLY AND STATE-MANDATED TESTS

Laws that mandate passage of proficiency tests may become a particular hurdle for students who are approaching their senior year of high school and who have failed to pass basic competency exams. As a result of No Child Left Behind, all states are required to administer assessments to all students attending public school. By 2005–2006, students had to be assessed in reading and mathematics in each of grades 3–8 and at least once during grades 10–12. By the 2007–2008 school year, students also must be assessed in science at least once in grades 3–5, 6–9, and 10–12. In many states, students must achieve a certain proficiency level on applicable standardized tests in order to receive a high school diploma. For some students, it is the source of a great deal of stress.

Case Example

Delsy, a high school senior, was 17. She came from a close-knit family with eight children. It was May of her senior year. She had just been told by the school counselor that she had failed the math portion of the statewide competency test for the final time and would not be allowed to graduate. Delsy had already sent out her graduation announcements. She was planning on attending the local community college in the fall. She had believed that she could pass the math test and was extremely disappointed when she learned that she had failed. She was talking to a friend in the hall when a teacher walked by and overheard the words "kill myself." The teacher knew both girls and called the friend in to talk to her during the next class period. The friend admitted that she was concerned because Delsy was very upset. The teacher called the school social worker. The school social worker went to the counselor's office, and they brought Delsy in from class. During the conversation it became evident that Delsy was beside herself and that suicide was truly the option she was thinking about. After talking to Delsy for a couple of hours, the school social worker asked Delsy to sign a "no-suicide" contract. Delsy refused to sign the contract. The school social worker and counselor then called Delsy's mother and explained the situation to her. The mother said she would check with her husband but did not want the social worker to leave Delsy's side.

The mother made arrangements to meet the father at school, and they drove Delsy to a local hospital for a psychiatric evaluation. Delsy was admitted to the hospital and spent 3 weeks in treatment. During her hospitalization, the school social worker, counselor, and school administration worked on a plan for Delsy to receive special tutoring during the summer. In July, she was able to pass the math test and receive her diploma. She began the community college in the fall as she had originally planned. The teacher was instrumental in overhearing the serious threat and in getting help from the school social worker to resolve Delsy's problem.

State-Mandated Tests for Special Education Students

The IEP for special education students should identify necessary modifications for state assessment and other standardized tests. Some of the modifications may include extended time or placement in a small group while taking the test. In many states, the local education agency has outlined forms of alternative assessment that schools may use to show student achievement. As an example, a student with multiple disabilities would keep a portfolio of his or her work during the school year that could show improvement (Friend, 2005).

DROPPING OUT

From 1990 to 2000, the high school completion rate declined in all but seven states ("Out in the World," 2005). School dropout rates have continued to increase in the last several years, to the point where the current dropout rate is one in every three students. Students also are dropping out at younger ages ("Out in the World," 2005). Children raised in poverty are more likely to drop out of school (Pecora et al., 2003). Males are 20 to 30% more likely to drop out than females. Hispanics and African Americans are more likely than whites to drop out ("New Study," 2003).

Intervention with at-risk students who are potential dropouts needs to take place on more than one level. First and foremost, students need to have the skills necessary to achieve the standards for graduation and academic achievement set forth by the schools. Many schools do not provide the instruction necessary for students to achieve (Jones, 2005).

Evidence demonstrates that a nurturing school climate has the power to overcome incredible risk factors in the lives of children (Benard, 1993). Student achievement can often be linked to the relationship that students have with their teachers. Students need to feel that someone cares about them. Teachers need to feel that students are trying to pass their class.

School social workers can intervene in situations where students are failing by connecting the student and teacher. Mediation between the student and teacher by the school social worker can often result in achieving a more positive relationship that may help the student feel connected to the teacher and the subject matter and pass the class. School social workers can help train teachers to interact more positively with students through teacher development and inservice classes.

Social workers are taught to develop understanding, genuineness, empathy, congruence, and respect in order to have a positive relationship with clients (Aspy & Roebuck, 1977). Most teacher training programs do not include this kind of training, although these qualities are essential for teachers in order to have successful classrooms. Teachers need empathy, congruence, and positive regard to build a relationship with students (Aspy & Roebuck, 1977). School social workers can train teachers to increase their capacity to develop empathy, congruence, and positive regard through the use of videotapes, role plays, and positive interactions with the social worker. The social worker must be a role model for these three behaviors or he or she will be unable to teach them to teachers. School social workers may want to review the curriculum from their practice classes and use some of the same methods used on them by their social work professors to teach these skills to teachers. For example, Hepworth et al. (2002) have provided helpful information on empathy and how to develop, teach, and use it as a skill.

Students benefit from a sense of hope and a belief that it will be worth their time to stay in school. Five criteria that help determine positive youth development are "(1) competence in academic, social, and vocational areas; (2) confidence; (3) connection to family, community, and peers; (4) character; and (5) caring and compassion" (Roth, 2000, cited in Morrissey & Werner-Wilson, 2005, p. 72).

Extracurricular Activities

School social workers can help students build positive connections to others by finding activities that will increase their interest in school and enhance their self-worth. The positive aspects of sports participation are well known (Wooten, 1994). Students who participate in school-related activities feel more of a sense of belonging and have additional incentives to achieve in school. It is expensive for students to take part in some activities such as band and cheerleading. However, athletics and many clubs are free of cost and demand only the students' time. Also, sometimes students can become trainers for athletic teams if they do not have athletic abilities.

School social workers should become acquainted with coaches; teachers of debate, drama, art, and choir; organization sponsors; and administrators in charge of extracurricular activities who will help match student abilities and interests to the right club or organization. School social workers should work with administrators to assure that cost is not a factor in limiting student participation for those from any socioeconomic group who want to become involved in school activities. Many school administrators have discretionary funds that can be used to pay dues or the costs of traveling to activities for students who are unable to pay on their own. The school social worker needs to serve as an advocate for students who want to participate in school activities.

Youths benefit from participation in constructive leisure activities (Morrissey & Werner-Wilson, 2005, p. 67). "Young people's self-perceptions, values, and skills are influenced by their relationships and the contextual constraints or opportunities available to them" (Leffert et al., 1998, p. 213, cited in Morrissey & Werner-Wilson, 2005). When youths take advantage of the opportunity to participate in extracurricular activities, they may also build relationships with caring adults. Children help build resilience through positive connections to supportive teachers, clergy, neighbors, and other adults outside the family who care (Benson, Leffert, Scales, & Blyth, 1998, p. 139). Resilience helps troubled children counteract the problems in their lives. Leffert et al. describe ideal activity for youths as consisting of at least 3 hours each week in creative pursuits, at least 3 hours per week in youth programs, at least 1 hour per week in religious activities, and at least 1 hour per week in service to others (1998, p. 212, cited in Morrissey & Werner-Wilson, 2005).

School social workers should work with students and their families to find available resources for students after school between the hours of 3:00 P.M. and 6:00 P.M., while parents are still at work. More criminal and delinquent acts are committed in this time period than at any other time of day. For example, the period between 3:00 P.M. and 4:00 P.M. on school days is when violent crime by juveniles peaks (Snyder & Sickmund, 1999). If students have positive activities through a YMCA, youth services organization, or work, they are going to be less likely to be involved in crime and other counterproductive activities. School social workers can advocate with community leaders to create programs and services for students during these hours.

Case Example

A school district in Texas has placed community centers next to many school campuses. The director of youth services in the city served by the district, a social worker, has made arrangements for students to be involved in sports, games, and various activities at the community centers. Students are placed on a point system that rewards them with a certificate for free pizza, drinks, or French fries from local businesses when they attend a certain number of activities during a month. The school counselors and school social workers work cooperatively with the director of youth services to help distribute the attendance cards and encourage students to participate. Many older youths stay involved and help mentor the younger ones in basketball, ping-pong, and various games. It is a positive partnership between the school district and community on behalf of school-age children and adolescents.

ALTERNATIVE PROGRAMS

Many school districts meet the needs of at-risk and failing students through alternative programs. Nearly 4 million students per year attend alternative programs. The goals in most alternative programs are to prevent students from dropping out, improve academic progress, and enhance performance outcome for students (Lange & Lehr, 1999). School social workers are often involved in the decision to place students in alternative programs. Some alternative programs for high-school-aged students are housed away from the high school campus and include evening classes for students who only want to complete the General Education (GED) exam, while other alternative programs are located on the high school campus. School social workers can support these alternative programs by facilitating groups for the students, responding to administrative requests for special counseling of students, working with pregnant teens, and assisting those who have mental health needs. Social workers also can provide support to the faculty of alternative programs by offering inservice classes to teachers on communication skills, behavior management, mental health issues, or other needs identified by the teachers. School social workers should make special efforts to establish rapport and a working relationship with the directors of school district alternative programs.

STUDENTS LIVING IN FOSTER CARE

Between 1980 and 2000, the number of children in foster care doubled. Fifty percent of the children leaving foster care are unemployed, and 19% of the young women have given birth. Fifty-five percent are African American and Latino children. The relatively young age of the majority of recent entrants to foster care, combined with the high probability that a significant proportion will not return home or be adopted, suggests that a high proportion of youths leaving foster care for independent living during the early years of the 21st century will have spent nearly all of their childhood in out-of-home care (Courtney & Barth, 1996).

Adolescents make up an increasingly large portion of the children placed in foster care. Approximately 20,000 adolescents leave the foster care system annually (Courtney, Terao, & Bost, 2004). As foster children begin to age out of foster care and become emancipated, their outlook for the future has become increasingly bleak. These youths already have lost parental support, and with the loss of state support, they are on their own. They also are leaving the support offered by the public school system (Maluccio, 2006).

Thirty-seven percent of former foster children did not finish high school (Pecora et al., 2003). School social workers can help meet the challenge to keep foster children in school and help them with transition planning when they have graduated. The school social worker should target this population throughout high school, and particularly during their last 2 years, to assure that they stay in school.

Youths transitioning out of foster care are faced with the predicament of having to live independently without support and without being fully prepared to do so. Youths are taking longer to transition to adulthood than at any other time in U.S. history (Furstenberg, Kennedy, McLoyd, Rumbaut, & Settersten, 2004). Non-foster care youths usually receive ongoing emotional and financial support as they transition into adulthood. Youths aging out of the foster care system find themselves trying to transition without the benefit of these supports (Maluccio, 2006). They need a continuum of formal, comprehensive, and concrete support services, including educational, medical, and psychosocial support and help with practical living skills (Pecora et al., 2003).

The John Chafee Foster Care Independence Program (CFCIP), included in Title I of the Foster Care Independence Act of 1999, allows the use of federal funds to match state dollars for the support of youths transitioning from foster care to independent living (Pecora et al., 2003). Between one-third and one-half of youths approaching discharge from the foster care system have not received services aimed at fostering independent living. Good predictors of success after leaving foster care include completion of high school while in care; access to postsecondary educational opportunities, such as college or vocational training; training in life skills and independent living ; not being homeless within 1 year of leaving care; participation in clubs or organizations while in care; minimal academic problems; and minimal use of alcohol or drugs (Pecora et al., 2003).

Team Approach

The most effective treatment strategy for students leaving foster care is a team approach, which includes foster parents, teachers, and the adolescent all working together to create a unified plan. Because education is the leading predictor of adult success, it is critical to provide a positive academic atmosphere that will keep foster children in school (Pecora et al., 2003). Failing to reach their educational potential is one of the most serious risks faced by foster children, and it has the most serious long-term effects. A recent survey found that 38% of foster children received special education services; more than 36% repeated a grade in school; and more than 67% attended three or more elementary schools, with half of those attending five or more elementary schools (Garcia, 2004).

Schools that establish high expectations for all children and give them the support necessary to live up to those expectations have amazingly high rates of academic success (Benard, 1993). Teacher support has been linked to the attainment of educational goals (Wilson & Wilson, 1992). Proactive practices from teachers include the establishment of clear rules, an organized routine, reinforcement of positive behaviors, and consistent consequences for inappropriate behavior (Lynn, McKay, & Atkins, 2003). The school social worker can create interventions such as uniform behavior management strategies across all classrooms to reduce students' behavioral difficulties (Lynn et al., 2003). Social workers can assist teachers by working individually with foster children and teaching social skills, emotional awareness, social problem solving, and peer relations (Lynn et al., 2003). School social workers also can help the students establish goals for their future.

Life Skills/Independent Living Training

A key aspect in ensuring post-foster care success for foster children is the cooperation of the foster parents. Caregiver support is critical as youths prepare to leave foster care. One of the best ways a foster parent can help a child is to help him or her develop communication and problem-solving skills, self-reliance, the personal integrity to accept the consequences of one's own behavior, and a sense of self-worth. These attributes can help the child become more resilient in responding to the stressors in his or her environment. As discussed in Chapter 5, resilient children usually demonstrate social competence, problem-solving skills, autonomy, and a sense of purpose and future (Benard, 1993). These attributes help assure success in school, work, and life.

The skills that are needed to be successful in school also will serve the students when they join the workforce. To be gainfully employed, a person needs not only job skills but the maturity to show up for work every day and assume various responsibilities. Foster parents can teach responsibility by making students accountable for themselves. They should have specific jobs at home and standards for school performance.

School social workers should be skilled in writing behavior management plans and can impart information about this skill to foster parents. A good behavior management plan is simple and comprehensible. Changes in behavior must be reinforced by factors that matter to the individual affected by the plan. The plan should reinforce small steps toward the desired behavior. Reinforcements should come often and soon after the desired behavior. Parents and foster parents should spend enough individual time with each adolescent to know the things that can serve as positive reinforcements, such as extra phone time, extra individual time in the bathroom in the morning, or extra time watching their favorite TV programs. (See Appendix 8.3 for a sample behavior management plan for an adolescent.)

Alcohol or Drug Abuse: Law Enforcement Guidance

Many school districts provide guidance classes on drug and alcohol abuse. Some programs, such as the Law Enforcement Teaching Students (LETS) program, are partnerships between law enforcement and the schools that teach students about drugs and alcohol. These programs provide excellent information and are geared toward young children to serve as a preventative measure.

Participation in Clubs or Organizations While in Foster Care

School social workers can assist foster parents in setting up peer mentoring or service-related activities for the adolescents in school. Civic participation also helps youths to seek goals other than material wealth and yields well-rounded adults (MacArthur Research Network on Transitions to Adulthood, 2005, p. 3). There are many volunteer clubs and organizations in the schools. The school social worker can be a link in assisting foster children to become involved in service organizations and may even offer to serve as the sponsor of a service organization. Likewise, the social worker can help the youths organize specific service projects to meet community needs, such as collecting school supplies for victims of natural disasters.

Training for Parents/Foster Parents to Help Them Recognize Cognitive and Emotional Problems

School social workers can work with foster parents and train them to look for cognitive and emotional difficulties in their foster children. About 20% of adolescents suffer from a diagnosable mental health disorder in a given year, and a significant majority of these disorders will continue to affect them as they age into adulthood (MacArthur Research Network on Transitions to Adulthood, 2005). Problems identified have ranged from relational and coping difficulties and school failure to emotional and behavioral disturbances causing moderated to severe impairment, with conduct disorder, attentional disorders, aggressive behavior, and depression the most common disorders (Pilowsky, 1995). About one-half of the youths in the juvenile justice system have mental health problems, yet only 15% to 20% receive help. Foster parents must be trained to recognize and seek help early for cognitive and emotional problems.

It is often difficult for minority families and foster families to seek outside help in dealing with mental health issues. Many foster children were living in low-income households prior to their removal. A background of poverty often includes family disruptions, disconnected parents, stress, and social problems. In addition, foster children are susceptible to emotional and cognitive problems as a result of the in utero and environmental exposure to drugs and alcohol common to youth entering the foster care system (Leslie et al., 2000).

Maltreatment, neglect, and entry into the foster care system all present emotional and psychological challenges for children. Entering the foster care system also may place children at significant risk for behavioral problems (Leslie et al., 2000). Maltreatment and neglect have also been linked with emotional problems. Entering the foster care system presents a psychological challenge; children must cope with the effects of traumatic events precipitating their entry into foster care, face the temporary or permanent loss of one or both parents, and adjust to new families and living situations. Experiences such as multiple foster placements and unclear length of placement may contribute to psychological problems.

The Adoption Act and Assistance and Child Welfare Act of 1980 (Public Law 96-272) mandated the need to preserve placement of children in their own homes whenever possible. This has led some to sug-

for independent living as they are transitioning out of the foster care system. Finally, school social work services can provide parents with a link to alternative programs and optional support, such as GED preparatory classes.

Discussion Topics

1. What positive incentives can school districts provide to high school students so they have a desire to stay in high school?
2. How can schools address issues of competency without standardized tests?
3. Where can school social workers obtain funding to help pay for extracurricular activities for students?
4. What solutions can you think of to help youths transition out of the foster care system?
5. Role play: Practice a role-play situation in which you would show a teacher how to use empathy, congruence, and positive regard.

APPENDIX 8.1. Daily Student Progress Report Form

Class period	Attended class on time (yes or no)	Grade for day	Teacher comment	Teacher signature
1				
2				
3				
4				
5				
6				
7				

APPENDIX 8.2. Weekly Student Progress Report Form

Class period	Daily attendance	Grade for week	Teacher comment	Teacher signature
1				
2				
3				
4				
5				
6				
7				

APPENDIX 8.3. Sample Behavior Management Plan

Susan's Homework Plan

Susan will come directly home from school and do her homework for 2 hours each night. When Susan completes her homework, she can use the telephone for 30 minutes without interruption. If she does her homework each day, she can go out with her friends on Friday night.

Place a check next to each day that homework is completed.

Monday ______ Tuesday ______ Wednesday ______ Thursday ______ Friday ______

______________________________ ______________________________
Susan Date

______________________________ ______________________________
Parent Date

9

Group Work in the School Setting

Group work allows school social workers to reach a wide range of students having a variety of needs in an efficient manner. The effort involved in setting up and leading groups is considerable, but this effort is worth it because groups have immense power to move people in positive directions (Corey & Corey, 2006; Malekoff, 2002).

Children and adolescents are particularly responsive to treatment in groups because peer support and acceptance are so important to them. Children and adolescents frequently seek advice from peers before asking adults what they should do. Thus, groups can provide a positive forum for them to receive peer support. Groups can help students deal with problems related to change, such as being a new student in school with a need for support and information. Groups also can be utilized to help teach and develop new skills, such as problem solving, anger management, and social skills.

Groups help children and adolescents deal with special issues, like parental separation and divorce. Grief groups can help with the aftermath of a school crisis, like a death or suicide. Groups can teach specific skills to students who want to learn to become peer counselors. They are also helpful in educating students about substance abuse, gangs, sexual harassment, and bullies and can be used to help children deal with eating disorders and obesity.

Group work in the schools can create positive changes in behavior for both students and faculty. School social workers can use group work skills in contexts such as IEP meetings, which facilitate placement in special classes, and to help the school administration and faculty develop goals and mission statements. School teams can work together in many ways to strengthen individual schools and faculties. They can be proactive toward future problems by teaching team building and group work skills so that when a problem arises an existing group that already has established rapport and trust can work together to solve the problem.

This chapter focuses on strategies for developing and running effective groups in the school.

BEGINNING A GROUP IN SCHOOL

Beginning a group requires thought and planning. The process of establishing and conducting groups varies significantly, depending on the type of group and the specific purposes to be achieved (Zastrow, 2006).

Purpose and Objectives

In order to use group work effectively, the school social worker must first clarify the purpose of the group and then determine which group model will best fulfill that purpose. Along with clarifying the purpose of the group, the social worker should clarify the objectives to be accomplished through the use of the group. It is essential that the objectives and purpose of each group be established at the beginning because they have a significant impact on membership selection (Zastrow, 2006).

Leadership

Group leadership issues should be resolved before beginning a group. Leadership should be based on group membership, purpose, and goals. Some groups need tight structure and an authoritarian, adult leader to keep the group under control and to accomplish group tasks. Other groups may do better under a laissez-faire leader who participates very little and leaves group members to function on their own. Some groups may need a democratic leader who works to involve each member (Zastrow, 2006). Leadership should be discussed during the first session to assure that members of the group understand why things happen as they do.

Five professional qualifications have been identified as important for those leading groups with children and adolescents. These include (1) an understanding of the developmental tasks and stages of the particular age group, (2) good counseling and group work skills, (3) knowledge and skills to assist in working with children from diverse backgrounds, (4) supervised training in working with children and adolescents prior to the group experience, and (5) knowledge from research and literature regarding counseling children and adolescents (Corey & Corey, 2006).

The school social worker should determine whether or not the group would do better with one group leader or two. Sometimes it is wise to have a cotherapist who can help observe the interactions in the room and assist in matters that a single therapist may miss. There are many benefits from coleadership, including a source of support for the leader, a different perspective on group activities, assistance during interventions and difficult group moments, and extra security for group members if one of the members becomes angry or upset. The cotherapist also can serve as a model of positive communication between the leaders and can help set group boundaries and enforce group limits and structure (Toseland & Rivas, 2001). However, cotherapists can be a hindrance in situations where there is a small group of shy students who are intimidated by too many adults or where the two adult leaders do not have the same goals and purposes for the group.

School Authorization

The school social worker should receive support and permission to provide group counseling during school time from school counselors, teachers, and administrators in the school where the group will be held. If the school staff members are informed and involved in helping determine group membership and purpose, they will be supportive of the process and will assist in student selection, secure teacher support when students leave class to attend the group, and find an appropriate room for the group meetings.

The room in which the group meets should be a private space that will be free from interruption for the allotted meeting time. School buildings have very few available rooms or spaces that are appropriate for group meetings. Specifically, the school library is not a good location for group meetings because it is not private, and there are too many interruptions from those using the library. Likewise, the school cafeteria, auditorium, or "cafetorium" (a combination cafeteria and auditorium with a curtained stage) are not adequate. There are many distractions in the cafeteria while meals are being prepared, served, and cleaned up, even if the group is being held behind a curtained stage. Classrooms that are unused during a particular class period work well as long as the teacher for that room has someplace else to work so the group can have privacy.

Parental Consent

Before a child or adolescent participates in a group, it is necessary to obtain the written permission of his or her parent or guardian. (A sample consent form is included in Appendix 9.1.) After parental consent has been received, the school social worker should discuss with each child referred to the group his or her level of interest and commitment to becoming a member. Children and adolescents will be much more willing to become a part of the group if they feel they have control about joining.

Sometimes the school administration will require students to attend a group as a means of alleviating student difficulties with issues such as truancy, anger management, social skills, or drugs and alcohol. When there is a need for an involuntary referral, it is a good idea to meet with the student and a parent prior to beginning the group to discuss group goals and format. This discussion will help alleviate some of the fear that accompanies attending groups and will give the child a chance to express any anger or frustration before actually beginning the group.

Confidentiality

School social workers must set clear parameters about confidentiality at the beginning of the group. The social worker should be aware of the school district's policies and procedures regarding confidentiality (Corey & Corey, 2006). The social worker should also be aware of state laws regarding confidentiality and its limits. Group members should be informed about the social worker's limits of confidentiality, such as reporting abuse and neglect. This information should be given to the child and parent in writing as a protection for the social worker. (See Appendix 9.2 for a Limits of Confidentiality form.)

The group must be made aware of the importance of confidentiality among group members. Developing trust allows members to feel comfortable with each other and gives them the freedom to discuss personal issues. The social worker should help the students to understand the value of confidentiality and the need for it.

Younger children do not fully understand the need for confidentiality. One activity that helps teach younger children how information can be altered as it is retold is the "gossip game." The school social worker whispers a one- or two-sentence secret to the nearest child. He or she then whispers the story to the next child until everyone in the group has heard it. The last person to hear the secret then must repeat it out loud to the group. The school social worker then tells the group what was whispered to the first member of the group. The sentence usually has become very distorted. The social worker can use this example to tell children that when they discuss things that other group members have told them, others will retell them inaccurately. (See Appendix 9.3 for group contract form.)

Group Structure

Groups need to be structured around their purpose. If the purpose of the group is to help new students adjust to the school environment, it may be wise to keep membership of the group open to accommodate the continuous possibility of new students moving into the school. On the other hand, if there is already a large group of new students, it may be overwhelming to continue adding more students to the existing group. The purpose may be better served by beginning a new group at the beginning of each report card period.

Other considerations for group structure are the length of each session and the total number of sessions. Likewise, how will each session be structured? Will there be icebreakers and closing activities each time? Will the students have homework? Will the school social worker be opening the session and then turning it over to the students? Will the social worker use the group as an educational resource and provide information, with the students just responding to what is being taught? It is important that the social worker think through all of the reasons for each activity and clarify how the group will run in order to avoid unexpected events that will upset the students. The school social worker needs to plan and consider all of the possible options before the group begins.

Group Size

The size of the group is also a major consideration. It is often determined by the population and the amount of time set aside for each group session. For example, teaching social skills to a group of special education students with emotional problems that make them angry and explosive will be most effectively accomplished in a small group with a cotherapist to assist if a fight breaks out. These sessions should probably be scheduled a couple of times a week for 30 minutes or less. The group could be much larger if the goal is to teach social skills to a group of third graders who don't interact much with their peers because they are shy. This particular group could meet weekly for a full class period (but no more than 40 minutes) in order to give the students a chance to practice peer interactions through role plays.

Group size will influence the success or failure of the group. The number of participants should match the group purpose and objectives. A large educational group may do very well because its purpose is simply to provide information, whereas a therapy group, in which all members need to interact, should remain small. Five members are considered the most effective size group when dealing with an intellectual task in which data must be collected, exchanged, and analyzed and a group decision made (Slater, 1958). In a group of five members, a number of different relationships can be formed with a moderate level of intimacy. Several individuals can act as "buffers" to help deal with stressful situations rather than letting each individual respond to his or her own individual pressure (Zastrow, 2006).

Group Length

The length of individual sessions and the number of group meetings should be predetermined by the school social worker. The social worker should decide if the group will have a set number of sessions (a closed group) with a particular topic to be covered each week or will be ongoing and end when the members feel they have reached their goals. The ideal length for a time-limited group is six sessions.

It is always important to remember that students who are attending groups are missing other classes, and it is not a good idea to keep them from a particular class for an extended period of time. Students in self-contained classrooms who remain with the same teacher for the school day have more flexibility. However, even these students may miss a particular subject repeatedly if the group is held at the same time each week.

Group Rules

When students or group members help establish group rules, they usually become more involved in making the group a success. The school social worker should clarify the purpose and goals of the group and explain his or her goals and plans for the sessions. The members should then work together to establish five or six rules of their own. These may include such things as each member arriving on time or attending each session. The number of planned sessions and whether or not the group will be open or closed also should be discussed.

Pregroup Assessment

Before beginning the group, the social worker should complete an assessment for each member of the group. Background information on group members will be an asset to the social worker in helping to understand the members and their individual needs. Social workers should remember that the group is made up of individuals with their own needs. Even though they meet as a group, they will not stay committed to the group if their individual needs are not taken care of. A social worker cannot meet each of these individual needs without knowing what they are.

Planning for Termination

When planning a group it is necessary to consider termination, follow-up, and outcome measurement to determine whether the group was effective in meeting the predetermined objectives. Termination should be discussed at the first session and in the individual meetings prior to the beginning of the group. Termination should never come as a surprise to members.

Group members should be allowed to share their feelings about the ending of the group. In addition, members of the group should have a say in determining that the group tasks have been accomplished and should be able to discuss what will determine group effectiveness for them. Termination should be an official activity in which students receive a certificate or some kind of formal acknowledgment of the work they completed in the group. It is a good idea to give some positive reinforcement to the students for their participation and encourage them to continue the work they did in the group.

Follow-Up

Support should be provided for students once the group is terminated. The school social worker should provide information to the students' teachers so they can help reinforce and support the skills that students learned in the group. Teachers can help bridge the transition from the group back to the classroom. The social worker should act as a support to teachers so that the skills students learned in the group will transfer to the classroom. When time allows, it is good for the school social worker to check on the students approximately 1 month after the group has terminated to give additional support.

CRISIS INTERVENTION AND PREARRANGED GROUPS

School social work practice requires flexibility. School social workers are often called on to assist in situations that are the result of a crisis or trauma. The ideal situation for running effective school groups is to have time to plan, preassess members, and set size and time limitations. However, it is possible to lead groups successfully without much time to organize and plan group membership and curriculum.

Sometimes school social workers are asked to provide group counseling in situations that are preestablished or consist of students from an entire classroom. The social worker should utilize the classroom teacher to assist in groups whose membership consists of an entire class. Because students need some monitoring and incentives to behave, and because school social workers do not have any leverage with children who do not know them, it is wise to ask the teacher to stay in the room and assist with student behavior.

Case Example

A school social worker was assigned to teach social skills to students in a self-contained special education class for emotionally disturbed students. The group was comprised of eight middle school students between the ages of 12 and 15. The students were placed around a table so they could write during some of the group activities. The school social worker was alone with the students and did not have a previous relationship with any of them. During the first session, the students kicked each other under the table and pushed each others' arms throughout the entire session. The next session, the social worker removed the table and put the students' chairs in a circle. The chairs were far enough apart to keep the students from touching each other. The group session was moving along when one student insulted another. Immediately, the student who was insulted jumped out of his seat and tried to hit the person who had made the comment. The school social worker jumped up and stood between the two students and was almost hit. Afterward, it was extremely difficult to get the two students and the rest of the group to calm down.

For future sessions, the social worker had the special education classroom aide remain in the room and keep track of inappropriate comments and actions from the students. Each time the students behaved inappropriately, the special education aide would write it down. The students were on a level system in which they could earn points for good behavior and lose points for inappropriate behavior. Therefore, the point totals mattered to them. When they reached enough points for each day, they could have spare time to play games or use the classroom computer. Each time the aide would write down an inappropriate action, the student would lose points for the day. The classroom aide helped keep the students' behavior under control, and the group was able to work on learning social skills. The school social worker was much more successful after she became familiar with the students and had the help of another adult who had leverage over the students.

When groups are formed quickly to assist students who are in crisis, the group members should be assured of group privacy and confidentiality. Even in crisis situations, parental consent should be obtained or parents should be notified that the school is providing group counseling. When students have been exposed to a traumatic situation, such as a natural disaster, suicide of a classmate, or violence, the school social worker should assist children in dealing with the fear and insecurity created in the aftermath of these situations. Crisis intervention groups should be made up of children who have been directly affected by the situation. The children should be matched in age whenever possible. The group should not be larger than 10 students to allow time for each student to talk out his or her feelings. When a school social worker is working with trauma and crisis situations, it is most important to allow the students to talk and release their feelings. When students have a chance to tell their stories repeatedly, they adjust to the traumatic events over time and their feelings in response to those events become less intense. Also, hearing stories from their peers helps students to become more comfortable with their own feelings. Most crisis groups will probably need to meet only one or two times. (Crisis debriefing is discussed in more detail in Chapter 10.)

ICEBREAKERS

Icebreakers, or warm-up activities, are a useful tool in helping group members to loosen up, forget about themselves, and join the group. A school social worker should begin each group session with an icebreaker. Most warm-up activities should take only 5 minutes, but they are excellent tools for helping members become acquainted with each other and learn what they have in common. Icebreakers should be presented as nonthreatening but mandatory. There may be some part of the activity in which a group member may not wish to participate, but the main activity should always include everyone in the group.

Following are some icebreakers that are particularly fun for children:

Two Truths and a Lie

Group members write two true statements and one false statement about themselves. The others in the group have to decide which of the statements is the lie.

Boundary Breaking

Each group member asks a partner a series of questions. The partner reports the answers to the group. The members may answer each question truthfully or make no comment. Some sample questions are:

1. What was the last movie you saw?
2. What was the last book you read?
3. What is your favorite sport?
4. What is your favorite thing about yourself?
5. What is your least favorite thing about yourself?

School social workers can write their own questions that may fit the group more completely.

Name Game

Each group member must make up a gesture that represents him or her. Members tell their name and gesture. The activity starts with one person and moves around a circle. Each group member must repeat the name and gesture of all the group members before him or her. The last person will be giving the name and gesture of all members of the group.

Who Is Your Neighbor?

This is like musical chairs, with one chair less than the group membership. A person stands in the middle of a circle and asks, "Who is your neighbor?" The speaker says things like "My neighbors have on blue shoes," at which point all of the group members with blue shoes must leave their seat and sit in a different chair. The person in the middle is also trying to get a seat. The one left without a chair then has to identify his neighbor with a statement such as "My neighbors have brown hair."

These fun activities help members to relax and become comfortable with each other so they can work in the group. There are many icebreakers that can be found in books and on the Internet to assist school social workers and group leaders. (The activities listed here are in the public domain and I could not find a source that lists the original author.)

TYPES OF GROUPS

School social workers should understand the various types of groups and determine which one will help accomplish their particular goals. Many of the groups listed in this chapter have been implemented in schools, some with a greater degree of success than others. The only way to become skilled as a group leader is to facilitate groups. Sometimes, things will not go as planned, and sometimes there will be unexpected outcomes. School social workers need to continue trying to facilitate new groups because group work skills can only be learned though practice and trial and error. Children are usually flexible and enjoy it when things do not go as planned. Children and adolescents are a wonderful population to work with to improve group work skills because they like the unexpected. School social workers can have a good time with children in groups.

When high school students need group counseling, it is difficult to find a meeting time during the school day that does not interfere with their required classes. Most high school students are in five to seven classes per day, and each student's schedule is unique. It is hard to find an ideal time for the group to meet. Therefore, it is a good idea to rotate the time the group meets weekly so that the students will not have several absences in one class (Fast, 1999). If the social worker needs to rotate the group meeting times, it is a good idea to make a printed copy of the schedule for each student and teacher. It also helps to contact the students the day before the group and remind them to attend the next day.

One way to assist with the scheduling of groups is to hold them during study hall periods (Fast, 1999). The school social worker could ask for students to sign up for group attendance during their study hall if they want to work on specific issues such as improving relationships, learning to write a résumé, or planning for college. Self-referral assures that students are motivated and willing to work in the group.

Education Groups

Education groups teach specialized skills and knowledge (Zastrow, 2001, p. 5). Some of the common skills taught in schools groups are communication, anger management, and conflict resolution. The format described below for teaching social skills should be used in teaching each type of education group.

The school social worker should be sure that all education groups are small and time limited, and that students who attend are close in age and have similar issues. The social worker should always begin a group by letting the students know what skills or information they can gain from participating in the group. The social worker should help the children want to attend and learn from the group. Curriculum development should begin with identifying some areas in which potential group members have difficulty.

The first session should allow children and adolescents to discuss some of their problems that relate to the topic of the group. This initial discussion helps students identify with others who are experiencing the same difficulties and helps them see that they are not unique in their struggles (Corey & Corey, 2006). Once the children can find some common ground and decide that the group discussions might help them, they will be more willing to continue. Education groups should always include role playing and practice of the new skill to help the children utilize the new skill correctly and become comfortable with it.

Social Skills Groups

Social skills are "the ability to interact with others in a given social context in specific ways that are socially acceptable or valued and, at the same time, personally beneficial, mutually beneficial, or beneficial primarily to others" (Combs & Slaby, 1977). Social skills include many verbal and nonverbal actions and responses to others. The responses one makes will either create a positive or negative reaction from the other person, either increasing or decreasing the social interaction between the two people (Spence, 2003).

Many children today do not have a good repertoire of social skills. They are said to have an acquisition deficit if they do not have a particular social skill in their behavioral repertoire. Performance deficits refer to a situation in which the child is known to have acquired a social skill but does not perform it appropriately. Children with anxiety and cognitive difficulties often struggle with the appropriate performance of social skills. Inappropriate social performance may be the result of cognitive deficits in information processing (Spence, 2003). These skill deficits create difficulty at school both with peers and adults.

Learning social skills and becoming socially competent helps children perform more effectively in any social interaction whether at school, home, or with others in the community. A child's ability to interact with others in a positive way affects every aspect of his or her life and will be a determining factor in later success on the job. School social workers should determine which social skills seem most needed by the students who will attend the group. The social worker should plan on teaching one skill per week for 6 weeks. The group should last for no more than 30 minutes. Groups should be structured with an even number of students (no more than 10 total) so there will be partners with whom to practice the social skills through role playing. Students who need social skills training usually have a difficult time dealing with frustrations. The school social worker should plan the group so that there is plenty of room between students. The students should be seated at a table, but it should be large enough so that they cannot hit or kick each other underneath the table.

As each session begins, the skill from the previous week should be practiced. An example from the Boys Town social skills curriculum is that during the first week students would learn to follow instructions: "1) look at the person, 2) say 'okay,' 3) do what you've been asked right away, and 4) check back" (Dowd & Tierney, 1995). The next week the social worker would ask the students to repeat and model the steps for following instructions before beginning to learn the next social skill, which is "accepting criticism or a consequence." The steps to accepting criticism include "1) look at the person, 2) say okay, 3) don't argue" (Dowd & Tierney, 1995).

Students should have a chance to tell stories about how they have used the last skill learned. Then the skills from all of the previous weeks should be reviewed. This review should take about 10 minutes. As the school social worker introduces a new skill, he or she should give background information about when this skill is used and how it will benefit the students if they use it. Then the new skill should be introduced, discussed, and practiced. The group time should consist of role-playing situations utilizing the new social skill. Role playing helps group members learn how to express themselves more effectively, test reality, and practice new behavior (Corey & Corey, 2006). The school social worker should have the role-play situations or vignettes ready in advance. The students should act them out in pairs, then each pair may volunteer to show the group how they have utilized the skill.

When teaching social skills, about 15 minutes of practice time must be given during each session. A necessary group rule for role playing to be effective is that students must be supportive and must not criticize or make fun of others.

Peer group pressure pulls a person to conform to the standards of friends (Corey & Corey, 2006). Sometimes the need for acceptance is so great that children and adolescents will behave in a way that is harmful to them. The group leader must be skilled in keeping the other members as a source of support rather than criticism. One of the best ways to implement the source of support is to ask the students how they want others to behave toward them. Answers should be typed and handed out to the group. The typed rules serve as a contract for members and help the leader reinforce the rules when there is a need to remind the members about them. (See Appendix 9.3.) The rules can also be placed on a poster that the group leader brings each session. A good reminder of the need to learn social skills occurs when students violate the rules. When that happens, the leader must stop the group and ask what skill has been violated, how it can be corrected, and what must happen to make everyone feel better.

Students should also be given homework assignments to keep them thinking about the social skill during the week. Students with severe social skills deficits should attend more than one social skills group in order to cover a wide range of skills. Social skills training must include instructions, modeling, behavior rehearsal, feedback, and reinforcement. In order for behavioral changes to become permanent, interventions such as cognitive restructuring, which can help the child or adolescent think about a situation in new ways, may be required. Along with cognitive restructuring, the child or adolescent must learn to self-regulate and control negative behaviors (Spence, 2003).

Social skills training alone cannot produce lasting change without the use of self-restraint and reinforcement from outside sources when the child or adolescent makes a positive effort to use the new skills. This means that the school social worker must involve the parents and teachers to help reinforce the skills that are being taught in the social skills group.

Self-Help Groups/Peer Counseling

Peer counseling and self-help groups are effective because teens value the opinions of their peers. Many schools have implemented peer counseling and peer support groups to help with issues such as new student orientation, drug and alcohol problems, fights at school, truancy, and disruptive behavior.

Some peer support programs focus on helping students improve their interactions with others. One approach to improving peer relations is to use creative drama in the classroom. This approach utilizes group work principles through improvisational role playing of invented themes that reflect the students' problems (Walsh-Bowers & Basso, 1999). Students are usually willing to act out a situation that is similar to one of their problems as long as they are not really revealing their true situation. However, as group cohesiveness develops, the students become able to confront their strengths and weaknesses directly (Walsh-Bowers & Basso, 1999). This approach gives children and adolescents a safe way to learn problem-solving skills for situations with which they are struggling. It also helps them learn how to cooperate, take turns, understand the feelings of others, and solve disputes (Walsh-Bowers, 1992).

Problem-Solving Groups

Group work principles can be utilized with school organizations and clubs. Sometimes a school organization is not functioning well because members do not get along or do not have the same goals. School social workers can be an asset to school organizations if they let the group sponsors know of their ability to facilitate groups.

Case Example

A large urban high school had a cheerleading squad of eight boys and eight girls who were in the 11th and 12th grades. The cheerleaders did not get along well and were constantly fighting with one another. The sponsor of the organization approached the school social worker for help. The social worker conducted team building activities and goal setting with the cheerleaders to help them find common ground. These activities took place after school and lasted for one evening. The school provided dinner for the students and social worker.

The goal setting involved having the cheerleaders write three individual cheerleading goals and three group goals for the cheerleading squad. Each goal was written on a sticky note and pasted on the wall. The social worker clustered together the goals that were similar. The 16 cheerleaders were then divided into four subgroups of four members each. Each subgroup was given the sticky notes that had been clustered together according to similarities (approximately 12 per subgroup). Each subgroup had to choose one individual goal and one group goal that all the members of the subgroup could live with from among those written on the notes. The four subgroups reported to the entire group on the goals they had selected. The entire group then discussed the goals and had the option of adding one or two additional goals if something that was important to the entire group had been deleted.

The process of selecting goals helped the cheerleaders to talk with each other and find some common ground.

The next phase of the group involved writing action plans that would set guidelines for accomplishing the group and individual goals. Each subgroup developed a framework for accomplishing their goal, including who was going to do what, and when and how it would be done. The four subgroups reported to each other and decided in what order they would work on the four goals.

The final phase of the group process was to allow the cheerleaders to do "strengths bombardments" with each other. The cheerleaders had to go around the room and say positive things about each other. After working so hard to find common goals and make plans to accomplish them, they were able to interact in a positive way, which set the tone for the rest of the year.

Faculty School Teams

School social workers can be an asset to the faculty as well as the students. School teams can be designed to build rapport among faculty members and to solve school problems. The format for working with school teams fits closely with the model used to build relationships with the cheerleaders discussed previously. The faculty is usually divided into small groups. The teams should be composed of teachers who do not normally work together so they can build new relationships. It is best to break up departments so that all of the fifth-grade teachers, or English teachers, or coaches are not on the same team.

The school social worker should conduct the school team meetings initially to explain rules of group work, define purpose, determine rules, and set a time frame. Sometimes, the school teams can be utilized as a task group to accomplish a specific task. The team concept can be used to set goals for the school year or to build rapport with new faculty members as each team provides mentoring and support. The teams should always set an agenda and determine an action plan for who will do what, and when and how it will be done. The school social worker should always be available to use his or her group work skills with any team to help the team members keep moving in a positive direction.

Truancy Groups

Students who are truant have unexcused absences, which are usually unknown to parents (Teasley, 2004). Reasons for absenteeism include lack of community support, unsupportive school environment, disorderly family life, inclement weather, transportation problems, personal deficits, and poor health. Reported juvenile court cases for truancy increased 85 percent from 1989 to 1998 (Baker, Sigmon, & Nugent, 2001). It is especially difficult when students are truant because of skills deficits or lack of interest and motivation. Truancy seems to compound these students' problems.

School social workers can help by determining the root cause of the students' truancy. Support groups that provide tutoring from peer mentors can be a helpful tool to assist truant students in returning to class. Mentoring has proven to be a useful method of reducing truancy rates (Teasley, 2004). School social workers who are interested in using mentoring programs with at-risk youths can review program information on the Internet through the U.S. Department of Justice's Office of Juvenile Justice and Delinquency Prevention (OJJDP) website at *www.ojjdp.ncjrs.org*.

Alternative Program Groups

Many school districts are utilizing alternative education programs to reach at-risk students. Group counseling is usually included in these special programs. Some of the types of groups include support groups for teenage pregnancy, parental education groups for teenage mothers, and drug and alcohol awareness groups. Students in special programs may need groups that teach life skills, such as how to write a résumé or how to conduct oneself at a job interview. The possibilities are unlimited if the school social worker will take notice of the needs in his or her school and try to respond to them by utilizing group work skills.

Groups for Children Who Have Been Traumatized

Traumatic events such as natural disasters, homelessness, school violence, suicide of a friend, or moving to a new community can create stress for children. Homelessness has severe effects on children's development and academic progress (Moroz & Segal, 1990). They cannot be expected to perform at their full academic potential shortly after a traumatic event (Williams, 2004). Children cannot function until they have been able to express their feelings. A group setting can give children the opportunity for peer and adult support and an opportunity to express their feelings.

Groups are particularly helpful when the situation to be dealt with is a disaster or has affected a large portion of the school population. Strategies that can be incorporated into a group include oral storytelling (with the leader providing the first sentence of the story), photos, poems, videos, creative writing, journal entries, art projects, puppets, and dramatizations (Williams, 2004). Children need to talk about the crisis, receive factual information, and be debriefed. Groups provide the perfect venue for all of these activities.

Children and adolescents who thrive after a traumatic event have built-in resilience that helps them cope. The dimensions of resilience include (1) the personality disposition of the child, (2) a supportive family milieu, and (3) an external support system that encourages and supports a child's coping efforts (Walker, 1995). The school can serve as the external support system just by recognizing the child's difficulties and not expecting full performance until the child has worked through the trauma. Placement in a support group can be extremely helpful to encourage the child to discuss his or her fears and normalize the situation. (Debriefing groups are discussed in Chapter 10, which deals with mass trauma and violence.)

Interdisciplinary Team Groups

School business is often accomplished by people working in groups. Most special education placements and dismissals are decided by groups. These groups consist of educators from several disciplines, such as special education teachers, school psychologists, social workers, administrators, regular-education teachers, and parents. The school social worker is an integral part of these teams and can assist in helping the team function by utilizing group work and communication skills when the team members seem unable to resolve issues. Often, the use of mediation techniques may keep the problem within the school, eliminating the need to seek outside mediators. The school social worker can use problem-solving skills to help both sides clearly define their main concerns. After both sides clearly state the issues in the conflict, they can begin to negotiate. Each side needs to brainstorm alternatives to the problem and then find a solution about which both sides can agree (Blades, 1985). The social worker can help the school district and parents reach agreement by helping facilitate the group through the use of mediation skills.

MEASURING SUCCESS IN A GROUP

Children and adolescents are the best monitors of their own success in a group. If the group purpose, goals, and contract have been clearly stated at the beginning of the group, it is easy to determine when the contract and goals have been reached. If the group is time limited, some of the goals may not be completely finished, so it is important for the school social worker to help the students recognize the progress they have made.

Parents also should be notified about the progress that students made during the time they spent in the group. (See Appendix 9.4 for a form to help notify parents about student progress.) If the group is long term or ongoing, it is helpful to send a letter to parents intermittently (such as every 6 weeks) to let them know that their student is continuing to make progress in the group. This written notification helps keep parents involved with the student and his or her school activities.

CONCLUSION

Group work is a valuable practice tool for school social workers. Almost any kind of problem can be addressed through group work. The possibilities are unlimited if a school social worker will make himself or herself available to students and faculty. The social worker must obtain parental consent to begin groups with students. For groups to succeed, the social worker must plan the size and purpose of the group to fit the developmental level of the students attending. It is never a good idea for the ages or interests of children and adolescents in a group to cover too great a space. Success also depends on having a private location for the group that is free from distractions. The social worker should plan ice-breaking and closure activities for each session. When groups function according to plan, wonderful things can happen.

Discussion Topics

1. With what kinds of groups do you have experience?
2. When working with groups, do you prefer working alone or with a coleader/therapist? What do you think would work better in a school: working alone or with a coleader/therapist?
3. What social skills do you feel are most important?
4. Discuss the various types of groups that schools need for (a) students and (b) faculty and support staff.
5. Role play: Practice trying to model and teach a social skill, such as how to accept criticism.

APPENDIX 9.1. Parent/Guardian Permission Form

The school social worker, ______________________________, is starting a group to teach social skills. Your son/daughter has been recommended for membership in the group. The purpose of the group is to teach social skills and practice the new skills in the group. Each week a new social skill will be taught and practiced with role plays. The group will meet for 6 weeks, and each session will last 30 minutes. The skills the group will teach are:

1. How to ask for help
2. How to show respect
3. How to accept consequences
4. How to give and accept compliments
5. How to accept criticism
6. How to manage anger

If you have any questions, please contact: ______________________________

Phone number: ______________________________

I give my permission for ______________________________ to participate in a group at school designed to teach social skills for 6 weeks.

______________________________ ______________________

Signature and relationship (mother, father, guardian) Date

Appendix 9.2. Limits of Confidentiality for Group Counseling Form

Student Name: ______________________________ Date: ________________

It is necessary for student group members and the school social worker to keep information they hear from other members of the group confidential. It allows group members to establish trust in one another, and makes it possible for members to share important information. The school social worker will address any breaches in confidentiality from other students but cannot guarantee that group members will keep all information confidential. Students are asked to keep all group activities and writing that they may do about the group focused on their own information and not information obtained from another group member.

The school social worker will not share information about the group without written consent from the student and his or her parent or guardian, except under the following circumstances:

1. If student threatens to harm self or others
2. If abuse or neglect is reported
3. If school social work records are subpoenaed
4. If parents request information about their own child

I agree to these terms:

______________________________ ________________
Student signature Date

______________________________ ________________
Parent or guardian signature Date

APPENDIX 9.3. School Group Contract Form

I agree to become a member of the ____________________ group during ___________ period for 6 weeks beginning ____________________. I will honor the following commitments:

1. Keep information I hear in the group to myself.
2. Attend each session on time and participate in group activities.
3. Show respect for other group members and the group leader.
4. Tell the truth.

____ ______________________
Student signature Date

APPENDIX 9.4. Group Progress Report

Date: __________

Dear Parent/Guardian:

Your student has successfully completed the __________________ group.

The goals that he/she set at the beginning of the group are as follows:

1. Meet other students.
2. Learn school rules.
3. Find out about extracurricular activities.
4. Become acquainted with school surroundings.

It has been a pleasure to have your child participate in the group.

Thank you for your support.

Sincerely,

____
School Social Worker

10

Violence and Trauma

Violent acts in the school and community cause trauma for children. Children and adolescents increasingly are exposed to violence across many settings in which they are innocent victims (Sieger, Rojas-Vilches, McKinney, & Renk, 2004). Children's reactions to violence range from mild to severe, including symptoms of posttraumatic stress disorder (PTSD). According to Bruce Perry (2004a, 2004e), a traumatic experience "activates an individual's stress response for an abnormally long period of time." An event is considered traumatic if it is threatening and overwhelming and involves a threat to one's life or the life of a close associate.

This chapter discusses the various types of violence and other traumatic experiences to which children are often exposed and also provides an overview of school-based interventions used to relieve the stress and trauma that result from exposure to violence.

OVERVIEW OF THE TYPES OF VIOLENCE TO WHICH CHILDREN ARE EXPOSED

Violence at Home

Children who live in violent homes experience both the direct and indirect effects of family violence. Direct effects include physical abuse and/or neglect. Indirect effects include irritability and inconsistent or negative discipline by caregivers as a result of stress, depression, or apprehension about future violence (Jaffe, Wolfe, & Wilson, 1990;

Jouriles & Norwood, 1995). Witnessing violence in the home can result in trauma similar to the trauma of actual physical abuse. Behavioral, cognitive, and social problems also result from witnessing violence. Children who witness violence experience some or all of the following behavioral problems: withdrawal; aggression against peers, family members, and family property; cruelty to animals; tantrums; acting out; immature behavior; truancy and delinquency; hyperactivity; impulsivity; sleep disorders; headaches; stomachaches; diarrhea; enuresis; and depression (Jouriles & Norwood, 1994; Openshaw & Halvorson, 2005).

It is critical for school social workers to establish a therapeutic relationship with children who are exposed to violence and neglect at home. School must be a safe place for the child, where the potential for embarrassment or threats is minimized. School social workers should notify teachers of warning signs of abuse and neglect so that teachers can help identify children who appear to be at risk. Social workers should partner with teachers to help keep the classroom and school a safe and stress-free environment for a traumatized child.

School Disasters

Unfortunately, children and adolescents are sometimes exposed to school disasters, which may occur in diverse ways. Some occur away from school, such as student car accidents and deaths of students in a school bus accident as they travel to games or field trips or to and from school. Other disasters, such as school shootings, may occur on campus during the school day.

Each student responds uniquely to school violence and disasters. Even students who were not directly involved or who do not know the victims often feel fear, anxiety, and a sense of vulnerability.

Altercations

Sometimes students are exposed to less extreme forms of violence at school, such as fights. These events, even where relatively minor, can still trigger anxiety and fear in those students who witness them. School administrators can reduce fighting by creating strict penalties for those involved in fights. The duration and intensity of school altercations can be decreased by penalizing those who watch the fight. When there is an audience, fights tend to last longer and become more violent. However, fights may occur in spite of efforts to prevent them when students respond spontaneously and violently to negative interactions before school officials can stop them.

Case Example

Duanne was 18 years old and was repeating his senior year of high school. He was classified as emotionally disturbed and was in special education classes. His parents did not want him in a self-contained special education class designed to help him with his behavior. He had a history of violence and had just returned to his home school after a 6-month stay in the district's intervention program, which he had entered because of a violent fight at school.

Within the first couple of days after his return to school he had jumped out of his seat and yelled at a teacher, telling her to "back off and leave me alone–or else." The school administrators called a meeting to review his individualized education plan (IEP), after which they decided to send him back to the intervention center. The parents refused to accept this change and hired a lawyer. Upon the conclusion of hearings on his situation, Duanne was allowed to continue attending his regular high school, but the school district hired an aide to accompany him throughout the day. It was the aide's job to keep Duanne out of fights.

One day, Duanne and another student who had not stepped out of his way got into a loud cursing and shoving match in the hall. They pushed and yelled at each other in the crowded hall, and the students who were trying to pass them in order to get to class were unable to pass through the hallway. Before the altercation was stopped, several students had been knocked down or shoved into lockers. Some of the students who were knocked down were hurt and very frightened over the intensity of the altercation. However, all of the students went to class after the fight had been stopped. Duanne and the other student involved in the fight were suspended for 3 days.

The students who had witnessed the fight were shaken for the rest of the day by the intensity of the violence and found it difficult to concentrate. No intervention or debriefing was conducted with these students. They essentially lost a day of school because the school did not respond to their needs. Later that day, the teachers talked among themselves about how students were affected by the fight. They determined that there should have been an in-school group discussion for the students who had been exposed to the fight, particularly those who were injured. The school administrators and school social worker should have briefly visited each classroom to meet with students who were affected by the fight. They should have asked if students were physically and emotionally all right. Then the school administrators should have provided reassurance that those who were fighting would experience consequences and that the school was a safe place and would not tolerate violent interactions between students.

Community Violence

Some children and adolescents are surrounded by violence. It is estimated that approximately one-third of junior high and high school students witness violence in their communities (Schwab-Stone et al., 1999). Exposure to violence in inner-city areas is very high. Mazza & Reynolds (1999) reported that only 12% of youths in these areas stated that they had *not* witnessed any violence.

Children living in communities in which violence is ongoing may experience more severe reactions to trauma than children who experience a one-time traumatic event. This is because they have learned to be on guard for violence. The longer and more severe the traumatic event to which a child or adolescent is exposed, the more likely he or she will experience severe emotional stress and reactions. Accordingly, some children experience long-term effects from trauma because of chronic violence in their home or neighborhood.

Children and adolescents who are exposed to community violence display a wide array of psychological symptoms, ranging from depression and anxiety to antisocial and suicidal behaviors. Exposure to community violence has emerged as a major risk factor in the development of emotional and behavioral problems in children and adolescents (Sieger et al., 2004).

PTSD symptoms are common in children and adolescents who are exposed to violence in their communities. Children who live with chronic violence experience difficulties at school, including poor concentration because of lack of sleep, difficulty avoiding thoughts about the violence, and anxious attachment to their mother. Likewise, children exposed to violence may be aggressive in their play because they are imitating behaviors they have seen, or they act tough to deal with their fears (Sieger et al., 2004).

Case Example

Juan, age 16, was a junior in high school. His father was in prison for murder and had been incarcerated since Juan was 10 years old. Juan and his mother visited his father in prison at least monthly. Juan had difficulty in school, with many absences. He was diagnosed as emotionally disturbed and was receiving services from special education.

Some of Juan's school-related problems involved his girl friend. Juan would yell at her, and on a couple of occasions he had hit her. The girlfriend's parents called the school frequently to complain about the situation, but the girl continued to date Juan in spite of the disapproval of her family and friends.

Juan was a member of a gang and was often involved in altercations with other gangs. One evening, his gang participated in a violent encounter with another gang, and Juan's best friend died in his arms from gunshot wounds. When he returned to school, everyone in the school building was talking about the gang shooting. Juan was withdrawn and would not talk about the shooting with either the school social worker or counselor. Most of the students on campus were afraid of him, so he received very little peer support. The other members of his gang gave him emotional support, but he would not allow himself to confront the grief he felt over the loss of his friend or the fear he felt over his father's potential execution. He remained aloof. The school social worker was unable to offer assistance in spite of continued efforts to provide nurturing and create a feeling of trust and security.

Natural Disasters

Natural disasters create trauma for children, particularly if they are displaced. Hurricanes Katrina and Rita gave many U.S. schools outside the hurricanes' paths the opportunity to help children and families who were displaced by the flooding and destruction they caused. Many of the families experienced a complete loss of personal property and community connections. Most of those who escaped had no personal belongings and, in some cases, no information about friends and family members, including pets. The trauma from the initial feelings of fear and loss seemed to become worse over time as more information about the degree of destruction and loss became known.

Case Example

Marcus, age 12, and his mother were displaced when Hurricane Rita uprooted their community. Marcus was a special education student. He and his mother left their home on the Gulf Coast with only the clothes on their back, their dog, and their extended family members. Marcus and his mother stayed with relatives in another city for 3 weeks until they could get settled in their own apartment. Because of the extended stay, Marcus was placed in school in his new location so he would not fall behind while he was away from home. The first day he attended school, he wanted to talk about his loss and fears. When pictures of the damage were released, he wanted to discuss the pictures and his experiences with his classmates. He talked about where his home was and what he thought had happened to it. He was finally able to visit his home after a month. After he had visited his home, he again needed to talk about the disaster with his classmates.

Marcus and his mother struggled with a variety of problems, like where to put their dog, who could not stay in their new apartment. They needed food and personal items, and Marcus needed clothing for school. These were important concerns for Marcus and his mother before they could begin to cope with their other losses.

School social workers can assist on an emotional level, as well as providing information about community resources for clothing, food, and cash. It usually takes a few weeks before those who have been misplaced by a natural disaster receive any cash from the Federal Emergency Management Agency (FEMA) or the Red Cross. School social workers can help solicit donations of money, clothing, and household items from the school and community. This, of course, assumes that the entire community has not been affected by the disaster. When assisting victims of natural disasters, it is necessary for school social workers to "start where the client is" by taking care of basic needs, such as food and shelter.

REACTIONS TO TRAUMATIC EVENTS

Traumatic events cause those affected to cope with feelings of fear, anxiety, and loss, as well as dealing with rebuilding their lives. When people are exposed to highly stressful situations, they may fall back on a variety of coping mechanisms (Milgram & Toubiana, 1996), including externalizing behaviors, such as aggression and confrontation, or avoidant behaviors. Confronting behaviors include attending funerals and memorial services, whereas avoidant behaviors are characterized by withdrawal and drawing inward to deal with the grief.

Traumatic grief can be different from normal bereavement because of the nature of remembering and reexperiencing and the extreme intensity of the symptoms (Nader, 1996). Grief can be described as sadness, whereas the major reaction to trauma is terror. Traumatic events may include natural disasters such as tsunamis and hurricanes or violent acts that create multiple or unanticipated deaths. Personal disasters such as house fires, drownings, or car accidents may create trauma for the surviving family members. Mass trauma includes situations such as multiple deaths at school, school bus crashes, plane crashes, and acts of terror. When a youth is severely traumatized during a violent event, it may be necessary to process a few or many aspects of the traumatic experience, emotions, and impressions before grieving is possible (Nader, 2001). Important elements to consider in assessing a child who has suffered a traumatic loss include:

- Level of anxiety/fear
- DSM-IV-TR diagnosis (especially symptoms of PTSD)
- Past experience with loss/trauma/crisis
- Specific meaning of this trauma (Webb, 2002, pp. 374–375)

Both teachers and students experience severe reactions to trauma. Vicarious or secondary traumatization occurs as adults "listen to children's stories, watch their play, and witness the accompanying painful feelings of rage, anguish, and fear" (Cunningham, 2006, p. 327). Teachers may become overly concerned or have anxiety and fears about future violence, which prevents them from concentrating.

Elementary school children may have stress and anxiety as a result of trauma that manifests itself in somatic complaints, such as headaches or stomachaches. They may also worry about death and the possibility of other violent acts or experience changes similar to those shown with depression, such as withdrawal, trouble concentrating, and difficulty sleeping or eating. Some children show signs of regression, such as baby talk, tantrums, and enuresis. Other children may become angry and defiant (National Education Association, 2000).

Older children may exhibit school-related problems such as increased absences, falling grades, and lack of interest in activities or friends. They may also become preoccupied with the details of the traumatic event. Common reactions are to dissociate and withdraw or to become hypervigilant or hyperactive (Perry, 2002a). Boys may also discuss the need for revenge or express hate and anger. Older students may blame themselves or distort reality. They may need to discuss the event repeatedly in order to rebuild reality (National Education Association, 2000).

Typical reactions to violence and trauma include recurring thoughts about the event accompanied by guilt for surviving. Trauma produces many symptoms similar to attention-deficit/hyperactivity disorder (ADHD), and a misdiagnosis of ADHD may prevent the child from receiving help in dealing with the trauma. Traumatized children will focus on nonverbal information, such as facial expressions, which makes it possible for them to misinterpret or misunderstand the responses of others. Some people talk about the event because their feelings are intense and need to be expressed in tears or anger. Others avoid the topic as much as possible. Anxiety and fear of recurring violence often lead to an inability to concentrate. Likewise, behaviors may be inconsistent and regressive. A preoccupation with death may also persist.

Continuous violence creates more pervasive symptoms and chronic problems. The following are extreme reactions to trauma:

1. Trouble sleeping or being alone
2. Eating disorders
3. Depression
4. Easily startled (anxious)
5. Hypervigilance (scanning the environment, or living in a constant state of fear)
6. Looking for safe spots in the environment ("scoping out" a room)
7. Wishing for revenge
8. Risk taking, acting on impulse
9. Violent behavior
10. Regression
11. School-related problems (absenteeism, failing grades)
12. Development of pessimistic attitudes
13. Substance abuse
14. Relationship problems
15. Dissociation (blocking of normal emotions)

Reactions to trauma require intervention from appropriate professionals, such as school social workers. Without professional intervention, there is a strong chance that the effects of exposure to trauma will not go away, resulting in poor performance at school and work, as well as an inability to form and maintain relationships. Trauma, if untreated, can create a lifetime loss of potential (Perry, 2002b).

An individual who remains isolated has an increased chance of burying the traumatic memory, which may create dissociation. When an individual suffers from dissociation, there is always the chance for resurfacing of the trauma through something that triggers the memory. Dissociation may be manifested through behaviors such as daydreaming, fantasy, distraction, pretending, and depersonalization (Perry, 2002a). School social workers need to be available to talk with children and help defuse and debrief those students who have been exposed to stressful situations.

Trauma can interfere with grieving. Initially, the child's primary emotion is fear. This may prevent mourning the lost loved one. During the second phase, the primary emotion is sadness. Discussing the traumatic event at this time is critical because children will model their responses after their caregiver. Children should be allowed to discuss the traumatic event as often and whenever they choose. The school social worker should then listen to the child and answer the child's questions the best way possible (Perry & Rosenfelt, 1999).

School social workers should be aware of the symptoms associated with PTSD. Posttraumatic stress disorder is a normal response from a healthy brain to threat (Perry, 2002e). DSM-IV-TR describes it as "the development of characteristic symptoms following exposure to an extreme traumatic stressor involving direct personal experience of an event that involves actual or threatened death or serious injury" or witnessing or hearing about violent threats or death to loved ones or associates (American Psychiatric Association, 2000, pp. 463–464). Other symptoms of PTSD include reexperiencing the stressful event,* avoiding and numbing of responsiveness, increased arousal, and a clinically significant change in functioning (American Psychiatric Association, 2000, p. 468).

The diagnosis of PTSD is used if the symptoms have been present for 1 month. An individual may be diagnosed with delayed onset of PTSD when there has been a 6-month lapse between the traumatic event and the onset of the symptoms (American Psychiatric Association, 2000, p. 465).

SCHOOL-BASED INTERVENTIONS FOR TRAUMA

School social workers need to have the skills to work with groups of children who have been exposed to traumatic events. As Nancy Boyd Webb (2002) has observed, "When large numbers of children have been exposed to a trauma, schools provide the ideal setting for group intervention as soon as possible after the event. Different helping interventions include 'classroom presentations,' 'debriefing,' and 'defusing' " (p. 377). Accordingly, school social workers can assist with classroom presentations on grief and the stages of mourning. The social worker should also learn debriefing skills and assist with debriefing large groups and with individual interventions, depending on how closely related to the event or victims the students were. Debriefing is discussed in detail by Williams (2004) in *Mass Trauma and Violence*: "A defusing should take place shortly after a traumatic incident occurs in a one to one conversation that is designed to help a person talk out the incident and receive some objective support, generally from a peer" (p. 131).

Defusing

School social workers should work with school counselors to present information on grief and the stages of mourning during classroom guidance sessions. This information can be presented to grade levels K–12. If the school social worker has created visibility by visiting classes, then after receiving parental permission, the social worker can invite students to meet with him or her individually if they feel there is a need to discuss the traumatic event and their reactions to it.

---

*Intense psychological response to cues that symbolize or resemble the event.

"A defusing occurs very shortly after a traumatic incident occurs in a one to one conversation that is designed to help a person talk out the incident and receive some objective support, generally from a peer" (Williams, 2004, p. 131). School social workers can help teachers and administrators defuse students if the social worker, teachers, and administrators process the event together first before working with the students. Defusing is most effective when done soon after the incident, has an expectation of recovery, and is brief and simplistic (Snelgrove, 1998).

Debriefing

Those who have experienced a crisis need to talk about it (Poland & McCormick, 1999). Discussing and processing the traumatic event with someone who has professional training can help eliminate feelings of isolation and help the traumatized individual avoid symptoms of PTSD (Poland, 2002). School social workers can help debrief those who have experienced trauma either in large groups or individually, depending on how closely related to the victims the students were. Debriefing begins with an introduction to explain the purpose, format, and rules of the meeting. During the second stage, the traumatic event is reconstructed from beginning to end in a factual manner. The third stage focuses on the children's thoughts about the trauma. The fourth phase provides the children with the opportunity to talk about their emotions related to the trauma. In the fifth stage, the school social worker should help draw similarities between the thoughts and feelings of the various children to help normalize their reactions. At the end of the session, advice should be given on how to cope with future thoughts and feelings related to the trauma (Stallard et al., 2006).

A stabilization plan should include (1) identification of the different groups that need support services; (2) stress management activities; (3) support at victims' funerals, wakes, and memorial services at school, if applicable; (4) identification of those in need of counseling and referral to mental health providers; and (5) planning of outreach support and stress management for the various circles of survivors (Macy et al., 2004).

Group Debriefing

Some traumatic events occur on such a large scale that it is not possible for professionals to meet individually with each person who was affected by the event. When a tragic event occurs on a large scale, group processing is a viable alternative. School social workers should be trained in both defusing and debriefing activities in order to assist in the process of helping students and school personnel who have been exposed to traumatic events. Feedback given during an intervention for a person who is grieving or in crisis must not focus on maladaptive patterns but rather should focus on client strengths that can help restore equilibrium, hope, and trust (Chen & Rybak, 2004).

A model developed by Nancy Stanford (Wong, 2000) and based on Jeffrey Mitchell's model (Mitchell & Everly, 1998) can be very helpful to high school students (Poland, 2002). The ground rules from that model–which include small groups of four to six, confidentiality, mandatory attendance, and equally timed periods for each member to speak (or remain silent)–can help set the stage and develop a positive group atmosphere for debriefing and defusing (Poland, 2002, pp. 3–4). The following are processing questions (Poland, 2002, p. 3) that should be asked in the order set forth below to help the group work through each stage of grief:

"Introduce self, and tell where you were when you first became aware of the tragedy. What were your initial sensory perceptions? What did you see, hear, taste, touch, or smell?"

"What thoughts or reactions have you been having since the tragedy?"

"What is your biggest concern or worry about the immediate future?"

"What would help you feel safer right now?"

"What has helped you cope when you have had to deal with difficult things or losses in your life before? What can you do to help yourself cope now?"

The leader should summarize the results after each session to help group members realize they are not alone. Emphasis should be placed on the fact that this is only a starting point and that if members need more time to talk, they are invited to stay (Poland, 2002). Poland also recommends that faculty be allowed to go through this process before students. The same process can then be utilized with students.

Elementary school students can draw pictures about their experiences and share them in class. "Art therapy interventions help children by promoting their positive expectations about the future and making overt the coping skills they used to manage ongoing stresses" (Mapp & Koch, 2004, p. 114). Poland also recommends that high school students write out some of their answers to the processing questions and send them to the principal as a way of letting the school administration know what students have experienced and if additional help is necessary (Poland, 2002).

Many respected mental health professionals maintain that there is "no evidence" that debriefing works, and some think it upsets certain people. Sometimes the effects of stress may impede the functioning of those who are trying to help. Staff may become dysfunctional after hearing and dealing with so much trauma that they develop vicarious secondary traumatization. "Regardless of the professionals' role in the school system, they will not be able to escape the impact of trauma on themselves" (Williams, 2004, p. 139). After the attacks on the World Trade Center, a program in New York City focused on coordinating community volunteer services in the schools. It is helpful to utilize debriefing and defusing techniques in order to allow students and staff the opportunity to express their feelings. However, school social workers must "take time for themselves and talk about their own feelings" (Williams, 2004, p. 140).

CULTURAL AND RELIGIOUS FACTORS

Beliefs and attitudes must be understood in a cultural context. Cultural influences determine what is passed on to each generation. Cultural attitudes about seeking help may prevent a traumatized child or adolescent from asking for help or receiving it, and certain behaviors by children who have been traumatized may be perceived differently when viewed within the appropriate cultural context. For example, children from Asian American families may feel stigmatized as "immature, weak, and low in self-discipline" if they admit to emotional problems (Fang & Chen, 2004, p. 236). Likewise, in the Asian culture "mental disorders are considered as hereditary flaws" (Fang & Chen, 2004, p. 236), so children and adolescents may not seek help in order to help the family save face. It is more common in Asian cultures to express emotional distress through somatic complaints and thus access the mental health system without stigmatization (Akutsu, 1997; Fang & Chen, 2004, p. 237).

Religious and spiritual beliefs provide support for many families. They are, for many people, a primary response to life—a reason for, and focus of, existence and a means of making sense of the world (Kudlac, 1991, p. 277). When DSM-IV incorporated problems related to spiritual matters in 1994, it opened the door for social workers to consider spirituality as part of client treatment. In order for a school social worker to view a student holistically, spiritual issues must be considered as an integrative force that is not isolated from that student's physical state, feelings, thoughts, or relationships (Hawkins, Tan, & Turk, 1999). School social workers must always take cultural and spiritual factors into consideration and help create awareness among school personnel about all the ways that children may manifest effects of trauma.

SCHOOL SOCIAL WORK INTERVENTIONS WITH INDIVIDUAL STUDENTS

Children cannot be expected to perform at their full academic potential shortly after a traumatic event (Williams, 2004). Children cannot function until they have been able to express their feelings. Whenever circumstances or events create trauma, there is a need for positive interactions and self-expression to help the victims normalize their feelings. School social workers are necessary to help children and adolescents express and understand their feelings. Following are recommendations for school social workers to use in working with a traumatized child.

1. Discuss the traumatic event with the child.
2. Provide structure and a predictable pattern for the day.
3. Provide nurturing and comfort within the appropriate context.
4. Discuss expectations about behavior within the appropriate context.
5. Talk with the child about topics other than the traumatic event.
6. Watch for signs of reenactment.
7. Protect the child.
8. Give the child choices and a sense of control (Perry, 2002b, 2002c).

Play therapy is a useful intervention method for individual students. "The term 'play therapy' refers to caring and helping interventions with children that employ *play* techniques" (Webb, 2003, p. 149). Because school social workers do not usually see children in their own offices but rather at the children's schools, the use of play therapy is somewhat more restricted than in a fully equipped office. The most useful tools are portable, such as clay, Play-Doh, paper, crayons, colored pencils, markers, small dolls, and puppets. "Plain white paper, colored paper, and colored markers are the most useful of all play therapy supplies" (Webb, 2003, p. 150). Play-Doh and clay can allow children to pound out frustrations, make all kinds of figurines, and tell stories to help work through their feelings. Puppets and dolls also allow children to tell stories and express feelings.

Some of the most useful art therapy techniques involve letting children draw a picture of their feelings or create a thought page. If the thoughts a child expresses in a picture are troublesome, it sometimes helps to let him or her tear up or wad up the picture and throw it away as a symbolic gesture to help get rid of the disturbing thoughts. If the child is struggling to start the picture, the use of the "squiggle-game" (Winnicott, 1971a, 1971b) can help get them started. In this game, the child and social worker take turns closing their eyes and making a "scribble/squiggle" line on the paper. The other person has to make an object out of the squiggle. "Each drawing receives a name, and after several have been completed, the child is asked to pick his or her favorite and make up a story about it" (Webb, 2003, p. 151).

Another useful technique is to play games such as mock basketball and football. A small ball can be made by wadding up a piece of notebook paper. Hands can substitute for goal posts or baskets. Students try to make goals or baskets created by the social worker's hands. Each time they miss, they have to answer a question or tell the social worker a feeling they are experiencing. If they make a point, they may ask the social worker a question.

The use of play and art therapy to help children express their feelings and emotions provides a safe vehicle for them to express some very difficult feelings and emotions. School social workers should not be afraid to use these techniques, even if they have had only limited training, because it helps the child to relax and open up and allows the therapeutic relationship to develop. As Nancy Boyd Webb (2003) has said, "We do not know initially whether our work with children is helpful. We do know that it will not harm children to spend time with adults who are interested in them. Just as in adult therapy, the relationship is the key to being helpful, not whether a worker invariably makes the 'right' response" (p. 154).

SCHOOL SOCIAL WORK INTERVENTIONS WITH GROUPS

Some of the group interventions discussed in Chapter 9 can be utilized with children who have experienced trauma. These include crisis groups, education and skills groups, anger management groups, and grief groups. Group work provides a vehicle for treating many students at the same time and often provides the opportunity for feelings to become normalized after hearing that others are experiencing similar reactions.

Groups are particularly helpful when the situation to be dealt with is a disaster or has affected a large portion of the school population. Resources that can be incorporated into group work include oral storytelling (with the leader providing the first sentence of the story), photos, poems, videos, creative writing, journal entries, art projects, puppets, and dramatizations (Williams, 2004). Children need to talk about the crisis, receive factual information, and get debriefed. Groups provide the perfect venue for all of these activities.

Crisis Groups

Through group work, school social workers can assist large numbers of students who have experienced trauma. Ideally, school social work group interventions should be planned by preassessing members and setting size and time limitations. In crisis situations, however, school social workers must respond quickly without much time to plan the group. The key ingredient in such groups is to provide an opportunity for students to discuss their feelings and feel validated and safe. School social workers should utilize their relationship-building skills to create trust so that students feel comfortable about discussing their fears and anxieties. If social workers are asked to provide group counseling to an entire classroom, the teacher should remain in the room to assist with the group as a coleader and to monitor student behavior and provide positive incentives for good behavior.

Support Groups for Students Whose Parents Are Separated or Divorced

Parental separation and divorce are often traumatic for a child or adolescent. Some children may express their emotions more readily at school than at home, where there is already conflict. School social workers must be equipped to deal with the frustrations and pain the child expresses.

Children and adolescents who thrive after a traumatic event have built-in resilience factors that help them cope. As noted in Chapter 9, dimensions of resilience include a child's disposition, the family milieu, and the external support system (Walker, 1995). School interventions that place students in support groups with peers who have similar experiences provide ongoing support that will help the child or adolescent achieve optimal performance at school.

School-based programs that are based on peer support groups, such as the Banana Splits program, can help children and adolescents express their feelings in a supportive, empathic environment. "Banana Splits" groups are intended primarily to support children whose parents are separated, divorced, or deceased. School social workers can implement the groups and use social work interns or parent volunteers to assist with them. "Children clearly stand to benefit from this validating and supportive program" (Webb, 2003, p. 181). (Additional information about the Banana Splits program may be found at the website for the Banana Splits Resource Center, *www.bananasplitsresourcecenter.org*.)

Grief Groups

The school social worker can be instrumental in helping students confront their grief and process the loss that is felt after a traumatic event or a school disaster. School social workers should keep in mind the differences between the short-term goals of grief work, which are to offer support and empathy, and the long-term goals, which are to help the members confront the issues of unresolved grief through emotional integration and healing (Chen & Rybak, 2004). Some of the following objectives and tasks should be planned and accomplished during a grief group:

1. Receive information about the process and tasks of grief.
2. Experience the opportunity to express emotions and concerns about the grief process and one's personal experiences.
3. Participate in activities to assist in working through grief, such as reviewing how the losses and events have changed their lives. Express feelings of anger and guilt. Develop commemorative activities.
4. Learn about current support systems and ways to use those systems or expand them if they are ineffective.
5. Develop understanding of available resources of both materials and support from peers, family, and community members (Williams, 2004, p. 136).

School social workers should be sensitive to the emotions and concerns expressed by children and adolescents in these groups. Social workers should also emphasize that all feelings are acceptable and there is no one timetable for grief responses.

SCHOOL SOCIAL WORK INTERVENTIONS WITH FAMILIES

School social workers should talk to parents and give them suggestions for helping their traumatized child. If the parents are also experiencing trauma, the school social worker should help parents understand what constitutes a normal reaction to trauma and when they should seek professional help. The school social worker could provide the parents with names of professionals in the community who could help them debrief.

Parents need to be taught to understand trauma and what they should expect from their child. They should be taught to patiently nurture and support their child and to allow the child to ask questions and discuss the traumatic event as often as the child seems to need reassurance. Parents should be taught to keep routine and structure in the home, such as regular bedtimes, the same as before. Prior to bedtime the child should be given time to relax and unwind. Short naps throughout the day may need to be encouraged. Parents may help with appetite problems by making sure some of the child's favorite foods are served. They must be taught to be nurturing and reassuring so the child will feel safe. The child should be repeatedly told that he or she is safe. Because traumatized children experience fears, new experiences should not be introduced to a traumatized child for several weeks, and the child should not be exposed to anxiety producing situations. The family routine should be as normal as possible.

School social workers can assist parents in responding to symptoms that result from trauma. Anger is a normal reaction to trauma. However, children should not be allowed to express their anger inappropriately. Parents should be encouraged to be firm and not rejecting of the child's anger. In addition, they should teach the child how to express feelings of sadness, fear, and (perhaps) guilt in appropriate ways through talking about their feelings or writing out or drawing pictures to express their feelings. Cognitive restructuring can be taught to parents by school social workers to help the parents reframe negative comments a child may make about himself or herself. Children should not be allowed to take on guilt related to their misconception that they could have controlled or altered the event in any way. Social workers should encourage parents to continually discuss the realities of the situation when the child wants to discuss it and help to alleviate any misconceptions the child may be carrying.

School social workers can assist parents and teachers in understanding the differences between nurturing behaviors, safety behaviors, and corrective actions. Adults should use safety behaviors to help monitor and protect a traumatized child. Corrective actions include nonthreatening discipline, clear behavior expectations, and positive and negative consequences for behavior. These should be carried out with respect and patience. Nurturing actions include touching, cuddling, direct eye contact, soothing, and consistency (Perry, 2002a).

School social workers should be nurturing in their interactions with traumatized children, showing consistency, caring, attention, respect, and compassion (Perry, 2002a). Social workers should answer questions, help reestablish structure in the school, and prepare the child ahead of time for known changes.

GUIDELINES TO HELP VICTIMS OF VIOLENCE AND TRAUMA

The individual characteristics of the traumatized person and the recovery environment affect the cognitive processes that help with the adaptation to the traumatic event (Green, Wilson, & Lindy, 1985). Webb

(2004) also includes the nature of the traumatic event as part of a tripartite crisis assessment, which is discussed in detail in Chapter 2. School social workers can be instrumental in establishing security and safety for the students at school and in helping teach parents how to reestablish a feeling of security and routine at home.

Students who survive traumatic events need to focus on recovery. The first 4 to 6 weeks after a traumatic event are critical. Often, those who have been traumatized have problems sleeping. To avoid sleep deprivation, short naps should be taken throughout the day. This is easier when the child is in special education classes and the teachers can adapt the curriculum to meet the child's needs. However, the school social worker can recommend that teachers allow for rest periods in which students in regular classes can lay their heads on their desks and listen to the teacher read stories related to the subject matter of the class.

School social workers should encourage staff and students to get regular exercise and teach them how to use self-relaxation exercises, such as deep breathing, muscle tightening and relaxing, and thoughts of happy places to substitute for unhappy or frightening memories. Social workers should encourage teachers to lighten up on both in-class assignments and homework following a traumatic event. They should also encourage students and teachers to eat whenever they feel hungry and to take time to relax and care for themselves. It is not a time to take on additional responsibilities.

Research from Father Flanagan's Boys' Home (1998) indicates that children need structure, predictability, and consistency. These conditions are particularly necessary after a traumatic or violent event. Children who have experienced trauma need a sense of normalcy and structure to help rebuild feelings of security. Children should return to school routines as soon as possible, with a regular class schedule and assignments. However, teachers should be informed that even classroom bells and unusual noises may trigger a reaction in traumatized students.

School social workers can help by reinforcing the concepts of safety and security. Social workers should visit each classroom and ask students if there is anyone who would like to talk about the trauma. They should describe both normal and unhealthy reactions and help students understand when their own reactions may be extreme. The social worker should ask teachers and students to make referrals to them if they feel a need to talk individually and privately. Students should be allowed to discuss the traumatic event, and adults need to provide reassurance that things will be okay.

If the event is covered by the media, students may need to discuss the differences between their perceptions and the coverage seen on television or in the newspaper. Students may express rage and feel anger toward those they feel created the event. They should listen without reacting to the content of the conversation and, instead, focus on feelings. School social workers should respond in a calm manner that establishes trust and rapport. Students may ask the same questions repeatedly, and it is critical that the questions be answered calmly each time with the same truthful answer. Continued support is necessary for as long as students and teachers ask for help.

CONCLUSION

Children and adolescents may be exposed to violence and other traumatic events. The reaction to these situations can have a devastating effect on a child or adolescent if an incorrect diagnosis is given or if the child is not treated correctly. School social workers need to become aware of the effects of violence and trauma on children and adolescents. They can be instrumental in helping children, adolescents, and school staff who have experienced trauma. It is critical for the home and school environments to remain places of safety and security in which the traumatized child can discuss and be nurtured through his or her difficult reactions to trauma.

Discussion Topics

1. Describe some coping mechanisms you have seen children and adolescents use as they deal with grief.
2. Discuss the merits of using defusing techniques.
3. Discuss the merits of using debriefing techniques.
4. How might a school social worker engage parents in helping children who have experienced a loss?
5. Practice relaxation techniques by using them on a partner. Begin with deep breathing and muscle tightening and relaxing.

CHILDREN WHO HAVE BEEN REMOVED FROM THEIR HOMES BECAUSE OF ABUSE OR NEGLECT

School social workers are often the first professionals to notice and report child abuse. When a child has been reported as a victim of abuse or neglect, child welfare personnel will usually make the first contact with him or her at the school. Because teachers are often uncomfortable with the idea of making a report to child protective services, they may ask the school nurse or social worker to help with the report. Social workers cannot file a report for someone else who is an "outcry" witness, but they can assist teachers or other school personnel and support them through the process of filing a report.

School social workers can help train other school personnel about potential warning signs of abuse or neglect. Bruises and welts, teeth marks, burns from cigars or cigarettes, multiple fractures, abdominal bruises, and genital lacerations are all symptoms that social workers should be aware of (Ryan, 2003, p. 73). Often the explanation given by the abused child for his or her injury does not fit the injury.

Once there is a sign or report from the child that he or she has been abused, a report must be filed with the appropriate child protective service agency. Protective services will usually assign a case number to the report, and the school social worker should keep that case number for future reference. Most school districts have additional forms connected with referrals to child protective services that should be completed and filed (usually with the school nurse).

Once child protective services has intervened, the child may be removed from the home. However, the family preservation model, which most protective services follow, helps ensure that families will stay together if possible. Children placed in foster care as infants have been found to develop attached relationships within 2 months after placement (Stovall & Dozier, 2000). Children who have positive emotional ties to foster parents and who receive physical affection from them are better adjusted psychologically and academically than other foster children (Marcus, 1991).

DIVORCE

Approximately 40% of all marriages end in divorce (National Healthy Marriage Resource Center, n.d.). Children are affected by the breakup of their parents' marriage and are concerned about what will become

11 Parental Absence

Parental absence creates stress for children. Life becomes increasingly difficult for a child when a parent is away for an extended period of time. Parental absence can be brought about through the parent's voluntary actions, such as military service, or involuntarily, such as when a parent is ill or incarcerated. A critical factor for children is the type of care they receive while the parent is away. If the child is placed in a caring environment, with structure, consistency, and predictable rules, he or she will thrive. School social workers can help caregivers and classroom teachers create an environment that will provide the needed support for the child whose parent is absent.

Rutter and Quinton (1977) have identified six risk factors related to child psychiatric disorders, three of which are connected with parental absence. These include paternal criminality, (maternal criminality was not studied), maternal psychiatric disorder, and admission into the care of local authorities. School social workers should be familiar with each of these factors and be aware of children in the schools they serve who are at high risk because of them.

PARENTS IN THE MILITARY AND DEPLOYMENT

Children whose parents are serving in the military experience a different level of stress than most children in civilian families (Hardaway, 2004). Most military families move frequently and many live abroad. Military families must deal with personal risk and family separation.

Military children do not have the advantage of growing up in a community in which they can establish roots. As a result, these children often have a hard time developing close relationships and keeping commitments (Wertsch, 1991). As Wertsch (1991) has noted

> Growing up in the military is difficult even in the most loving and close-knit families; the frequent moves, the threat or the reality of war, and the requisite masks of secrecy, stoicism, and denial will see to that. In dysfunctional military families—the ones poisoned by alcoholism or abuse or stifled by an authoritarianism so rigid it allows no room to breathe or grow—the difficulty is increased geometrically.

Deployed U.S. Navy personnel and their spouses reported greater emotional distress, increased life stress, and lower family functioning than did nondeployed families. Families who reported the highest levels of stress reported less family cohesiveness, expressiveness, and organization (Eastman, Archer, & Ball, 1990).

Over the past two decades the number of women serving in the military has increased until today approximately 212,000 active-duty personnel are women (U.S. Census Bureau, 2006). This constitutes 14.4% of overall active-duty personnel. John Bowlby's attachment theory suggests that it is important for a child to have a warm, sensitive caregiver who is available and responsive to his or her needs and able to provide comfort in times of distress (Bowlby, 1980). Considering the importance of sustaining strong attachments and support throughout childhood, it is easy to understand the kind of strain deployment would put on a child and mother. Deployment affects all members of a family—those who go and those who stay behind—because of the stresses caused by the unpredictable (Ender, 2002).

The stress experienced by a child whose parent is deployed to active duty is manifested in many ways. In one study, children whose mothers were deployed exhibited higher levels of internalizing behavior than children whose mothers were assigned to shore duty. These internalizing behaviors are manifested in younger children with symptoms of anxiety and sadness. In many cases, the maternal grandmother is the child care provider during deployment. Child care providers report that children exhibit slightly higher levels of externalizing behavior when their parents are deployed. These behaviors include aggression and acting out. Older children with deployed mothers often experience behavioral improvements, while younger children did not (Kelley, 2002).

School social workers should have some method of identifying

children whose parents are in the military, especially those who parents are deployed, in order to give them emotional suppor School social workers should work closely with school personne in order to identify military families. Teachers, school counselors administrators, or registrars can provide the names of students who have military parents. Because school social workers cannot work with children without parental permission, the social worker should send out a written announcement at the beginning of each semester listing the types of services he or she provides. Children who have just moved to a campus benefit from a peer support group in which the students get to know the school rules and culture from other students.

Because deployment affects the entire family, school social workers may serve the children most effectively by offering family support. If the children are left in the care of a grandmother, the grandmother may need to have access to the school through the social worker. School social workers should make the effort to reach out to families with deployed military parents and offer both emotional and community resource support as needed. Special attention from the school, such as sending a care package to the deployed parent from the students' classmates, can have a powerful impact in helping the student whose parent is away.

Case Example

Kim's older sister was deployed to serve in Iraq. Kim, age 12, talked about her sister constantly to her friends and would always bring her letters to school to share. The teacher and school social worker asked Kim if it would be okay with her and her family for the other students to send a package to Kim's sister, Jennifer. The family was excited. The teacher asked Kim to write to her sister and find out the kinds of things she and her fellow troops needed most. When the list arrived, the teacher printed it out and sent it home with each student. Students were told not to spend more than $5.00 on an item and to contribute only one item. The students' response was overwhelming. They brought candy, Handi Wipes, gum, and books. Each student wrote a letter to Jennifer and her friends. The teacher packaged all of the donations, and the school social worker mailed them to Jennifer. Jennifer sent back several thank-you notes from herself and other military personnel thanking the students for the treats. The notes were posted in the classroom. It helped Kim to see how much her fellow students cared about her and her family.

of them. They struggle with guilt and feelings of being disloyal if they side with one parent. Children sometimes become caught in the middle of custody disputes. Some children are even denied the opportunity to spend time with one parent on a regular basis. The number of children living apart from one of their parents has increased from 12% to almost 40% since 1982 (McLanahan, 1997). Half of the children born in the United States are going to spend a part of their childhood being raised by a single mother (Bumpass & Raley, 1995). Divorce and single parenthood usually affect a child's school performance and behavior.

Case Example

Jimmy's parents had been divorced for about 2 years when he began working with the school social worker. The custody dispute had been bitter, and Jimmy was no longer allowed to visit or talk with his father except on holidays. Jimmy, age 10, was grieving and would often have angry outbursts at school. The school social worker was assigned to work with him weekly for counseling sessions as part of his individualized education plan (IEP) through special education. Jimmy brought up his dad almost continually, so the social worker allowed him 10 minutes of each session to talk about his dad. These 10 minutes were spent with him doing a "thought page" in which he could draw or write out all of his feelings for 5 minutes. He would then tell the social worker about what he put on the picture. It became a positive outlet for him to discuss the hurt and loneliness he felt about his father's absence from his life.

PARENTAL DEATH

Children are often not acquainted with death, and American society has set up boundaries around death that prevent people from dealing with it in a positive way. School social workers and counselors are equipped to deal with loss and grief, but this knowledge should also be imparted to classroom teachers who deal with children on an everyday basis. Teachers should begin by modeling caring behaviors to their students (Shaw, 2004). Teachers must learn to recognize that angry outbursts are the way some children manifest depression and sadness. They also should recognize when the grief seems overwhelming to a child and call in the social worker or counselor to give the child individual attention. School social workers should alert teachers to the signs of clinical depression so that they can detect any signs that a child is sinking into depression. Teachers and school social workers should work together to offer support for the student.

PARENTAL INCARCERATION

A child whose parent has been incarcerated faces a myriad of difficulties. First and foremost is the concern about what the child was exposed to before the parent was arrested. Were drugs use, illicit sex, domestic violence, or neglect taking place in the home to traumatize the child? Were the police frequently coming to the house? These factors alone create a sense of fear and instability for children. This is compounded when one or both of the parents are taken away and children are uncertain about their own future and who will take care of them. There are approximately 1.3 million children in the United States whose parents are incarcerated. Approximately one-fourth of these children end up in the child welfare system. The others are usually in the care of relatives, particularly grandparents.

The traumatic effects of parental incarceration are usually manifested at school. Many of these children end up in special education because of emotional problems. Some of the problems may stem from attachment difficulties. Changes in family configuration, such as divorce, adoption, and foster care, have implications for attachment security, particularly if the changes occur in infancy or early childhood (Johnson & Waldfogel, 2002).

Children of incarcerated parents have multiple risk factors, and theories of cumulative risk suggest that it is not just one risk factor that affects child outcomes but an accumulation of them (Rutter, 1987; Davies, 2004; Sameroff, Bartko, Baldwin, Baldwin, & Seifer, 1998). The greater the number of risk factors in a child's life, the greater the potential for difficulties. A key factor is not only whom the child stays with during the incarceration but whom they lived with prior to it and what risk factors they were exposed to (Johnson & Waldfogel, 2002).

Case Example

Sean's father was in an out-of-state prison for drug trafficking. Sean, age 13, in seventh grade, was an only child and lived with his mother, who had many emotional problems. He was often hit and threatened by his mother. The two of them made bimonthly visits out of state to see his father. When the school social worker met Sean, his father had been incarcerated for 5 years and had at least 5 more years on his sentence before he would be released. Sean was extremely moody and violent at school. He would often explode into loud, name-calling outbursts, or spend an entire school day with his head on his desk refusing to do any work. He was placed in a special education classroom for emotionally disturbed students. Sean was good-looking and had good social skills. His classmates all liked him, but he treated his teacher and classroom aide with disdain. Whenever he had an outburst at school, the teacher would try to have his mother help with the problem. However, during one school meeting, the mother hit Sean and tore his shirt in front of the teacher.

The school social worker tried to intervene. On most visits with the social worker, Sean would talk openly about his life and how hopeless he felt. The social worker helped Sean to focus on his strengths and commit himself to passing his classes. He would do well in school until he made a visit to see his father, then the depression would start all over again. Child protective services was involved to help the mother stop hitting Sean. She did not seem to make much progress, even though the agency intervened more than once.

The social worker referred Sean to the community mental health agency, which provided medication for depression that helped him slightly. However, he was never fully committed to continuing the counseling sessions, and his mother refused to see the counselor. The school social worker advised his teacher to stop calling the mother whenever there were school problems and, instead, to deal only with Sean. Sean seemed to appreciate the control he was given over his own situation at school and improved over the course of the social work intervention.

PARENTAL MENTAL ILLNESS

The mental illness of a parent creates a great deal of stress for children. It can lead to homelessness, instability, and inconsistent relationships as well as disciplinary problems. Approximately one-third of the homeless population is mentally ill. Many have co-occurring disorders with substance abuse. Parents with these difficulties struggle trying to raise children. It is difficult for school personnel to deal with parents if they are not receiving treatment for their mental illness. The parent will be very inconsistent and often hard to reach.

School social workers can offer support to the children once they realize the kinds of difficulties the child is experiencing. Children with mentally ill parents often do not know that the parent has problems. The child thinks the whole world lives the way that he or she does. School social workers can help assure that there is consistency, stability, and structure during the school day. They can work with the child individually to provide emotional support and make sure the child has the needed resources, such as school lunch, bus rides to and from school, and adequate clothing. It is most important for these children to have positive role models at school. Social workers should help with scheduling and teacher selection to assure that these children have teachers who will give them the care and support they need.

Case Example

Walter's mother had bipolar disorder. He was 10 years old when he was referred to the school social worker because he had many tantrums and acted out frequently at school. The social worker learned that Walter spent every evening alone and had to make his own dinner of cold cereal every night. The mother worked the swing shift on her job. They lived in an apartment. Walter was an only child, and he did not know his father. Whenever the school contacted the mother, she would usually scream at the teacher over the phone or come to the school and pull Walter out of class so that she would not have to miss work later in the day. Walter always became embarrassed if his mother came to school.

He told the social worker that the social worker would hate to be living his life. He was placed in special education, where he could receive a very structured school environment. The school social worker met with him daily for the first few weeks of his special education placement. The special education teacher did not call the mother unless she was reporting positive behaviors. The social worker arranged for Walter to be involved in an after-school program at a nearby recreation center.

With the support of his special education teacher and aide Walter's behavior improved. The school social worker helped teach him social skills and provided an outlet for his frustrations. She also taught him how to problem solve and deal with his frustrations in a more positive manner. He eventually worked his way out of special education, and by the time he entered high school he was doing well.

HOMELESSNESS

Children make up about 39% of the homeless population. Most homeless children are under the age of 12. They are often homeless because of parental mental illness, co-occurring mental illness and substance abuse, or family violence. About 43% of homeless children do not attend school on a regular basis, and about half of them have failed at least one grade (Hicks-Coolick, Burnside-Eaton, & Peters, 2003). Many homeless children live in motels, without adequate laundry facilities. They are often made fun of by their peers. Nearly half of homeless children have at least one developmental delay, such as language skills, fine/gross motor coordination, or personal and social skills (Webb, 2003).

School social workers should make visits to the places where homeless children are staying to try to connect them to the school. Many school districts have shoe, clothing, and eye-glass centers available for children in need. The school social worker should link the family to as many community resources as possible. The social worker can be sure that the child receives school breakfast and lunch. Many school districts also have after-school day care sponsored by organizations like the YWCA, in which volunteers spend time with children. The school social worker should help arrange for tutoring and have the children screened for special education and Section 504 services. Sometimes the school social worker needs to arrange special transportation to assure that the children attend school. Even if the time spent with a child in school is minimal, it may still prevent the developmental delays from becoming more severe and may increase the child's sense of well-being to see that someone cares for him or her.

Case Example

Lana was 13 and began attending school midway through the school year. Her attendance was erratic, so she was referred to the school social worker. The social worker made a home visit to the address that Lana was using. It was a local motel. Lana was living with both her grandparents. The day the social worker made the visit, a man in his twenties was just leaving as the social worker arrived. Lana's grandparents were very defensive about the social worker's visit and gave her very little information.

Lana returned to school the next day, and the social worker met with her. She did not come forward with much information. She did give some specific indicators to the social worker that she was sexually active, so the social worker called child protective services (CPS), which made a visit to the motel. They found that Lana was being sold out for sexual acts and that the grandparents were making the arrangements. The family moved after the initial CPS investigation, and the school social worker lost the ability to work with and help Lana. Sometimes school social workers are unable to intervene on all of the levels necessary, and it is very frustrating.

GRANDPARENTS RAISING GRANDCHILDREN

Some of the most common reasons for the increasing number of grandparents raising grandchildren are the use of drugs and alcohol, the spread of HIV/AIDS, parental abuse and neglect, divorce, death of a parent by illness, suicide, or accident, and parental mental or physical illness or incarceration (Dunn, 1992; Kelley, Yorker, & Whitley, 1997).

In *Youakim v. Miller* (1979), the United States Supreme Court held that federal foster care benefits could not be denied to kinship caregivers who were otherwise eligible solely because they were relatives. Many states interpreted this decision liberally and made funds available to encourage grandparents to care for their grandchildren if the parent was not available or capable (Roe & Minkler, 1999).

Schools have not been adequately utilized in meeting the needs of children being raised by family members other than their parents (Rogers & Henkin, 2000). Children raised in kinship care often face a combination of academic, developmental, health, and emotional problems. Primarily, these children are dealing with loss and possible rejection from their parent, which makes it difficult for them to concentrate and behave appropriately at school. Many children mask their anger with depression and withdrawal. Some children, particular boys, act out aggressively without much provocation. Some of the loss these children experience is related to the fact that the grandparent is now the disciplinarian and not just someone who adds support to their lives.

Research has shown that children being raised by grandparents have significant health-related problems, including high rates of asthma and other respiratory problems, weaker immune systems, poor eating habits, inadequate sleep, physical disabilities, and ADHD (Dowdell, 1995, p. 222).

In order to help cut down on the chaos these children are experiencing in their lives, the school social worker must help provide structure, predictability, consistency, and skills training within the school environment (for skills training, see Pratt, Ford, Burke, & Hensley, 2005). This can be accomplished by placing the student in the classroom of a well-organized teacher who uses consistent disciplinary techniques. The classroom must be free from clutter, and student work expectations must be very clear and explicit. The school social worker can provide additional support through individual counseling to help the student express his or her feelings. The student must have the opportunity to express his or her grief and anger in a safe environment. The school social worker can assist the student in learning positive outlets for anger and problem solve about the most appropriate time and place to deal with frustrations. The social worker can also assist the student in social skills training to alleviate any deficits.

Case Example

Dennis, age 8, was being raised by his paternal grandmother. His mother was incarcerated for drug dealing, and his father was an alcoholic and around only occasionally. The grandmother had limited financial support for Dennis because the father was the legal guardian and would not relinquish his rights to Dennis's mother. Dennis was in third grade and was placed in a behavior adjustment classroom through special education because he was classified as emotionally disturbed. He threw frequent tantrums at school and often refused to do his schoolwork.

The school social worker met with him weekly to help work on his social skills, give him an outlet for his frustrations, and a chance to talk about the world from his point of view. He was often worried about his father. He resented it when his father came home drunk and would not spend time with him. His grandmother was in good health and was not working, so she was available to help with Dennis's schoolwork. The social worker and Dennis's teacher often spoke with the grandmother on the phone to let her know when he was doing well at school. Both the teacher and social worker had a good relationship with the grandmother and provided support to her regarding school-related issues. When Dennis threw tantrums at school, the social worker or teacher would deal with him rather than sending him home to his grandmother. The main goal was to try to keep the relationship with the grandmother positive regarding school issues. The teacher and social worker took responsibility for dealing with Dennis regarding his school behavior and did not call the grandmother or upset her each time he had a problem. The school invited her to classroom parties, field trips, and school assemblies. The grandmother became familiar with Dennis's classmates and built a positive relationship with them. She expressed her concerns to the social worker, and the social worker and teacher would try to address the problems.

The problems faced by children being raised in kinship care are closely connected with the issues facing their caregivers (Rogers & Henkin, 2000). Because the grandparent experiences problems similar to those of the student, the school social worker should offer family support. Weekly phone calls from the school social worker or information sharing with the grandparent can help him or her feel more connected with the school.

If the school social worker sets up a weekly contact with the grandparent in which positive information is shared, it will help decrease the feeling that the school is only calling to report bad news. Often parents and grandparents whose children are having academic and emotional difficulties at school express the feeling that they don't want to hear from the school because it is never positive. The school social worker can change this situation by creating positive contacts with the home.

Grandparents experience frustration over their inability to help with homework, so the school social worker could arrange for a tutorial period or a tutor to help the student after school hours. The social worker could also offer information to the grandparent about community resources and programs, such as private companies set up to assist with homework.

Grandparents raising grandchildren experience isolation because their time is taken up with child care, which keeps them from interacting with peers in social situations, but they will rarely seek help for their own emotional and mental needs (Roe & Minkler, 1999). For grandparents who are single, the isolation and difficulty of dealing with all of the household duties, additional problems from the grandchild, such as homework and discipline problems, and other issues experienced in child rearing can become overwhelming. African American and Hispanic grandparents report that there is a failure in their community and churches to understand the isolation and shame created by having to care for the children of their own children who may be HIV positive or addicted to drugs (Minkler & Roe, 1993).

School social workers can assist with the loneliness and isolation felt by the grandparent by helping the grandparent to become a volunteer at school. School volunteers can do any number of jobs from tutoring students, assisting teachers with making copies, and cutting out art projects for teachers to putting together bulletin boards. If grandparents are seen at school in a positive way, other students will get to know them and build a relationship with them. This positive interaction may decrease some of the stigma that students often feel when their grandparent is so much older than the parents of their peers.

Another area in which the school social worker can offer assistance is through staff development and training to help teachers and classroom aides understand the issues faced in kinship care and learn to deal more effectively with children and grandparents (Rogers & Henkin, 2000).

SCHOOL SOCIAL WORK INTERVENTIONS

Children who are exposed to the stress and trauma of parental absence can still live productive lives if they are given support and taught coping skills. The biggest difficulty school social workers experience is that the problems centered around the child's education can be maintained and handled at school, but if the child goes home to a negative, nonsupportive environment each day, many of the positive effects of the in-school interventions are negated. School social workers are usually able to work only with problems related to the child's educational needs. Although systemic interventions can be put in place, the social worker has very little control over the long-term effects of negative living environments.

The social worker should intervene at the levels that are most appropriate within the school environment. Social workers should make a point of finding out which students are at risk because of parental incarceration, deployment, foster care, kinship care, or parental death. Once the students have been identified, the social worker can find ways to track their progress at school. If at any point the student begins to fail or have emotional difficulties, the social worker can intervene, request weekly progress reports, and visit with the student regularly. The social worker can work cooperatively with teachers to alert them of warning signs of depression. He or she can teach effective interaction skills to teacher aides and other personnel so they will work in a compassionate, supportive manner with children who are at risk.

The school social worker should mobilize all of the resources available within the school, such as free lunch, clothes closets, school bus rides, and medical attention from the school nurse. The school system has many resources available that just need to be tapped by a knowledgeable social worker.

The school social worker should form support groups with the students to help them work through their anger and grief. He or she can advocate with the school administration to keep the students from being suspended or sent home to environments that would offer no support. The social worker can help set up study halls and tutoring sessions to assist the students with their schoolwork.

The social worker should help the caregivers become involved with the school, setting up communication channels that will make it easy for the caregiver to have access to the student's progress and not feel intimidated by the school system. School social workers can help explain terms such as "procedural safeguards" and other jargon associated with special placements in the schools so that interaction with the school system is not looked upon as demeaning and a negative experience for the caregiver. The social worker can help caregivers serve on committees or as volunteers at school to help them feel they are part of the system. The social worker can also assist the family and student with referrals to appropriate community agencies.

CONCLUSION

Children are vulnerable and need to be protected. When the home environment is unsettling it is necessary for schools to be safe havens. It is also necessary for children to feel they can turn to school social workers to discuss their fears and losses. Separation from parents because of military service, removal by child welfare, divorce, or parental death are all devastating to children and can affect school performance. School social workers should help teachers and school counselors who have identified children who are experiencing loss by giving them support. School social workers should also assist caregivers, particularly grandparents and others who are providing kinship care but may not have had children in their home for many years and who are unaware of potential resources. Caregivers often lack knowledge about the options for care available to them. Knowledgeable social workers can help them access these resources. In summary, the school social worker's multifaceted role can bring critical support to both students and their families.

Discussion Topics

1. Discuss ways in which school social workers can be more responsible to children of deployed military personnel.
2. Discuss the warning signs of abuse and neglect.
3. How can school social workers help students with mentally ill parents?
4. Can you think of a more effective way to help Lana besides involving child welfare?
5. Grandparents raising their grandchildren need support. What can school social workers do to help them become aware of social trends and things like dress and music, so they will understand the world of their grandchild?

12

Alcohol and Drug Abuse

WHAT IS SUBSTANCE ABUSE?

At any one time, between 2 and 10% of adults in the United States either abuse or are addicted to illegal drugs (Doweiko, 2002, p. 9). It is estimated that 40 to 60% of the risk of addiction is genetically influenced. The risk for alcohol dependence is three to four times higher in close relatives of people with alcohol dependence (American Psychiatric Association, 2000, p. 221). According to Mary Dufour, MD, former deputy director of the National Institute on Alcohol Abuse and Alcoholism (NIAAA), the results of a 10-year study indicate the discovery of "hot spots" on four chromosomes that indicate either a risk for, or protection from, alcohol dependency. These findings could pinpoint a predisposition to addiction. Perhaps notifying children of alcoholics about their own genetic propensity for the disease could serve as a preventative (Whitehouse, 2000).

This chapter discusses drug and alcohol abuse and how parental substance abuse affects children. It also discusses fetal alcohol syndrome (FAS) and some of the disorders associated with substance abuse.

The terms "substance abuse" and "substance dependence" are listed in DSM-IV-TR (American Psychiatric Association, 2000). Substance abuse "refers to a maladaptive pattern of substance use in its early phases, with danger signs such as not fulfilling major role obligations at work or home and continuing to use a substance despite frequent interpersonal or social problems caused by the substance's effects" (Webb, 2003, p. 288). Substance dependence refers to "a dysfunctional pattern of substance use leading to clinically important distress or impairment over a 1-year period, during which tolerance and withdrawal increase, use of and desire to obtain the substance also increase, and other activities are given up because of substance use" (American Psychiatric Association, 2000, p. 195).

PARENTAL SUBSTANCE ABUSE

Parental substance abuse and addiction is the chief culprit in at least 70%, and perhaps 90%, of all child welfare cases. Nine of ten professionals cite alcohol alone or in combination with illegal or prescription drugs as the leading substance of abuse in child abuse and neglect (Califano, 1999). In this country one child in eight under the age of 18 lives with an alcoholic parent. Fathers are three times more likely than mothers to be alcoholics (Whitehouse, 2000).

Crack cocaine and marijuana presently are the leading drugs of abuse in the United States. Crack cocaine addiction limits a parent's ability to respond to the needs of his or her children. "Most true addicts simply cannot take adequate care of their children. Without societal intervention, their children are condemned to lives of severe deprivation and, often, violent assault" (Besharov, 1996, p. 33).

Methamphetamine has become increasingly prominent as a drug of abuse, particularly in rural areas, where meth labs are a growing phenomenon. Methamphetamine is a form of speed that can be inhaled, snorted, or smoked. The ability to produce methamphetamine in meth labs contributes to high crime rates in once safe areas. Methamphetamine is considered to be the poor man's cocaine because it can be produced with legal and accessible products. The abusers become addicted to the energy rush and feeling of invulnerability it provides. Children whose parents are addicted to methamphetamine often suffer extreme neglect because the parents become very focused on their own continuing needs to obtain the drug.

How Does Parental Substance Abuse Affect Children?

Parental substance abuse is associated with a constellation of risk factors in children (Kelley & Fals-Stewart, 2004). The substance abuse is likely to take precedence over a child's basic needs (Tracy, 1994). "For many, the most insidious aspect of substance abuse and addiction is their power to destroy the natural parental instinct to love and care for their children" (Califano, 1999, p. 11). Alan Leshner, former director of the National Institute on Drug Abuse, has observed, "The addicted parent sometimes sees the child as an obstacle to getting drugs" (Califano, 1999, p. 11). Emotional absence is the primary and most subtle outgrowth of a parent's alcoholism (Whitehouse, 2000). When parents are emotionally and physically concerned about their own addiction, their children are at risk for both neglect and violent abuse.

Children of drug and alcohol abusers often exhibit both emotional and behavioral problems.

> Children of alcoholics are more likely to (1) exhibit elevated levels of aggression (Merikangas, Dierker, & Szatmari, 1998), (2) meet diagnostic criteria for conduct disorder (Muetzell, 1993), (3) engage in antisocial behaviors (Merikangas, Weissman, Prusoff, Pauls, & Leckman, 1985), (4) meet diagnostic criteria for one or more mood disorders, such as anxiety and depression (Chassin, Pitts, DeLucia, & Todd, 1999; Merikangas et al., 1998), and (5) abuse alcohol or other psychoactive substances (Sher, Walitzer, Wood, & Brent, 1991). (Kelley & Fals-Stewart, 2004, p. 621)

Because drug and alcohol abuse are costly, families with patterns of abuse often have financial difficulties, which may cause a family to live in lower socioeconomic status. Traditionally, the low-income neighborhoods where these families live have high rates of crime and drug abuse, few opportunities for learning and recreation outside school, and lower-performing schools. The children from these families are placed at risk because of the community surroundings. The social environment, including the family situation, school, peer culture, and societal unresponsiveness, all contribute to cause at-risk youth (Davis, 1999, p. 25).

Inconsistent and harsh disciplinary measures are potential problems in the homes of parents who abuse drugs and alcohol. Many studies have found a significant relationship between adverse family functioning and parental alcohol misuse (Grekin, Brennan, & Hammen, 2005). "Children whose parents abuse drugs and alcohol are almost three times likelier to be physically and sexually assaulted and four times likelier to be neglected than children of parents who are not substance abusers" (Califano, 1999, p. 10). Learning theory suggests that when they have children of their own the children of substance abusers who have been abused and neglected are at risk for copying the behavior of substance abuse, as well as the child abuse and neglect that was modeled by their parents.

Children born to mothers who were using drugs and alcohol during pregnancy have a high risk for birth defects, including mental retardation, developmental delays such as language lag, behavior disorders, lack of coordination, and physical abnormalities. Disruptive behavior disorders and specific language impairment may be found in children of substance-abusing parents. Children who are disruptive in school have a high risk of academic failure, delinquency, and early onset of substance abuse disorders (Wilson, Nunes, Greenwald, & Weissman, 2004). A possible explanation for the linkage between disruptive behavior and linguistic deficits is that language mediates behavioral regulation through "self talk" (Vygotsky & Kozulin, 1986). "Verbal deficits may be specifically related to disruptive behavior disorders or be nonspecific risk factors for general psychiatric impairment" (Wilson et al., 2004, p. 203).

Child welfare laws require the removal of children from abusive and neglectful homes. Many of the "seize the kids" laws in large U.S. cities have changed because addicts would not seek help during pregnancy to avoid potentially having their children taken away. Regulations that govern when child welfare agencies should take custody of a child vary from state to state. In many counties in the United States the biggest factor in determining whether or not the county takes custody of a child is the presence of a sober grandmother (Willwerth, 1991). Currently, grandmothers care for many high-risk babies (Willwerth, 1991). If there is not a family member to care for the children when they are removed from the home, they will end up in the foster care system.

According to Stephanie Brown, PhD, director of the Addictions Institute in Menlo Park, California, "children try to protect themselves emotionally by ignoring or submerging emotions" (Whitehouse, 2000, p. 155). Children will often be in denial concerning the problem, maybe because they truly don't understand what the problem is. A common coping response is to withdraw or to blame themselves. Children of alcoholics are confused and do not understand their parents' drinking or its consequences (Whitehouse, 2000). Children of substance abusers often become introverted and withdraw into their own world. Neglected children may have been forced to care for themselves at a very young age with tasks that were beyond their capabilities.

Parents who use drugs run the risk of being arrested and incarcerated, often as repeat offenders. During parental incarceration, the children are often placed in temporary kinship or foster care. There is always uncertainty and lack of predictability in these children's lives, particularly when the parent returns home from jail. Recidivism rates for drug addicts, particularly methamphetamine abusers, are extremely high.

Case Example

Stefano, age 12, was in seventh grade when he began meeting with the school social worker because of his emotional outbursts and fighting at school. His father was incarcerated for drug trafficking. Stefano lived with his mother, who also abused drugs and alcohol. Stefano constantly spoke about how much better things were going to be when his father was home. During the school year, Stefano struggled with accepting the reality that his father was not going to be home until he was grown. He was embittered and in denial about his father's drug use and angry most of the time. The school social worker tried to develop a relationship with him and to work on anger management skills. Stefano met with the social worker weekly, would usually avoid any discussions about his behavior, and seemed unwilling to accept help. The minimal amount of time the school social worker had available to work with Stefano, coupled with his continual absences, was not sufficient to make an impact on his life during the school year. What Stefano needed was full-time support in a residential treatment program, like Boys Town, to provide him with all the things that were missing in his life, like safety, security, love, support, consistency, and predictability.

THE EFFECTS OF DRUG AND ALCOHOL ABUSE ON THE COMMUNITY

Each year an estimated 75,000 to 100,000 people die from alcohol-related illness or abuse (U.S. Department of Health and Human Services, 2006; Lewis, 1997). An estimated 5,475 people die as a direct result of drug abuse each year in the United States (Evans, 1998). However, if drug-related infant deaths, overdose-related deaths, suicides, homicides, motor vehicle accident deaths, and the various forms of drug-abuse-related disease (such as hepatitis, HIV infection, pneumonia, and endocarditis) are included, the death toll may be closer to 20,000 or 30,000 ((Miller, 1999; Prater, Miller, & Zylstra, 1999; Doweiko, 2002) per year. One-third of all deaths in the United States may be attributable to recreational chemical abuse (Hurt et al., 1996). The cost of alcohol abuse in terms of criminal activity, motor vehicle accidents, and destruction of property, as well as the cost to social welfare programs and private and public hospitalization costs for alcohol-related illness totals between $99 billion and $166 billion per year (Olmedo & Hoffman, 2000; Doweiko, 2002).

FETAL ALCOHOL SYNDROME

Fetal Alcohol Syndrome (FAS) is caused by the impact of maternal alcohol consumption on an unborn child. "Children with FAS are smaller and slower than other children of their same age. Their eyes may be small, with drooping eyelids, the groove between the upper lip and nose may be absent, and the lower part of their faces may seem flat" (Friend, 2005, p. 291). FAS students may have mild mental retardation and a short attention span. They also may be characterized by hyperactivity, learning disabilities, and poor coordination.

"Fetal alcohol syndrome is considered to be the leading cause of mental retardation that is preventable" (Friend, 2005, p. 291). Mental retardation impacts several levels of cognitive functioning. The impairment may affect memory, resulting in the inability to remember what one is supposed to do, particularly in tasks with multiple steps. "Students with mental retardation have difficulty with generalization[1] on academic tasks, on behavior expectation, and in social interactions" (Friend, 2005, p. 295). Children with mental retardation have difficulty with metacognition, or thinking about thinking, and in making judgments about what to do next. These students also struggle with motivation and learned helplessness. They become frustrated easily and ask for assistance or wait for help rather than trying to figure things out on their own (Friend, 2005, p. 295).

Case Example

Kevin was born with FAS. He was in the first grade when the school social worker met him. He had the physical appearance of a child with FAS, particularly a slightly enlarged forehead and flattened lower face. He lacked coordination and always had cuts and bruises on his head from falling off his bike or skateboard, or just falling. Kevin was living in a foster home. His father was incarcerated for drug abuse, and child welfare had placed him in foster care until his mother could rehabilitate herself from her drug and alcohol abuse. Kevin was placed in a special education class for children with behavior disorders. He was temperamental and had tantrums at school. He would often refuse to do his schoolwork when it was too difficult. He was in the process of being tested for cognitive deficits because his skill levels in language use and reading were below average. He was struggling with writing and reading. Kevin also had difficulty controlling his emotions at home. He often threw tantrums, which caused him to get into trouble with his foster family.

[1]Generalization is the ability to learn a task or idea and apply it in other situations.

He was referred to the school social worker to learn social skills and anger management skills. He was a loving child and would often draw pictures for the school social worker as they talked. The pictures Kevin drew were usually hearts saying he loved the social worker and his teacher too. He was receptive to counseling because he seemed starved for attention. Kevin was responsive to behavior charts and graphs that the school social worker and his teacher used. He was given short-term behavior goals and rewarded each time he accomplished the goals. Kevin helped pick out his rewards, which were usually the chance to lay his head down and rest for 5 minutes when he completed his goals. The school social worker often bought him new "designer" pencils when he accomplished his goals.

Some of Kevin's behavior goals at school were to stay in his seat for 15 minutes and work and to raise his hand and ask for help rather than throwing a tantrum when confused about the school assignment. Whenever he met his goals, he was given immediate rewards by his teacher.

He was disruptive in his foster home and expressed fear because he was threatened with removal from the foster home and placement in a children's home. He had some anxiety and uncertainty about leaving his foster home. He would often say that he was going back to live with his mother.

The school social worker contacted the foster parents and wrote behavior management plans to help with Kevin's tantrums at home. The behavior plans would work temporarily, but it seemed that the foster family's commitment to offering rewards was not consistent. To succeed, behavior plans must have the commitment of both the child trying to make the changes and the adults who are providing the positive feedback and rewards for positive changes in behavior.

Kevin was placed in another foster home out of the social worker's school district before the end of the school year. It was heartbreaking for both the social worker and teacher. They feared that Kevin was at the beginning of a possible lifetime of change and uncertainty that would hinder his abilities because he would have to spend so much time making adjustments and learning new rules rather than having the stability he needed.

HELPING CHILDREN OF ALCOHOLIC PARENTS

Many researchers have concluded that the effects of growing up in an alcoholic home often last beyond the individual's childhood years (Doweiko, 2002, p. 313). Woititz, an early researcher on the effects of alcohol on children, reported that the adult children of alcoholic parents exhibit a number of characteristics that include:

1. Trouble with intimate relationships because of "guessing" about normal adult behavior.
2. Difficulty following a project through from beginning to end.
3. A tendency to lie in situations where it is just as easy to tell the truth.
4. A tendency not to be able to "relax," but always to judge themselves harshly, and to feel a need to keep busy all the time.
5. A tendency not to feel comfortable with themselves, but rather to constantly seek affirmation from significant others (1983).

A school social worker needs to be aware of these characteristics and work to help children develop confidence in themselves and trust in their own instincts. This could be accomplished through developing a positive relationship with the children and teaching by modeling normal adult behavior. Also, school social workers should try to create positive peer relationships through groups and peer mentoring programs that help validate the child as a person.

Children of alcoholic parents need to have an understanding that alcoholism is an illness that is causing their parents to behave differently from other children's parents. Children need to be told what is going on in an age-appropriate way (Whitehouse, 2000). A simple explanation of the problem is usually helpful. One of the most crucial needs for children is a safety plan if the alcoholic parent is volatile or violent. Family members are often in denial or are contributing to the substance abuse by making excuses for the substance user. Often family members can serve as enablers by making excuses to those outside the family for the substance abuser.

School social workers can assist children of alcoholic parents by talking to them about the problem and helping them understand that the alcohol dependence is not their fault. They need an explanation about alcohol dependence in clear, uncomplicated terms. School social workers should help children develop a safety plan for themselves and, if possible, their siblings. School social workers can teach problem solving and social skills to children who live with substance-abusing parents. These children may not have a repertoire of decision making skills other than using violence or trying to avoid problems as they have seen their parents do by using drugs and alcohol. Social workers can help teach anger management skills to allow children a healthy way to express their frustrations over their lives at home.

According to SAMHSA Administrator Charles S. Curie, "too often when we concentrate on providing treatment for the affected adult we forget the heavy burden that substance abuse lays on the children of those in treatment. Often when the needs of the children are ignored, these children grow into substance-abusing adults" (Substance Abuse and Mental Health Services Administration, 2003).

By treating children and helping them find effective solutions to their problems rather than turning to substance abuse themselves, social workers can help prevent the continuation of the intergenerational cycle of addiction. School social workers may also assist a child by offering a support group at school and offering assistance to the family by providing referral information for interventions, since the issues related to substance abuse are difficult to handle alone. The social worker also can encourage the family to continue family rituals and activities–particularly at bedtime so the child falls asleep peacefully, help children become involved in extracurricular activities, and try to get the substance-abusing family member into treatment (Whitehouse, 2000).

School personnel must understand that addressing the personal problems of children of alcoholic parents increases their chances of succeeding in school (Torchia, 2003). Early detection of these at-risk children is critical. Interventions that can address their academic, behavioral, and emotional problems need to begin early in the school years. It is important for the children in substance-abusing families to feel that their needs are important and that it is okay to take care of themselves. The National Association for Children of Alcoholics (NACoA) and the U.S. Department of Health and Human Services (DHHS) have collaborated to create the Children's Program Kit to assist in teaching age-appropriate alcohol education to children from first grade through high school. This program is called the STARR program. (See Appendix 12.1 for contact information.)

The STARR problem-solving model teaches problem-solving skills to children who may not learn how to make decisions in alcoholic homes where "rigid behavior prevails" (Torchia, 2003, p. 4).

> The program also includes social skills training and help with self-esteem in order to develop competence, autonomy, and a sense of purpose. The problem-solving steps in the STARR program are:
>
> 1. Stop: Ask, "What is the problem?" Name it.
> 2. Think: Ask, "How do I feel? How can I solve this problem?" Identify options.
> 3. Act: Choose the best option that helps me stay safe and allows me to take good care of myself.
> 4. Resources: Ask, "Who can help me? Where can I find assistance?" Find safe people and places for help.
> 5. Review: Ask, "Would I try to solve this problem the same way again? What would I do differently next time?" (Torchia, 2003, p. 4)

HELPING CHILDREN OF DRUG-ADDICTED PARENTS

Parental abuse of drugs is harmful to the entire family. As a result of drug addiction "family cohesion is often damaged, relationships between family members are undermined, there is an increase in violent behavior along with economic hardships, health, and social problems, and often a clash with the legal authorities" (Peleg-Oren, 2002, p. 245). Children's lives are affected by both emotional and physical instability. There are often feelings of emotional and social loneliness (Peleg-Oren, 2002). Hyperactivity and antisocial behaviors are also common among children of drug-addicted parents (Peleg-Oren, 2002). Because these children have a lower perception of their own abilities, often their test results will be lower than those of peers with equal intelligence, the result of a self-fulfilling prophecy (Murray, 1989, p. 859).

If a school social worker encounters a child with drug-addicted parents, the social worker may need to work with the local child welfare agency to help stabilize the child's life. School social workers should support child welfare agencies as they try to intervene with the family. The following are possible interventions that may come from child welfare:

1. Intensive–and prolonged–child protective supervision
2. Formalized kinship care program
3. Adoptions
4. Long-term substitute living arrangements
5. Family planning (Besharov, 1996)

Group intervention is a recommended tool to assist children of drug-addicted parents. Children respond to support from peers in elementary school, and it becomes increasingly important as they mature. The group can give children a chance to discuss their frustrations with a sympathetic audience with similar difficulties. Also, the children can develop a sense of belonging, which may help to eliminate the feelings of isolation and loneliness that often are associated with children of substance-abusing parents.

School social workers should provide information to each teacher about behaviors that can help identify children with substance-abusing parents. The social worker should then work in conjunction with the school counselor to present short vignettes to each class about alcohol and drug abuse and what it feels like to live in homes where such abuse takes place. Then the social worker should ask students to self-refer if they would like to talk about their feelings. Groups may develop naturally from self-referrals. Once a student has self-referred, the school social worker should inform the student's parents about the nature of the group and obtain written permission from the parents for the student to attend the group.

Children whose parents abuse drugs will need structure and security from the school. Often, their homes may be very chaotic, with no meals or a regular time to eat whatever food may be in the house, no regular bedtime, unclean surroundings, dirty laundry, and no assistance with homework. Many of these children may be providing their own self-care. Coming from a chaotic environment, there is a need for order and predictability. The school social worker can help assure that children have order and structure in their school day by working with teachers to make sure that assignments, tests, and in-class activities are not surprises and that the children have been able to complete the things that are expected of them.

These children also need to feel that the school is a safe environment. School social workers should provide a peer support group for them where they can discuss their fears and difficulties at school and receive validation from their peers. The social worker should model openness and provide a feeling of acceptance and positive regard for the students. Interactions with the school social worker should focus primarily on the child's strengths and create a positive feeling for the child.

Many children of substance-abusing parents have a negative attitude toward authority, particularly police officers. Children can become immersed in the paranoia toward police officers that their parents display. Likewise, the children can adopt some of the fears and delusions the parents may exhibit at home about being caught with substances. Many methamphetamine addicts become afraid that others are out to get them. This fear is manifested as hypervigilance. Their children may exhibit the same fears by becoming hypervigilant, or the fears may be internalized within the child. The school social worker can help alleviate this fear by inviting police officers who serve as school resource officers or other police officers to attend group sessions and befriend the children. Meeting and talking to police officers can help the children learn to see the officers in a positive light.

One of the most helpful activities for these children is a homework assistance group. These children usually do not have parental support with homework, which may include purchasing supplies for extra projects. The school social worker can ask the school principal for discretionary funds or approach the parent–teacher association (PTA) for funding to help with school supplies for these children. The social worker can also help set up a program of volunteers to assist with tutoring.

EXTRACURRICULAR ACTIVITIES

Involvement with activities outside the family gives the child another reality from which to draw (Whitehouse, 2000). Children who have been traumatized by parental substance abuse will thrive better if they have the support of other adults, such as scout leaders, church leaders, coaches, and teachers (see Perry, 2002d). Time spent with other children can help ease the sense of isolation and loneliness that children of alcoholic parents often feel (Whitehouse, 2000).

Case Example

Max, a 10th grader, had an alcoholic father. When he entered high school, he wanted to be involved in athletics. However, he was not selected for the football team when he tried out. He had many frustrations because of the violence in his home and would often explode at school. He wanted to be treated as a normal student but was placed in a special education program for emotionally disturbed students because of his emotional outbursts. He worked closely with a school social worker to learn anger management. He also worked with the social worker on his self-esteem, which was damaged from the violent aggression that his father would demonstrate toward him and his mother.

With the encouragement of his special education teacher and the school social worker, he decided to take a drama class. He was given a small part in a school play. He did very well in spite of his anxiety about the part. He was extremely disappointed when his parents did not attend the play, and it almost ruined his performance. However, the teacher saw his potential and encouraged him to continue trying out for other school plays. He was able to act in several different programs and to find a small group of friends who were also interested in drama. His involvement in drama became very important to him and gave him the incentive he needed to graduate from high school.

SETTING UP A SCHOOL PROGRAM

Group work seems to be the most effective treatment method for children of alcoholic and drug-abusing parents. The size of the group is dependent on the age of the children. The younger the child, the fewer children should be in the group. School social workers should work hard at the outset to provide a private setting and to build a group that has age similarities. It is difficult to assure the use of a private space in school buildings, but groups could be scheduled in spaces in the building that are not utilized during certain times of the day. Pre-enrolling children and providing them with enough information to come to the group prepared to talk about the problems they face is essential. Also, it is important that each child enrolled in the group have enough time to become acquainted with the other group members. The group sessions should be held at the same time each week and give children a chance to play physically active games, share private thoughts, and use play and art therapy to express their feelings (Torchia, 2003).

Programs for children of alcoholic parents, such as the Maplegrove Children's Program in Detroit, are successful in part because of the simplicity of the rules and program. The group rules include the following:

1. One person talks at a time.
2. Members respect each other.
3. Members use "put-ups," not put-downs.
4. Everyone has a right to pass.
5. What we say here stays here (Torchia, 2003).

School social workers can utilize the same rules in school support groups for children of alcoholics.

School social workers may find helpful concepts for children who have substance abusing parents in John Gottman's 1997 book *Raising an Emotionally Intelligent Child.* Gottman found that good emotional coaches validate children's emotions and encourage them to trust their feelings and solve problems by giving them choices. These coaches use a child's negative emotional state, such as anger, sadness, or fear, as an opportunity for learning. They treat the child with patience and avoid criticism, and they listen with empathy and verify the child's feelings (Gottman, 1997; Corley, 2005).

If school social workers decide to intervene through group therapy, they need to decide the purpose of the group, such as support, anger management, problem solving, or increasing self-esteem. The age range of the students included in the group should be narrow, with no more than a 1- to 2-year difference in ages. The gender of the group should also be predetermined–parental drug and alcohol dependence often affects girls differently than boys. A high level of depression and low self-esteem is found among girls (Peleg-Oren, 2002).

Three group goals identified by Neta Peleg-Oren can address the problems faced by children of addicts. These include:

1. Educational goals that give children knowledge about their parent's addiction.
2. Social–familial goals to help the children realize they are not alone and to teach social skills.
3. Emotion-dynamic goals to enable the children to interact with the school social worker in a positive adult relationship (2002).

Children also can be taught positive ways to express their emotions (Peleg-Oren, 2002). Social skills programs in both classrooms and groups should begin as early as possible for children of substance abusers. Children with early social skills deficits, such as having few friends, often have later problems in forming relationships and friendships with peers (Hussong, Zucker, Wong, Fitzgerald, & Puttler, 2005).

Developing social competence can help children achieve academic success and learn to deal with aggression, loneliness, and depression (Hussong et al., 2005). Peer support programs and peer mentoring programs are also a positive way to help build social competence. Most group programs for children of addicts have been short term. Long-term groups that meet weekly and last throughout an entire school year (8–9 months) offer a vehicle for support and structure that could help children of substance abusers succeed in school. A clearly defined group intervention can help children learn to relate to others, acquire interpersonal communication skills, and develop emotional awareness (Peleg-Oren, 2002).

CONCLUSION

Parental substance abuse is related to emotional, physical, and mental risk factors for children. The risks may be present indirectly through neglect and the modeling of deviant and paranoid behaviors. Other risks are direct, in which the child is a victim of violence or is a witness to parental violence. Parental drug and alcohol abuse may force a child to provide his or her own self-care or possibly turned over to child welfare services. Often the effects of parental substance abuse are evident in school, where children cannot concentrate, may be tired and want to sleep, and may display behavioral problems, inadequate social skills, truancy, and academic failure.

School social workers need to identify which children may be living with parental substance abuse and intervene as early as possible with social skills training, peer support groups, mentoring programs, help with homework, and any other programs the school social worker can create. Social workers should strive to build positive relationships with the children of substance abusers in order to provide a positive adult role model. They need to create a relationship that will help the child learn to understand the home environment and feel safe in discussing his or her fears. They also need to help children create a safety plan and help provide structure and safety at school. Intervention early in the child's school years may prevent the patterns of failure and feelings of inadequacy that often lead to substance abuse later in life. The school social worker can be instrumental in breaking the cycle of continuous addiction within a family.

Discussion Topics

1. What are the most common reasons for substance abuse?
2. How can school social workers identify students whose parents are substance abusers?
3. Discuss ways a school social worker can use group therapy to teach the principles identified by John Gottman for emotional coaching. (Some of these principles include validating emotions, validating feelings, responding with empathy, and giving choices.)
4. Discuss ways school social workers can help children develop positive feelings toward police officers.
5. Discuss ways that a school social worker can develop a program for homework assistance.

APPENDIX 12.1. Resources on Alcohol and Drug Abuse

1. Bureau of Indian Affairs
   www.doi.gov/bureau-indian-affairs.html
   12-step program
   White Bison, Inc. (an American Indian nonprofit organization)
   6145 Lehman Drive, Suite 200
   Colorado Springs, CO 80918
   719-548-1000 (voice)
   719-548-9407 (fax)
   www.whitebison.org

2. SAMHSA National Clearinghouse for Alcohol and Drug Information. Toolkits can be order by calling 800-729-6686. Faxed requests should be sent to 301-468-6433.

3. SAMHSA's report *Children Living with Substance-Abusing or Substance-Dependent Parents* can be ordered at *www.drugabusestatistics.samhsa.gov*

4. U.S. Department of Health and Human Services (DHHS) and National Association for Children of Alcoholics (NACoA) Children's Program Kit.
   http://ncadistore.samhsa.gov/catalog/productDetails.aspx?ProductID=17245

13

Death and Loss

Death and loss are difficult to face at any age. It is hard to know how well children have processed the death of a loved one because most younger children do not have a clear understanding of the permanence of death. Children do, however, understand the permanence of loss, which they manifest through behaviors such as separation anxiety.

Children express grief in many ways. Some become clingy, are fearful, and have nightmares. Some children grieve by becoming aggressive. Others alternate between sadness and their usual behavior (Brodkin, 2004). Some children do not grieve openly, whereas some become angry, others despondent.

Adolescents who are grieving may react in many different ways. Some may become argumentative. Some adolescents may act recklessly and turn to substance abuse (Christ, Siegel, & Christ, 2002). They also may seem unconcerned about a death and appear wrapped up in their own lives. This may reflect normal egocentric characteristics of adolescents rather than a failure to feel or cope with difficult emotions (Schlozman, 2003).

The reactions to loss and the process of grieving usually interfere with a child's ability to perform well in school. Because there are so many ways to grieve and so many types of responses, it is necessary for school social workers who are helping children work through their grief to understand the importance of any new behaviors manifested by a grieving child.

This chapter provides an overview of the various types of losses encountered by children and adolescents in school and the community.

These losses may include the loss of a teacher, a classmate, a parent, or a sibling. The chapter also discusses suicide and the ripple effect felt by all who had any contact with the person who committed suicide. Additionally, there are discussions about terminal illness and the death of pets. Deaths of community leaders also can be devastating to students and create feelings of insecurity. The ways that school social workers can assist in losses will be discussed.

School social workers should be aware of students who have experienced a loss. They should offer support that will allow the child an opportunity to grieve. It is critical for social workers to realize that the pain associated with grief and loss comes and goes. When consoling a bereaved child, school social workers should follow the child's lead. If the child seems sad, the social worker should respond with understanding and empathy. When the child is playful and oblivious to the loss, the social worker should respond playfully (Brodkin, 2004). Some children may deny the feeling of loss by blocking the grief.

School social workers also need to understand that children often grieve differently from adults. Children have not had many life experiences and are not cognitively able to understand death in the same way adults do. Their grief is without a complete comprehension of what is happening to them because they may not have experienced the finality that accompanies someone's death (Naierman, 1997). Nancy Boyd Webb (2002, p. 14) has identified the following characteristics of childhood grief:

1. Children's immature cognitive development interferes with their understanding the irreversibility, universality, and inevitability of death.
2. Children have a limited capacity to tolerate emotional pain.
3. Children have a limited ability to verbalize their feelings.
4. Children are sensitive about "being different" from their peers.
5. Children are able to express their feelings in play therapy.

Individual differences in a person's concept of death may be influenced by factors such as "family and cultural background, life experiences, and environment, which are often related to socioeconomic status . . . and race" (Morin & Welsh, 1996, p. 585). It has been hypothesized that because of their greater exposure, lower-class children are more aware of the concept of death than middle class children (Tallmer, Formanek, & Tallmer, 1974). Likewise, children who have experienced previous losses are often more aware of the concept of death than those who are experiencing one for the first time.

The support that friends, family, and neighbors give in abundance immediately following a death usually diminishes over time. However, the people most affected by the loss may only be barely recovering from the associated shock and trauma and just beginning to deal with the pain of grief as outside support declines. This is why it is so critical for school social workers, counselors, and teachers to be aware of students who have experienced the loss of a loved one and to offer continuing support for many months afterward. School social workers should find out if the child is exhibiting new behaviors that could be indicators of his or her grief response. These behaviors include a change in eating or sleeping habits, a change in appearance, an interest in or preoccupation with death, giving away prized possessions, a change in academic performance, school absences, and despondency.

School social work intervention can help children successfully deal with the loss of death before it overwhelms them. When students are not allowed to discuss the loss and their feelings, the ability to work through the grief is delayed. Sometimes it can lead to later depressive illness (Birtchnell, 1980).

DEATH OF A TEACHER

Children occasionally experience the death of a teacher. Because the death of a teacher is traumatic, students need to be helped to express their grief and ask questions. School social workers need to know each child well enough to be able to assess when the child has received a sense of closure. They should help students realize that even though they may have come to a sense of acceptance about the loss, future events may trigger the feelings of loss and sadness again.

Case Example

When I was in fourth grade, my teacher was killed in an airplane crash during Thanksgiving break. She was with her husband, son, and daughter, who were all killed. The only surviving family member was a married daughter who had not gone on the family vacation with them. I attended the funeral with another classmate and our mothers. It was the first funeral I remember attending. There were four gray coffins in the front of the church. It was very sad, and I remember feeling bad because we were told that she had taken our report cards with her, and many of them were found at the crash site. It made our entire class feel sad to think she had been working before she died. We also felt a sense of loss because we did not ever find out how well we had done in our classes during the first term of the school year. It was a part of the grief that made it hard for us to deal with.

We did not get a permanent teacher until about February, and it was difficult to have an array of substitutes. No one came into our class to provide any grief work for us. I remember that the school principal was in the classroom when we came back from Thanksgiving break. He told us that our teacher had died and about the report cards. No one else ever talked to our class about our teacher and about our loss. I was lucky because I attended the funeral and was able to hear more information about her death. In addition, my parents talked about it with me. I remember feeling very curious about who she was as a person, not just a teacher. Our class was expected to continue our schoolwork and did not receive any other intervention. There were many unanswered questions, and we all felt the emptiness that comes with not being able to say goodbye. The situation did not allow us to work through our grief and feel a sense of closure.

In retrospect, there were many needs that were not met. The students all wanted more information about the accident and how our teacher died. They wanted to know more about the teacher as a person. They wanted to know about their performance in school but were never given the grades or report on the first term of the school year. The students needed some way to say goodbye, and they needed stability and a sense of permanence as soon as possible to help them feel secure.

Fourth grade is a fairly young age to be confronted with the permanence of death. For most of the students it was their first encounter with loss. It would have helped to have someone explain what grief was, that it is normal, and that it is acceptable.

It is important to help children and adolescents understand the grieving process without using the term "closure" because closure may not be a reality for them. There is usually an expectation from adults that at some point a few months after a death, it is going to be necessary to put the grief aside and move on. However, children may not be able to verbalize the feeling of regret or guilt they experience in forgetting about the person who is deceased. "If closure means letting go of precious memories, I don't think we ever find closure when a loved one dies, nor would we want to" (Ufema, 2005, p. 24).

Case Example

Ian was in his late twenties and was a first-year special education teacher at a senior high school. He was an exceptional teacher who was innovative and able to make all of his students feel special and challenged. He also was a writer and would inspire the students to express themselves through their writing rather than taking their frustrations out on each other or keeping their feelings hidden. He went on a skiing vacation over Christmas break and was killed in an automobile accident on the way home from the ski resort. The students were devastated. Many of the students had just begun to feel connected to school through Ian, and now he was gone.

The school social worker, administrators, and special education director went to the classroom to inform the students about Ian's death during each class period. The school social worker talked to students, first as a group, and then individually for several days to help them express their loss. Many students wrote letters to Ian at the school social worker's encouragement as a way of coping with their grief.

The social worker also had to pack up all of Ian's personal belongings from his classroom. Many of the students were curious about Ian's personal belongings. The social worker let the students know what he had left at school and gave them a chance to learn more about Ian through some of his possessions. The students were very curious about who Ian was and tried to learn more about him for the first few days after his death. The social worker helped them learn whatever she could and let them ask anything they needed to know.

The school district immediately replaced Ian with a permanent teacher. The new teacher gave the students a chance to get to know her in their own time. She did not push them in any way but slowly became a part of their lives. She allowed them to tell her what was different about her teaching style and requirements and Ian's.

Adults must not be overlooked in the process of dealing with a school crisis. Ironically, during the writing of this chapter one of my graduate students was killed in a motorcycle accident. He was young, had a promising future, and left behind a wife and young son. Several of our faculty and students attended the funeral, sent flowers, and sent notes to the family letting them know how he had made an impact on their lives. The faculty members who were teaching classes in which he was enrolled took extra care to discuss the situation with the students and to allow students to have time to confront their grief openly. The faculty members also were supportive to each other during this time, and it was very comforting to share the loss with colleagues.

William Worden identified four tasks that mourners must accomplish (2002). The first task is accepting the reality of the loss, or, in the words of Joy Ufema, "acknowledging that the person is dead and reunion isn't possible in this life" (2005, p. 24). Worden's second task is experiencing the pain of grief. Third is adjusting to an environment in which the deceased is missing. Fourth is withdrawal of emotional energy from mourning and reinvesting it in another relationship. These tasks do not have a specific timeline, and there may be occasions months after a death in which the mourner will need to spend the day grieving. School social workers should help students recognize that there is no one prescribed way to grieve and that each person experiences grief in his or her own unique way.

DEATH OF SCHOOL PERSONNEL/FACULTY

School social workers may be helpful to staff and faculty as well as to students after the death of a school employee. "The relationship of the person who died to students and colleagues, the circumstances of the death, and the response of the school community to the death" all affect the grieving process for the school community (Stevenson, 2002, p. 194). There is always a need for adults to express their grief and receive emotional support after the death of a coworker or supervisor. School social workers should make a schoolwide offer of assistance to anyone who wants to talk. The month following the death is an opportune time for the school social worker to be in the faculty lunchroom and in an office on campus before and after school. Many teachers and staff members will casually drop in to talk about their feelings of loss. Of course, this may present a problem for the social worker who is also grieving. This may be a time to invite a social work colleague from a nearby school or district to provide consultation and assistance.

Case Example

Mr. Wilkes was a coach and driver's education instructor in a large high school. Early in the school year, he died of a massive heart attack over the weekend. He was in his fifties and very well liked by the faculty and staff. Many of them were able to attend his funeral. Those who went to the funeral and the viewing the evening prior to the funeral seemed to cope better with the death than those who were unable to attend those events. As the school social worker, I became aware that many teachers were dropping into my office or the offices of the school counselors for a couple weeks after the death. These school employees wanted to talk about Mr. Wilkes. Some told funny anecdotes, others described what a good person he had been, and others just said how sad they felt. The death was also discussed for several days in the faculty lunchroom. Mr. Wilkes had been teaching and coaching at the same high school for several years and had many friends on the faculty. Several of his peers who were close in age expressed their own vulnerability and fears about the possibility of their own sudden death. The school social worker and counselors served an important role in helping many of the school personnel express their grief and feelings of loss.

DEATH OF A CLASSMATE

There are an estimated 20,000 deaths annually of young people between the ages of 10 and 29 in the United States. The three leading causes of death are accidents, homicide, and suicide (Dyregrov, Bie Wikander, & Vigerust, 1999). Loss of a friend or classmate can lead to both short-term and long-term grief reactions (Podell, 1989; McNeil, Silliman, & Swihart, 1991; Brent et al., 1993; Webb, 2002). The death of a classmate is devastating to students. It is unexpected to have a young person die. It makes other children and adolescents feel vulnerable.

School social workers can help children understand that death is part of life, as they may be worrying that they might also die. Children should be told that "they are healthy and will probably be alive for several years, that most people live to be old" (Ufema, 2005, p. 24) and that the imminent death of any friend or loved one is unlikely.

School social workers should help teachers and other school personnel know that "children aren't just small adults either physically or emotionally. They mourn differently than adults and have emotions they can't understand and worries they can't express" (Ufema, 2005, p. 24). School social workers should spend time with the classmates of a student who has recently died. It helps the other students to discuss the loss openly and ask questions about the death. Likewise, "a life review of the deceased will often bring smiles and laughter when recounting anecdotes. The game of 'remember when' lessens tensions and helps the group accept the professional who is providing the group support" (Zinner, 1987, p. 500). However it is done, students must be allowed to have their questions about the death answered, express their grief, and say goodbye to their friend through attendance at the funeral or memorial service or through discussions, art therapy, or writing.

Case Example

Jeremy and Andrew were high school seniors. They were driving home from a party on a Saturday evening a month before the end of the school year. They were driving too fast, and their car spun out of control and hit a tree. Both of them were killed instantly.

The boys were students from a self-contained special education class. Their school attendance had been sporadic, and they had each been in many skirmishes with their classmates, teacher, and the school administration. The tragedy of their untimely death was felt quite intensely by the students who were in their class. Their teacher and some of their classmates attended their funerals. The day after the funerals, the teacher described to his students what had happened at the funerals and gave the students

> more details about the accident. He allowed the students to talk about the death and their feelings. The school social worker also spent time with each student individually to answer questions and to let the student express grief. The social worker helped teach the students how to write a "thought page" in which they expressed all of their feelings about the deaths in writing. (See Appendices 13.1 and 13.2 for examples of forms for written and art thought pages.) The students seemed able to cope with the deaths because they were allowed to express their feelings and have their questions answered. The teacher did an outstanding job of helping his students and appropriately enlisted the school social worker for additional support.

If a child continues to grieve longer than a few months, he or she may actually be carrying a secret or guilt surrounding the death. It is possible that the child did not like the person who died and feels bad about that. Likewise, he or she may have been in a fight with the deceased child and expressed hostility, or even a wish that the child were dead.

Children who carry secrets are afraid to divulge them for many reasons. Sometimes they don't want other people to know how mean they are. Other times they believe that their wish was granted and that their classmate is dead because of them. The continuing presence of a school social worker may help the child who is feeling guilty develop enough trust to open up about his or her guilt.

SUICIDE

Suicide is the second leading cause of death among children and adolescents (Pritchard, 1996). People who contemplate suicide are frequently ambivalent about killing themselves and usually respond to help. This is because people who have a suicide plan may not want to die, but only to be free from their current situation, and suicide seems to be their only viable option. Suicidal students often try to communicate their feelings indirectly prior to attempting suicide. Many people veil their cry for help so that others do not recognize it as a serious plea. Thus, afterward there is a great deal of guilt and feeling that the suicide could have been prevented "if only. . . . " Suicides trigger many emotions in fellow students, such as "poor self-concept, excessive self-demands, fear of loss, grief over previous losses, self-blame, and self-recrimination" (Alexander & Harman, 1988, p. 285).

Following a youth suicide a ripple effect affects everyone in a school or community who was remotely connected to the suicide victim. There also is a concern that suicides may be related to agreements or suicide pacts with other young people, who also will try to hurt themselves shortly after the first suicide. As one school counselor observed regarding her encounters with friends of a suicide victim, "They were experiencing the various grief responses and a pronounced fear that others would follow. Not only were they greatly afraid of being faced with the loss of yet another friend, but many also feared their own suicidal potential" (Alexander & Harman, 1988, p. 283).

School social workers can be instrumental in helping schools implement suicide prevention programs. These programs must focus on teaching awareness of the danger signals. Social workers must have the ability to teach prevention strategies and awareness of the warning signs of suicide to school personnel and students.

School social workers must also have the ability to deal with the aftermath of a suicide. The process of assisting students and school personnel in the aftermath of a suicide is twofold. First, the school social worker must help those who knew the deceased student express and work through their grief. Second, the social worker must try to minimize the likelihood of copycat suicides (Alexander & Harman, 1988, p. 283).

A positive approach to the aftermath of a suicide focuses primarily on the students who were in class with the deceased student and those who self-identify as close friends. As Alexander and Harman (1988) have noted, the appropriate response should not eulogize the deceased but should focus on the feelings of "grief, shock, loss, fear, and even anger" (p. 283). The act of suicide should not be glorified, but those associated with the deceased student should be allowed to express the fact that they miss him or her (Alexander & Harman, 1988, page 284).

After a student at her school committed suicide, a middle school counselor intervened with the student's classes in the following manner: "I entered each classroom and announced, I'm here today to help you say goodbye" to the deceased student (Alexander & Harman, 1988, p. 283). After telling students the deceased student had committed suicide, the school counselor then gave students the opportunity to tell their deceased friend goodbye and express all of the feelings they had, such as sorrow, grief, anger, abandonment, and frustration over not being able to prevent the suicide. Students who did not want to express their feelings openly were invited to draw a picture or write a letter to the deceased student. (See Appendices 13.3 and 13.4.)

The school social worker should help students express their grief and frustration about the suicide of a classmate and friend, yet at the same time the social worker should not focus on or eulogize the deceased student in a way that makes suicide seem like a viable option for other students. Short-term support groups within a school are a time-effective way for a school social worker to help students express their feelings of grief and frustration over a suicide. Suicide usually leaves others feeling a sense of guilt and helplessness because they were unable to prevent it. School social workers need to allow students to express their guilt and realize that many suicides are not preventable.

DEATH OF A PARENT

The death of a parent is one of the greatest traumas a child can suffer and is known to be associated with psychological problems for many children (Lyon & Vandenberg, 1989; Bentovim, 1986). However, it is important for school social workers to remember that "not every child who experiences either permanent or temporary loss grows up to be a disturbed person" (Bowlby, 1963, p. 527). The hope is that with timely, appropriate professional intervention, a child may be able to work through his or her grief and recover.

There are two points of view regarding a child's ability to recover from the loss of a parent. The first holds that "prior to adolescence, children are unable to mourn the loss of a parent. Instead, they seek to retain their union by clinging to an idealized image of the deceased parent, precluding the experience of the broad range of emotions that accompany grief" (Lyon & Vandenberg, 1989, p. 327). Some believe that the inability to mourn a parent's death during childhood leads to depression and a failure to achieve appropriate autonomy. Such individuals cling to attachment figures, shun dependence, and respond to threats of loss with excess hostility (Lyon & Vandenberg, 1989).

The second point of view regarding a child's ability to cope with parental death claims that "children after the age of four have developed a rudimentary understanding of the meaning of death, the capacity for comprehending person permanence, the ability to verbalize feelings, and sufficient ego maturity to enable them to mourn. In order to accomplish the work of mourning, however, children must receive extensive support from their environment" (Bowlby, 1980; Furman, 1983).

"Under the right circumstances, children can recover successfully from the trauma of parental death" (Lyon & Vandenberg, 1989, p. 327). The right circumstances include a family that communicates openly and the surviving parent's ability to maintain a strong parenting role. It also helps if the child had a positive relationship with the deceased parent (Lyon & Vandenberg, 1989).

School social workers can add support for a bereaved child by creating a supportive environment at school. The social worker should notify all of the child's teachers about the parent's death. He or she also should train teachers how to recognize and respond to grief so that they will be able to talk to a child about his or her loss. The social worker should also talk to the other students in the class and suggest possible responses to the child when he or she returns to school after the funeral (Naierman, 1997). However, it is important to realize that some children are embarrassed about the death because it makes them "different." They may not want a great deal of public attention paid to it (Webb, 2002). The school social worker should meet regularly with a bereaved child to allow the child the opportunity to talk privately and to build a supportive adult relationship. The social worker should follow the child throughout the school year and, if possible, into the next school year to assure that school academic performance and attendance do not become a problem.

Case Example

Ryan was in fifth grade when his father went into a diabetic coma and died. Ryan did not have a close relationship with his father because the father had been abusive on several occasions, and Ryan had been afraid of him. However, Ryan was very despondent at school about the loss. He received support from his special education teacher, the classroom aide, school administrators, and the school social worker.

The social worker's intervention centered around weekly time with Ryan. He was given the option to talk and ask questions. He wanted to talk about why his father had been mean to him. He felt he had been bad and that he had made his father angry.

The social worker helped by talking to his mother and grandmother to obtain additional family background. The social worker and family members helped Ryan understand that his father had a temper, but they talked to him about how much his father had loved him.

Ryan had many days at school in which he did not want to work but just laid his head on his desk. The teacher would allow him to do so for a limited time when he asked. He was angry on many occasions, and the school social worker was called to talk with him on those occasions. He was given the opportunity to write, draw pictures, and discuss his anger. However, he was not allowed to use the anger against another student.

It took several months before he seemed to accept the death and relax at school. Expressing his emotions to the teacher and social worker whenever he was overwhelmed helped him to release his grief and anger over his father's death.

DEATH OR SERIOUS ILLNESS OF SIBLINGS

The death of a child shocks and devastates the child's family (Soricelli & Utech, 1985). Siblings often are neglected as parents deal with their own sense of loss and grief. School social workers can be instrumental in helping students adjust to a terminal or serious illness of a sibling. It is necessary for social workers to let teachers and other school personnel know of the necessity of early intervention to help a student deal with the possible impending loss of a sibling. When a person is upset, he or she is more open to the influence of others than during psychological equilibrium. Crisis intervention is extremely helpful as an individual deals with a crisis situation, and a small amount of effort leads to a maximum amount of lasting response (Caplan, 1962, cited in Soricelli & Utech, 1985).

Families coping with a serious disease or terminal illness normally respond in four phases, which the school social worker can explain to the siblings of the sick child in discussing their reactions.

The first phase is *bereavement*, as the family begins to mourn the loss of a healthy child. During this phase, a school social worker should encourage the sick child's siblings to express their grief openly and should offer emotional support (Soricelli & Utech, 1985).

The second phase is *integration*, during which the family members integrate the changes resulting from the illness into their previous life. During this phase, the school social worker should monitor the stress level of the sick child's siblings and assist the family through resource networking.

Phase three is *renewed bereavement*, which occurs as the certainty of death becomes a reality. Siblings of sick children need continuous contact with the school social worker during this phase.

Phase four is *postdeath mourning*. During this phase the family is forced to learn how to live without the deceased child. It is important during this phase for the school social worker to help the surviving siblings establish connections with other students to help fill the void left by the deceased child. Likewise, the school social worker should meet with the surviving siblings regularly to help them express their fears and grief.

Case Example

Jessica, age 12, was in seventh grade when her 8-year-old brother was diagnosed with bone cancer. She had another brother who was 5 years old. The older brother's treatment for cancer required him to spend nights in the hospital. The mother would stay at the hospital with him during these times, while Jessica and her younger brother would stay with their grandmother. As the condition of her younger brother seemed to vacillate between good and bad, the parents, particularly the mother, focused more and more attention on him. Jessica began to become despondent at school. She did not do her schoolwork in class and did none of her homework. She would sometimes respond with hostility to her teachers' requests to complete her work during class.

The teacher called the school social worker to meet with Jessica. The girl was guarded during the first meeting, and the school social worker just talked about herself. During the second meeting, the school social worker had obtained written reports from each of Jessica's teachers. She showed Jessica the difference between her current school performance with her former academic record and asked her to talk about the changes. Jessica said she was afraid that her brother would die. She didn't care about school. This opened up the floodgates for future meetings in which the school social worker could help Jessica express her fears and sorrow. The social worker called the grandmother and obtained information about the brother's illness and prognosis, which actually was good.

The social worker continued meeting with Jessica weekly for the remainder of the school year. Jessica began to do her schoolwork, and her grades improved slightly. She was able to receive emotional support from the social worker and grandmother, with whom she had a close relationship. The health of Jessica's brother improved with his treatments, and his prognosis for recovery was favorable. The school social work intervention allowed Jessica to express her fears and grief and gave her some of the attention she was missing from her parents. It also was helpful for the social worker to keep in touch with the grandmother in order to encourage her to follow up on Jessica's homework.

DEATH OF PETS

Grief over the loss of a pet is very real for children. Most children who have pets are very attached to them. In many cases, the pet has been a member of the family longer than the child, and the entire family feels a great sense of loss at its death. It is important to allow children the opportunity to express this grief and work through it. It also may be the first time that a child has had to experience and understand death. School social workers can help with this grieving process and allow the child to grieve without feeling silly. The feelings of loss are deep and should be taken seriously and legitimized by school social workers.

Case Example

Kevin was in fourth grade when his dog died. He was in special education and was already being seen weekly by the school social worker to help him with emotional problems. He came to school extremely upset and crying the day after his dog was put to sleep. The teacher called the school social worker, who sat with Kevin and let him cry for quite a while. She asked him to tell her the details about his dog's death. Kevin told the social worker the story that his parents had told him. The social worker asked Kevin if he had been able to tell his dog goodbye, and he acknowledged that he had but still wished he could be with his dog. The social worker suggested a thought page in which Kevin could express all of his feelings. The social worker wrote the words as Kevin said them. Then Kevin drew a picture of his dog. The social worker gave the thought page and picture to Kevin and encouraged him to add to it throughout the week as he thought of additional things about his dog and his feelings about her death. The social worker visited with him two more times that week. By the end of the week, he was doing much better. The social worker suggested that he have his mother frame the picture he made of his dog and put it in his room so he could remember how much he loved his dog. This intervention kept Kevin from acting out in school, allowed him to express his grief, and legitimized his feelings about losing his dog.

DEATH OF EXTENDED FAMILY MEMBERS

When there is a death in the extended family, it disrupts the normal family routine. Even when a child is not acquainted with the family member who has died, he or she is aware of the loss felt by the parents or other family members. Social workers should be aware of the following factors that have been identified by Brown (1989, p. 458) as determining the degree of disruption that occurs in a family that has experienced a death:

1. The social and ethnic context of death.
2. The history of previous losses.
3. The timing of the death in the life cycle.
4. The nature of the death or serious illness.
5. The position and function of the person in the family system.
6. The openness of the family system.

The significance of the loss to the family should be discussed at home. Children should receive support from parents as well as school personnel.

School social workers do not always know when there has been a death of an extended family member. However, school social workers can inform faculty and attendees at PTA meetings about the necessity of helping children understand loss. School social workers can also ask teachers to notify them if a child returns to school after an absence with a note stating there was a death in the family. The social worker should obtain parental permission to talk with the child, but families often welcome outside intervention. The social worker can get information from the family on how well the family is coping and assess the need for ongoing support at school for the child. The social worker should then meet with the child, ask what he or she thinks and feels about the loss, and ask the child to complete a thought page or drawing expressing his or her feelings and saying goodbye. If the child is very young, puppets, stories, and storytelling about the death may help him or her.

Children sometimes feel that they should be able to help their parents and siblings. The school social worker can assist the child in understanding the realities of his or her personal responsibility. The fears and insecurity a child feels when the adults in his or her life are grieving must be addressed to help the child know that he or she is not responsible and that the relatives will return to their previous family roles and functioning in time.

DEATH OF COMMUNITY LEADERS

The death of a well-known national figure or well-liked local community leader usually affects children. If the death is traumatic, such as an assassination, the school personnel may need to help children understand the details of the event. I remember clearly when President Kennedy was shot and the anguish and horror that my friends and I felt. It helped to have our teachers discuss his death, to watch the events on TV, and to discuss them with our parents. Teachers and school social workers should allow children the opportunity to write about and discuss their feelings about such deaths. There should not be continuous exposure to the actual death, such as watching it replayed on television, particularly if it is a tragic death. However, children will be curious and should have their questions taken seriously and answered honestly.

School social workers should educate teachers about normal grief reactions and about extreme reactions. When the faculty becomes aware of a child who is experiencing unusual reactions, referral to the school social worker should be made. Unusual reactions may occur because the death reminds the child of other losses or because the death occurs too soon after a child has already experienced another loss or traumatic event. School social workers can help these children express their fears and give them support through discussions, play and art therapy, and thought or feeling pages.

SCHOOL RESPONSE TEAMS

Most large school districts have crisis teams of mental health professionals, such as school social workers and psychologists, who travel throughout the district and intervene whenever there is a crisis or significant event on a campus and can also provide backup to the school community when there are community tragedies. The teams have several purposes, but the main focus is crisis intervention. "Crisis response team leaders in the schools provide information in the form of handouts for teachers (and parents) about what to say to children and how to answer their questions. They can give examples of ways to provide that information to attempt to resolve children's distress" (Williams, 2004, p. 131). For example, if a student threatens suicide, the school social worker or counselor can call the school response team for additional support. The crisis teams also may serve a school in which there are student outbursts. In such cases, they may be able to calm an angry student. The team may serve the entire district at once if there is a community crisis.

Crisis response teams are an extremely effective solution for large school districts that may have only a few social workers assigned to specific campuses. The response teams ensure that students who need extra support will receive it.

CONCLUSION

All school districts must be prepared to handle issues related to death and bereavement. The support of a school social worker is invaluable in assisting students and school personnel. School social workers have the knowledge and skills to teach faculty the warning signs of suicide and the attributes of extreme grief reactions. They have the skills to provide grief groups and individual counseling to students who have lost a family member or teacher. School social workers also serve on crisis response teams to assist school districts in dealing with individual student outbursts and a community crisis. Social workers can offer timely, appropriate interventions that may assist students and school personnel to resolve grief and loss.

Discussion Topics

1. Discuss what you learned about a child's reactions to grief.
2. How can school social workers learn about parental, sibling, or family deaths so they can offer assistance to the child?
3. How do you think a school social worker could implement a suicide prevention program for students, parents, and school personnel?
4. How can school social workers offer long-term assistance to a child after the death of a parent or sibling?

APPENDIX 13.1. Thought Page

Write down all of the thoughts and feelings you have right now about the death of

_______________________. We will talk about it together when you are finished.

When we have discussed what is on the page, it is yours to keep or tear up as you say

goodbye to ______________________________.

APPENDIX 13.2. Art Thought Page

Draw a picture of your feelings related to the death of ______________________.

We will talk about your picture together when you are finished. When we have discussed your picture, it is yours to keep or tear up as you say goodbye to ______________________.

14

Working with Noncitizen Populations

JOYCE A. KELEN

Schools across the United States are witnessing changing demographics as a deluge of newcomers from every part of the world is entering our country. School social workers often work with so many culturally diverse populations that it is impossible to acquire knowledge about every noncitizen student. Therefore, it is critical that social workers develop competence in a cross-cultural practice (Caple et al., 1995; NASW, 2002, Standard 4). It also is important for school social workers to be able to distinguish between refugees and immigrants (documented or undocumented) because the resources and services they receive depend upon the student's immigration status.

DEFINITIONS

There are many types of immigrants to the United States today, including refugees, documented immigrants, and undocumented immigrants.

Joyce A. Kelen, DSW, LCSW, is a school social worker at Bennion Elementary School and Indian Hills Elementary School in Salt Lake City, Utah, where she works extensively with refugee and immigrant families. She has received several awards for her work, and has coauthored *Faces and Voices of Refugee Youth* with her husband, Les.

Immigrants come to the United States voluntarily to escape economic hardships and with hopes for better educational and employment opportunities. Documented immigrants have legal official documents allowing them to move from their place of origin, whereas illegal or undocumented immigrants have no official documents.

The distinction between documented and undocumented immigrants is important because an immigrant's experience before coming to the United States and the circumstances under which he or she comes to this country greatly affect his or her adjustment to the new surroundings (Fong & Wu, 1998). Undocumented immigrant students often come to the United States from impoverished environments because their parents want better lives.

According to the United Nations definition, a "refugee" is a person who has been forced to leave his or her home to escape danger or persecution because of race, religion, nationality, membership in a particular social group, or political opinion. Refugees are unable to obtain protection from their government. Refugees may become U.S. citizens in time if they are given refugee status from the United Nations High Commissioner for Refugees. Refugees often have experienced trauma associated with war and torture and need special attention to help them with their adjustment to school and their social surroundings. While legal refugee students can receive Medicaid, which allows them to receive medical care and eyeglasses, undocumented refugee students cannot.

Whatever their reasons for coming, immigrant students are here, and they should be given the best possible education, including culturally sensitive supports and interventions.

Case Examples

David, an 8-year-old third grader, was referred for being socially withdrawn, not completing his school work, appearing depressed, and needing glasses, having failed the recent eye exam. Five years earlier, the school social worker provided counseling for his mother and sister to help them cope with their grief and handle their financial challenges and emotional trauma after the unexpected death of David's father in a car accident. They were undocumented immigrants from Mexico and David's mother spoke no English.

Peter, a 5-year-old non-English-speaking kindergarten student whose family recently migrated from Sudan, was referred for appearing withdrawn, isolated, and nonresponsive to teachers or students. His teacher was extremely concerned about his numerous fainting spells and the frequency with which paramedics were called to the school to provide emergency care. One time he was taken by ambulance to the hospital. He would often be seen in his teacher's arms as he was brought limply to the office. No one knew if he was fainting from the food he was eating at school or from a medical condition he acquired in Sudan. After numerous medical evaluations and school consultations, it was determined that Peter was fainting at school because he was "paralyzed with fear."

Both David and Peter were recent arrivals to the United States. Although David was undocumented and could not qualify for Medicaid resources to pay for his glasses, the social worker was able to use a voucher from a local optical store for him. Since Peter was a declared refugee, his medical care was covered under the Medicaid program.

RESPONSE TO IMMIGRATION

Although the United States has often been described as a "melting pot," immigration policies have evoked much controversy. While this country was founded by immigrants, successive waves of immigration have resulted in fears that newcomers will become a drain on resources because of the costs of providing education, social services, and medical services. Many are against immigration because they fear loss of their jobs or reductions in their salaries because of competition from immigrant workers willing to work for lower wages.

These controversies are not new to our society. While the Burlingame Treaty of 1868 eased Chinese immigration because there was a high demand for Chinese labor, Congress later passed the Chinese Exclusion Act in 1882, when Chinese workers were no longer in high demand. At that time, it was declared that "the coming of Chinese laborers to this country endangers the good order of certain localities within the territory thereof." Congress later established an immigration quota system in 1921 and passed the Immigration and Nationality Act restricting communists and other supposed "undesirables" in 1952.

While legislatures have attempted to restrict the access of undocumented immigrants to services, recent court decisions have limited the effect of these laws, particularly in the educational sphere. In 1982, the Supreme Court ruled that school districts could not deny undocumented school-age children the free public education provided to children who are citizens of the United States or legally admitted aliens (*Plyler v. Doe*, 457 U.S. 202, 1982). As the court said, "We are reluctant to impute to Congress the intention to withhold from these children, for so long as they are present in this country through no fault of their own, access to a basic education."

ECOLOGICAL–DEVELOPMENTAL FRAMEWORK FOR PRACTICE WITH NONCITIZEN POPULATIONS

The ecological–developmental perspective sees each student as an integral part of various social systems (e.g., home, school, community, peer group, religious institution, and neighborhood) within which the student must learn to function. As a school social worker, one must address specific environmental situations in addition to helping the students develop coping skills. The ecological–developmental framework is especially critical for working with noncitizen students.

Case Example

Natalie, age 11, was referred to the school social worker by her sixth-grade teacher for crying uncontrollably in class after having returned from the weekly class visit to the computer lab. Natalie couldn't speak because of her uncontrollable crying. The school social worker asked Natalie to describe what happened. Natalie told her that the computer teacher was mean and that he was teasing her. When she teased him back, he got very angry and yelled at her. Natalie said she froze when he started yelling and ran out of the room. At that point, she starting shaking and got into a fetal position. Natalie was from Bosnia and PTSD was a possibility, as it often is when working with refugee youths. When asked who Mr. Brown reminded her of, Natalie went on to describe a man dressed in black who was the one telling them they had to leave their home in Bosnia. She was 4 years old at the time and remembered only the fear on the faces of her parents when this man in black confronted them.

Natalie was seen for individual counseling. She also was included in small group counseling with other refugee children led by the school social worker and a dance therapist. During the group, Natalie taught traditional Bosnian dancing along with the African dances taught by other group members. Her teacher was trained to work with refugee youths, and her parents were involved with the counseling. They were also provided with resources for additional counseling and support from refugee organizations.

School social workers often deal with students who are referred to child protective services, have special needs and learning problems, and have parents who are low functioning and/or distrust the system. In this case, all these issues occurred in one family, and the social worker was especially challenged. The language barrier also made this case unique. What is not unique, though, is that good school social work practice made this case successful. Those interventions included:

- Competence in cross-cultural practice: establishing an initial positive relationship, establishing rapport as an effective listener, understanding the client's definition of the problem, working with interpreters, and valuing diversity.
- Involving other agencies, including community health centers, child protective services, hospitals, special education services, and dental services.
- Parent involvement and counseling.

STUDENT-FOCUSED INTERVENTIONS

Working with noncitizen populations can be complicated. Therefore, it is essential that school social workers conduct thorough assessments, usually as part of an interdisciplinary team of school professionals including the school psychologist, speech pathologist, and resource teacher. The inclusion of a wide range of professionals allows the evaluation to include environment, learning patterns, health issues, and data on social and peer relationships, as well as information obtained from the family, school records, and previous testing. As explained by Caple et al. (1995), it is imperative to include cultural information and understand the client's definition of the problem (Caple et al., 1995).

In order to qualify for special education services, students of limited English ability must be tested in their native language in order to rule out learning disabilities or language problems. Parents must also complete a parent interview form in their native language.

Individual Counseling

Noncitizen students are often unaware of the reason for their referral to the school social worker. It is critical for social workers to develop a trusting relationship so these students will feel safe and will be comfortable expressing themselves. Play therapy provides avenues for children to explore their inner worlds. It enables these youths to express their feelings and unload the burdens they carry as well as create and dramatize their lives and cultural identities. That is why they often benefit from puppet and play therapy, sandtray therapy, and art and music therapy, where there is less focus on verbalization and more on nonverbal therapy. Children learn about themselves and their world through play. It is how they work through their fear, frustrations, conflicts, and anxieties (Webb, 1998).

Case Example

Almina, a 12-year-old sixth grader, was referred for counseling because she was cutting herself. She and her 14-year-old sister lived with their maternal grandparents because they did not get along with their parents. She complained that her parents and grandparents were incredibly strict and would not let her go to the malls, visit friends, or have any fun. She was expected to clean the house and follow their strict rules. She told the school social worker that she cut herself to release the pain she felt. She did not want her parents or grandparents to find out that she was cutting herself because they would get very angry and think she was "crazy."

Almina received individual counseling from the school social worker and worked on ways she could communicate with her parents and grandparents about her cutting herself and her need to have more fun with her friends. Almina would not tell her parents or grandparents about her cutting, so the school social worker, teacher, and translator met with Almina, her parents, and her grandmother to discuss the seriousness of her cutting herself. Since it was the end of her sixth-grade year and Almina would be going on to middle school, a referral to a mental health agency was made while they were at the meeting with the school social worker.

Sandtray Therapy

Sandtray therapy is a wonderful medium for working with noncitizen students. It can be used with all ages. A sandtray need be no more than 3 feet by 18 inches. Baskets filled with items such as people, furniture, animals, soldiers, fences, dishes, dinosaurs, plastic flowers, trees, and shells are placed next to the sandtray. Children are asked to choose from the items in the basket. Figures can easily be buried or moved around in the sand. The sand is very fine and feels wonderful to the students' touch. Children who are not familiar with sand often become excited and eager to try the sandtray. Children place the figures in a way that creates their world in the sand (Oaklander, 1988).

Games

Games are a great tool for teaching social skills and helping children learn to take turns, play fair, and become good losers and winners. The way children play games is an indicator of how they cope in life. Games help establish trust and build relationships.

Puppets

Puppets provide a creative, fun, nonthreatening way for youths to express feelings and yearnings, act out dreams, and send and receive messages. A reluctant or shy child can be approached in a nonthreatening way with puppets (James, 1989, p. 209). It is often easier for a child to talk through a puppet rather than to say directly what he or she is feeling (Oaklander, 1988).

Case Example

The school social worker at an elementary school was called to the office to help resolve a conflict between two third grade refugee students. Ilir, age 8, was from Kosovo, and Mihael, age 8, was from Croatia. Both spoke very limited English. As the social worker sat with the boys and the principal trying to piece together the reason for the fight on the playground during recess, it slowly became clear that there was a misunderstanding between the boys. Ilir thought that Mihael was Serbian and that he was urging him to fight. Mihael kept telling him that he wasn't Serbian but Croatian. In working with Ilir and Mihael, the school social worker explored the historical background out of which the boys' conflict arose. Ilir and his family were forced out of their home in Kosovo after the Serbs burned their house down. They were saved by NATO troops and eventually made their way to the United States. Ilir thought Mihael was Serbian, and thus indirectly responsible for his family's displacement.

The school social worker used conflict resolution strategies in helping Ilir and Mihael listen to each other's perspective. Puppets were helpful tools in working out their difficulties. They loved to create puppet shows from behind a desk. They knew exactly what story they wanted to tell. Usually, the puppet show involved hurting and fighting. These puppet shows gave them a safe place to act out their aggressions. At the end of the school year, Mihael moved back to Croatia with his family. Mihael left his basketball with Ilir since he couldn't take it back with him and he wanted Ilir to remember him when he was gone.

Art Therapy

Finger painting allows children opportunities to create, destroy, and recreate scenes, giving them permission to make mistakes (James, 1989, p. 201). Clay has an effect similar to finger painting. Children often prefer to draw or paint whatever they want rather than being told what to do (Oaklander, 1988).

Case Example

An art therapy group was conducted for refugee youths, ages 7–9, in second and third grades. The 10-week, 45-minute, weekly group included eight refugee children from Africa, Bosnia, and Albania. While one student from Sudan couldn't wait to get his hands totally covered with paint and had no inhibitions, a Bosnian girl would only dip her little finger in the paint. Eventually, as other students became bolder with the paints, she dipped a few fingers in the paint. It wasn't until the very end of the session, during preparation for cleanup, that she put her entire hand in the paints and let out with a full yell, "I did it." She later spoke of her fear of trying new things and her need to do everything "right." She didn't know how to finger paint "right."

Relaxation Training

Relaxation helps students reduce tension and teaches them control of their bodies. As Beverly James has stated, "it gives them a sense of mastery" (p. 210). Forced migration of refugees and immigrant youths often causes them to feel a lack of control over their lives; therefore, activities that permit them to take back control are fundamental to their development.

Small-Group Settings

Support groups give children an opportunity to talk about their problems and understand that they are not alone. Games, dance, music, drawing, painting, storytelling, and singing are appropriate (United Nations High Commissioner for Refugees, 2001, p. 42). Some of the support groups conducted with noncitizen students include art therapy and social skills groups.

Music

Music and song can teach children to work together and feel part of a group. Children enjoy singing; it is fun and a safe way to feel connected with others (James, 1989, p. 206). Providing traditional music that represents a student's culture helps the student integrate while maintaining a connection with his or her heritage.

Case Examples

Colorful African drums were used as part of a therapy group for a student from Sudan. When he entered the room and saw the drums, he immediately went over to them and started playing. All the members of the group joined him as he created and led an improvised African dance.

Lorenzo, age 6, a student from Mexico with limited English skills, was referred by his first grade teacher for problems with speech (articulation), inappropriate touching in class, poor social skills, and low reading skills.

Lorenzo was placed in a play group. His favorite game was duck-duck-goose. In that game, the children were arranged in a circle. One child outside the circle taps the children in the circle on the head, saying "duck" whenever he or she taps a person on the head. When the head tapper says "goose," the identified child and the head tapper run around the circle in opposite directions. When they meet, the chaser asks the other student if he or she wants a hug or a handshake. Most of the time, Lorenzo wanted a hug. This often satisfied Lorenzo's need for touch, but in an appropriate way. Lorenzo's teacher often commented that he couldn't wait for group to start and he seemed calmer when he returned to class.

Classroom Interventions

Classroom interventions include behavioral observation and specific behavioral management plans. The school social worker can work with teachers to establish behavioral contracts so that students complete tasks and demonstrate appropriate classroom behavior. It is important to build on the strengths of the students rather than focusing on their weaknesses.

Case Example

Jose, age 10, was referred for evaluation because of current academic difficulties in his fourth grade class. He was seen as very shy and rarely asked teachers for help or interacted with peers. According to information obtained in an interview with his mother, Jose was born in Mexico after a normal pregnancy, labor, and delivery. No head injuries were noted. Jose attended preschool and kindergarten in Mexico. When he was in the first grade, he and his family moved to the United States. When he was tested on the Woodcock-Munoz Language Survey, a Spanish/English language proficiency test, Jose's language scores in both languages were typically below the 4th percentile, again pointing to a language-based learning disability separate from second-language acquisition, although learning a second language was probably especially difficult and confusing for Jose. Although both sets of language performance scores were weak, Jose showed a relatively stronger performance in English than Spanish. Jose qualified for special education under the classification of learning disabled in the areas of reading comprehension and listening comprehension. Jose received 2 hours of special education services per day. The school social worker worked with Jose in a social skills group to help him express himself more in class with teachers as well as peers.

SYSTEM-FOCUSED INTERVENTIONS

Anti-immigration sentiment in society is reflected in the schools. Often, schools find it difficult to welcome refugees and immigrants.

Case Examples

At one elementary school, the school social worker ran a parenting class for parents of kindergarteners. Since many of the parents spoke only Spanish, the social worker had a translator assist with the class. Many of those who spoke only English resented the extra time taken up with translations and complained that because of them, the class was taught at a lower level.

When newer refugees from the former Yugoslavia began arriving in the same community, fights between students arose because of ethnic struggles and wars in their home countries. As Nenad, age 17, a Serbian student, explained, "The people who were at war against my people are here. My friend was beaten up by Bosnians, Muslim people. He had to go to the hospital. They beat him because of his religion." Nenad thought that generally the Bosnians and Serbs looked to avoid such confrontations. "We don't want to wake up the memories. We don't want to wake up the moments we had there, so we just stay quiet. We are never gonna love each other, but hopefully we will learn to respect each other. The best thing is if you can form a friendship with a different person. People are just people. It's only the different ways we were raised up, the different teachings, that make for different opinions. So it's okay if we are different. It would be really stupid if everybody in the world were the same" (Kelen & Kelen, 2002, p. 17).

Impacting the Culture and Climate of the School

One can often enter a school and, after a few minutes, feel whether it is inviting, open, and friendly, and giving off positive or negative energy. A school's culture and climate have tremendous impact on student learning and behavior, yet changing the climate and culture of the school is a tremendous challenge for school leaders (Dupper, 2003). School culture is defined as the "beliefs and expectations apparent in a school's daily routine, including how colleagues interact with one another (p. 28). Climate has been defined as the "heart and soul of the school" (Freiberg & Stein, 1999). Factors affecting school climate and culture include violence (Menacker, Weldon, & Hurwitz, 1990), racism (Pollard, 1989), and teacher expectations, number of suspensions, and educational engagement (Wehlage, Lipman, & Smith, 1989). Schoolwide programs can improve the school climate for noncitizen students and their families by creating welcoming spaces.

Including cultural dances and food festivals is a powerful way to introduce cultures to the school and excite students from those cultures to get involved and feel they are contributing something to their school community.

Case Example

An elementary school created an art gallery that displays student artwork, as well as traveling exhibits. As visitors enter the school, they often see their own children's artwork. They see faces from other cultures as well as their own.

Teacher Training

As more and more children of diverse cultural backgrounds enter our schools, they will be met with educators who are not of their cultural background (Caple et al., 1995). School social workers need to recognize the changing populations and needs of students and adjust their programs to meet these needs.

Increased Parent Involvement

School social workers can perform many valuable roles in increasing involvement among noncitizen parents. Many of these parents are intimidated by their children's schools and cannot communicate with teachers and staff because of language barriers. Schools with noncitizen populations must develop programs and methods to invite parents into the school and involve them with it. They can be encouraged to volunteer in the classroom or work as assistants. They also can be invited to serve on PTA and planning boards, attend English as a second language (ESL) classes, and teach the traditional dances of their culture.

Access to Health Care

Noncitizen youths often are in need of health care. Refugees from war-torn countries often experience trauma or stress-related symptoms and need mental health counseling. As the United Nations High Commissioner for Refugees has indicated, "protection and promotion of children's health requires that children have access to the essential services of a health system. . . . Special efforts are always required to address the unique health needs of refugee children" (United Nations High Commissioner for Refugees, 2001, p. 62).

Case Example

Belma, a 5-year-old kindergarten student born in the United States, was referred to the social worker by her teacher for not knowing the letters of the alphabet and not making any academic gains. Her parents were from Bosnia. Belma's father told the social worker and teacher that he would pull Belma out of school if they did any testing. When Belma's mother met with the school social worker, she was holding her mouth and appeared to be in excruciating pain. She explained in limited English that she had problems with her teeth but no money to go to the dentist. With the help of a translator it was discovered that Belma's mother didn't know her own telephone number, was illiterate (in both Bosnian and English), and was very low functioning.

The school social worker called the community health clinic immediately when she saw the mother's tears and her swollen face. The school's Bosnian teaching assistant served as translator. When the translator explained to the mother that the social worker would drive her to the nearby clinic, she told the translator that she had a baby home alone in the crib. While the mother returned home to get the baby the social worker arranged for a car seat to transport the baby, mother, and translator to the clinic. The baby turned out to be around 3 to 4 years old and severely handicapped (he couldn't walk or talk). When the mother was asked whether this child had received any prior medical care, she stated that her husband was angry at the pediatrician who examined him when he was 6 months old and would never take him to another doctor.

When the school social worker arrived at the clinic, she explained to the nurse that not only did the mother need intervention, but the baby needed to be seen and a referral to child protective services should be made to report medical neglect. It would have to be done in a gentle, tactful way, since the husband would not want any intervention.

The mother's abscess was treated with an intravenous antibiotic, and she was told to come back the next day for an antibiotic injection since her condition was life threatening. The nurse reported the parents to child protective services for medical neglect, and their caseworker referred the child to a medical center for a thorough evaluation. After many months of parent contacts, the child was evaluated, received the necessary medical care, and eventually was placed in a special classroom for severely multiply handicapped students.

The school social worker later arranged for dental care for Belma and her mother. The major intervention involved building a relationship with Belma's father so that he would allow the necessary care for his family. Belma was evaluated and eventually placed in a self-contained class for intellectually handicapped students.

ETHICAL DILEMMAS FOR THE SCHOOL SOCIAL WORKER

Confidentiality is a complicated issue when working with noncitizen students and their families. It often is difficult to decide what information can be shared and with whom. School social workers must often weigh the consequences of sharing confidential information. Therefore, they must become familiar with school district policies regarding confidentiality (NASW, 2002, Standard 7).

Confidentiality entails additional difficulties when translators are involved. When working with noncitizen students, it is common practice to utilize interpreters. These interpreters must have considerable skill to translate the often sensitive information in a way that transfers both the content and the speaker's tone. Caple et al. (1995) have emphasized the importance of preparing the interpreter for the purpose of the interview and the need for a skilled interpreter who can convey meaning across both linguistic and cultural systems (Caple et al., 1995).

The following are examples of the ethical issues school social workers face when working with noncitizen students.

An undocumented student from Mexico tells a school social worker that her father beats her mother when he is drunk. She does not want the social worker to report it for fear the family will be deported.

The lunchroom director informs the school social worker that a Somali student needs to fill in additional information on the lunchroom form in order to continue receiving free lunch. The parents speak a language for which there are no local interpreters and do not speak English.

A first-grade teacher brings a Vietnamese student to the school social worker because the student is complaining that her back hurts because her father did something to it. (In the Asian healing practice called coining, coins are heated and placed on a sick person's skin.)

The parent of an undocumented student from Mexico attempts to register a kindergarten child but has no birth certificate or immunization records.

A 16-year-old high school student from Kosovo has no records indicating previous classes taken and wants to graduate with her classmates.

CONCLUSION

School social workers must understand and address the individualized and complex needs of diverse student populations in the schools today. Working creatively and sensitively with noncitizen students in meeting their needs allows us to educate all students with similar needs for belonging, acceptance, and growth. In sharing the cultures, strengths, and struggles of the noncitizen student, we recognize our shared humanity and are challenged to transform our schools into welcoming places for all students and families.

Discussion Topics

1. Discuss the aspects of cross-cultural practice.
2. Discuss the differences in family stress and access to services for documented and undocumented immigrants.
3. Discuss the ecological–development framework and how school social workers can utilize it with immigrant students.
4. Discuss the advantages of play therapy, music, and art therapies with immigrant populations.
5. How does school culture impact student learning and participation?

15

Mental Health Services in the Schools

As early as 1909, a White House conference on children recommended new programs to care for mentally disturbed children (Tuma, 1989).

> The recommendations from various panels and study commissions have consistently found the need for a child advocacy system to coordinate federal, state, and local services in a comprehensive network to meet children's mental health, physical and social needs. The recommended system would include establishing prevention–family planning, prenatal care, and mental health services in the schools. (Tuma, 1989, p. 188)

School social workers often are required to assist in the implementation and delivery of services to students with special emotional needs, including assessment, early identification, or actual provision of direct services. School social workers will be more effective in their interventions with students with mental disorders if they have an understanding of the various types of mental disorders, knowledge about psychotropic medications, and information about the community resources available to serve those with mental disorders. Collaboration with students, their families, and other mental health care providers, both within the school and the community, is the key to successful interventions (Bentley & Walsh, 2006). School social workers must have the skills to work effectively with many professionals and systems in order to coordinate effective mental health services within the schools.

This chapter discusses mental health and mental disorders and describes some of the programs school social workers have used to help children with mental disorders and families who have children with mental disorders. The chapter also discusses how to apply a logic model to an individual child to provide outcome measures that will help school social workers clarify the kinds of interventions used with students and the success or failure of these interventions.

MENTAL DISORDERS

Mental disorders cause impairment in everyday life, such as poor school performance and difficulty in interpersonal relationships and in one's personal life. The term "mental health" means optimal functioning in the psychological and social domains, including interpersonal strengths that promote optimal functioning, with the absence of dysfunction in the psychological, emotional, behavioral, and social spheres (Kazdin, 1993). The American Psychiatric Association's (2000) DSM-IV-TR is designed to offer guidelines for making a diagnosis for each mental disorder, including anxiety disorders, depression, and psychosis. (See Appendix 15.1 for a list of resources on child mental health.)

School districts refer to students with mental disorders as having either an emotional or behavioral disorder. Emotional disturbance is one of the 13 categories of disabilities specified by the Individuals with Disabilities Education Act (IDEA). Special education laws contain core principles that ensure the rights of students with disabilities and their parents in the education system (Friend, 2005). A student may have a mental disorder, such as a personality disorder, that does not significantly impair school functioning. If the disorder does not cause extreme difficulty at school, the student may still qualify for services under Section 504 of the Americans with Disabilities Act. School social workers should be instrumental in explaining the acronyms used by special education staff to parents. School personnel typically use a different nomenclature than mental health practitioners for categorizing children with serious emotional difficulties. They identify a mental health problem as an emotional disturbance (ED), behavioral disorder (BD), or other health impairment (OHI) (Roberts, Jacobs, Puddy, Nyre, & Vernberg, 2004). Parents must understand the acronyms used by school districts in order to participate effectively in student placement meetings.

School social workers should offer support and help to students with dysfunctional behaviors. They should also teach students the skills needed to perform adequately at school. Social workers have the skills to intervene with both students and parents and to attack mental health problems at a preventative level. Successful prevention programs can avert and minimize maladjustment and clinical dysfunction in adolescence (Kazdin, 1993). Prevention programs that focus primarily on providing education are not as effective as those that provide education, teach appropriate behaviors, and provide emotional support.

Students with serious emotional disturbances are often the most difficult for schools to manage (Roberts et al., 2004). Several factors identify children who are at high risk for mental illness, including a reported history of physical or sexual abuse, substance abuse, running away from home, a suicide attempt, and sexual abuse of another individual. Family conditions that put children at high risk for mental illness include caregiver felony conviction, substance abuse, or psychiatric hospitalization, family violence or mental illness, having a sibling in foster care, or having a sibling placed in an institutional setting (Davies, 2004; Walrath et al., 2004).

Classroom teachers and school counselors usually refer students with mental disorders and behavioral problems to the school social worker for treatment or to the school psychologist for testing. Parents will sometimes ask for help from school counselors, social workers, or psychologists for their child's behavioral problems. "Minority parents are less likely to recognize and report mental health problems of their adolescents than are their majority group counterparts" (Roberts, Alegria, Roberts, & Chen, 2005, p. 3). This is because there are strong ethnic and cultural differences in what constitutes an emotional problem and whether one goes outside the family for help. These ethnic and cultural differences also can create barriers to services. "Federal law mandates that school districts assure that any assessment completed as part of a special education decision-making process is unbiased" (Friend, 2005, p. 15).

During the 1990s, research on the brain expanded the capability to diagnose, treat, and prevent mental illnesses and brain disorders and provided an understanding of how psychotherapeutic medication works (Donahue, 2000). However, in the midst of this new ability to serve those with mental disorders, support of public programs to fund services for mental disorders has continually decreased. This lack of financial support has affected school social workers because it has limited the number of community resources available for referral purposes and the number of programs that work in conjunction with schools.

COMMUNITY MENTAL HEALTH SERVICES COORDINATED WITH SCHOOL SOCIAL WORK INTERVENTIONS

Many students who are diagnosed with emotional and behavioral problems can benefit from the combination of psychotropic medications and support from a mental health professional. School social workers and counselors are usually among the few staff members in a school district who are licensed to provide ongoing counseling or who are able to connect students to community resources, such as mental health agencies. Usually school social workers have a large caseload and, therefore, cannot provide in-depth counseling for a long period of time. As a result, it may become necessary to refer students with mental health problems to other mental health professionals in the community. There is an ongoing need in schools to help connect families to mental health and social service providers.

School social workers are often in the position to act as consultants to students and families who are utilizing psychotropic medications. They must have the knowledge to determine when it is necessary to recommend that a student see a physician. School social workers can help prepare students and their families for consultation with a physician by explaining the reasons for the referral and giving information about the child's disorder and medications. The social worker can advise students and their parents to ask their physician about the side effects of their medications and can also be instrumental in linking economically disadvantaged students and their families to community agencies that can help fund the student's medications (Bentley & Walsh, 2006).

School social workers should be careful in the way they phrase a child's need for additional services to his or her parents. If a school social worker states that the child has a mental disorder and needs medication, testing, or counseling, the school district may become liable to pay for those services. School social workers should always check with their individual school districts to find out how to make appropriate outside referrals and to inform parents about community services without committing the school district to cover the costs of those services. Usually, the school social worker can convey the need for mental health services by saying something like the following:

> "It appears that your child is displaying characteristics that may indicate a mental disorder, which could be diagnosed correctly by a psychiatrist or psychologist. If such a diagnosis shows a mental disorder, medications can sometimes be very helpful. You can ask me

or the person who administered the tests to refer you to a psychiatrist who will discuss medication."

This statement identifies the child's need for services but does not constitute the school social worker's direct recommendation for testing or screening for medication.

School social workers also should be aware of the importance of their role as part of an interdisciplinary treatment team that includes community mental health professionals. School social workers have information about students' school performance, peer relationships, and home and family situation that can be useful to other mental health professionals who are working with students. Social workers should strive to create a shared vision of open and frequent communication, trust, adaptability, and respect with the other mental health professionals who also work with students (Bentley & Walsh, 2006).

"Wraparound programs" involve agencies outside the school system to assist in delivering service for needy children and their families. They provide family-focused, community-based mental health services that focus on family and child strengths and needs. Wraparound services are developed by community-based interdisciplinary services teams that will not deny services to any youngster regardless of the severity of his or her disability. Children between the ages of 3 and 17 are eligible if they have a serious functional impairment, are at risk for disruption of their preferred living or child care environment, and are enrolled in the school system's special education program with a diagnosis of emotional disturbance.

When an interdisciplinary team from the school and community agency determines that a child is eligible for wraparound services, the child is assigned to a service coordinator, who assists with monitoring and delivering services, including crisis care and links to doctors for prescribing medications and nurses for monitoring and supervising their use. Residential crisis care is available when necessary. Likewise, respite care is provided either in the home or at an agency to give the family relief from the stress of dealing with a child who is mentally ill.

Students who have difficulty in school because of emotional problems often feel disconnected. They also can become the target of other students' bullying and harassment. Linking schools to community agencies creates a support network for children and families who have unique needs that cannot be met in one place.

Some community mental health agencies provide services to schools by sending a staff member to do an initial screening and eligibility determination. When a school social worker is aware that a professional from a community mental health clinic will visit the school, the social worker should obtain parental consent in order to make a referral for community mental health services. This process can help waive the initial wait involved in scheduling an appointment and determining eligibility for services. Along with this initial assessment, the mental health professional often can complete the paperwork with the student's parent and set up the first appointment with the mental health center psychiatrist to help expedite the initial medication screening visit. This process is helpful to both students and parents, and when it is completed at school, much of the delay related to becoming a client at a mental health clinic is eliminated.

Case Example

John was a high school junior. He had only one friend. That friend, who was older than John, would play video games with him after school. John had a very peculiar affect, which made most students and teachers uncomfortable when he was around them. He rarely made eye contact with anyone, and his only conversations related to becoming a pro wrestler. He rarely said anything and would not respond to questions and conversation from others. His hair covered part of his face and he would look sideways through his hair at others when spoken to. He wore black shirts with wrestlers on them and the same denim vest every day. Many of his teachers thought he was putting on an act and did not try to get to know him. He did not do much schoolwork and was not passing his classes. He was referred to the school social worker to help him learn social skills and pass his classes.

After the initial assessment, the school social worker referred John to the school psychologist for testing. Those tests indicated severe emotional problems. The school social worker contacted John's father and asked if he would allow John to have a consultation with the psychiatrist from the community mental health center who visited the school district 1 day per month. The psychiatrist wanted the father to meet with him. The father and John met with the psychiatrist who, after a brief contact, informed the father that John appeared to have a diagnosis of paranoid schizophrenia and needed to be placed on medications immediately in order to keep him from hurting himself or someone else. The father was initially offended and said that John was really only behaving as the father had as a young man, but he did agree to let John try the medications. The medications immediately helped John improve his affect and school performance. The school social worker continued to meet with him weekly and worked on social skills and helped him problem solve about his school assignments. Without the easy access to a mental health assessment and consultation with a psychiatrist, John and his father might never have sought help on their own. However, because there was an intervention, John became able to handle the stress related to school.

Along with making community referrals, school social workers must be able to intervene by assessing and treating mental health problems. The techniques that appear to be most effective in treating adolescents with mental illness involve education, cognitive-behavioral interventions, and peer support (Lambert, 2004). For this reason, psychoeducational interventions, which combine education, behavior therapy, and peer support, are used frequently. The school social worker must have the capacity to conduct outreach that will engage reluctant students in treatment. Most classroom teachers are inexperienced and often desperate for help in dealing with children with severe mental health problems. The social worker must be able to intervene and provide initial crisis intervention and then ongoing intervention appropriate to the student's motivation to change his or her problematic behaviors.

FORMING FAMILY AND SCHOOL CONNECTIONS

To assure that schools are safe places for students with mental and emotional problems, school social workers should be instrumental in providing positive social and psychological anchors at school. Psychological anchors include a strong attachment to someone who will express kindness, concern, and warmth to the student; teach positive coping skills; assist the student in developing positive self-esteem; and find positive social support outside the family. Social anchors include other families, schools, organizations, agencies, and community and governmental programs (Boulter, 2004). When adolescents are comfortable with their roles at home and with their friends, they are able to accept and conquer discomfort in other environments (Blyth, Simmons, & Carlton-Ford, 1983; Simmons, 1987; Simmons & Blyth, 1987).

The school social worker may prevent mental health problems from evolving by assisting families to understand the importance of helping students feel cared for and connected to others. Social workers should send newsletters to parents when children enter school with information that will help them understand the value of being involved in their child's education. Likewise, social workers should assist teachers in teaching social skills to students who do not have positive peer relationships. Social workers should form relationships with students who are isolated to help them form a positive connection with an adult in the school. They should also help provide support groups for students who need friends and help initiate classroom discussions that will help sensitize students to the importance of treating others with respect. Many of the issues that contribute to emotional problems and acting out at school can be prevented with appropriate intervention at the onset of the problem.

CHILDREN LIVING IN SHELTERS

Nearly one-half of the children who are in homeless shelters show symptoms of depression and anxiety, with one-third meeting the criteria for clinical depression. Seventy-six percent of homeless children have a mother with major depression, schizophrenia, substance abuse problems, or high levels of distress (Hicks-Coolick et al., 2003). Within the homeless population, those with mental illness and other disabilities have been found to be the most isolated (Chinman, Rosenheck, & Lam, 1999). Homelessness creates multiple physical and mental health consequences. Homeless children and adolescents are at risk for emotional and behavioral problems, such as depression, anxiety, and substance abuse, and school problems including failure, nonattendance, and dropping out (Kazdin, 1993).

Homeless children are placed in schools, which gives the social worker the opportunity to form a relationship and make connections with them and to help them become part of the school environment. These students should be assigned to work closely with another student who is willing to serve as a mentor and help him or her establish relationships with other students. The school social worker should meet at least weekly with the students to assure that they do not disappear and that their needs are being met.

It is critical to intervene immediately after homeless children are placed in school. The very nature of their homelessness means that the placement will probably not be permanent. Therefore, school social workers must act quickly to help welcome a homeless child into the school, connect the child to a positive peer and teacher mentor, and help him or her negotiate the new environment. See Webb (2003) for an in-depth case example of a homeless child and her family.

USE OF A LOGIC MODEL IN PRACTICE TO ASSIST IN FUNDING NEW PROGRAMS AND INTERVENTIONS

Funding restrictions have limited the options of residential and long-term outpatient care in both the public and private sectors. Consequently, schools are the de facto mental health service provider because school systems have a mandate to serve children (Roberts et al., 2004). Because of the challenges of meeting the mental health needs of students in public schools, school social workers are often placed in a position of writing grants and developing new programs to help maximize their services. If funding sources provide for social work interns, they can be utilized to work part time with other agencies, such as juvenile probation. Many school social workers write grants to utilize interns in their schools as additional support staff. Most external funding sources require a well-organized process to demonstrate the effectiveness of the interventions and programs that are being funded.

School social workers should become familiar with evidence-based practice and models that have demonstrated program effectiveness. One of the effects of managed behavioral health care has been increased pressure to demonstrate the rational use and anticipated outcomes of mental health services (Lyons, Libman-Mintzer, Kisiel & Shallcross, 1998). Many social service agencies have adopted the use of logic models to demonstrate their effectiveness.

Logic models are excellent tools for clarifying goals and evaluating whether or not programs and interventions reach their desired outcomes. A logic model describes the logical links among program resources, activities, outputs, community resources, and outcomes for a particular program or situation (Chen, Cato, & Rainford, 1998–1999; den Heyer, 2002). Logic models have typically been used for program planning and evaluation. They have become increasingly popular for these purposes among funding agencies (United Way of America, 1996). Social work practitioners can use logic models to evaluate their practice and illustrate that interventions are effective and create positive outcomes.

Social workers should become familiar with logic models and use them for planning and evaluating practice interventions. They must be able to utilize tools showing that their interventions with students and their treatment plans have been effective and contributed to lasting change. Logic models provide a clear strategy to help organize planning, goal setting, and delivery of service and measure the effectiveness of the intervention. The value of a logic model is that it provides a systematic way to evaluate each step of the process and to integrate the parts into a holistic picture related to the desired outcomes.

Although the terminology used in connection with logic models may differ depending on the systems model used, logic models address three system elements: (1) inputs, (2) outputs, and (3) outcome. Inputs are resources or, for the purposes of social work practice, social work practitioners. Outputs are the product, which is the client, family, group, agency, or community. Finally, outcome addresses the effect of the intervention or program on the client, agency, program, or community. Logic models apply short-term, intermediate, and long-term outcome measures to assess effectiveness of interventions and to set goals (Lewellen, Openshaw, & Harr, 2005).

School social work can be evaluated by determining if the actual short-term and long-term outcomes match the stated goals and objectives. The goals and objectives should be established following an assessment that clarifies what treatment goals should be established and acted upon. If the short-term or long-term outcomes are not achieved, the model provides a clear path that can be followed to determine where a problem may exist. The amount and type of input to accomplish the goal should be examined. Was the investment sufficient to support the outputs? The outputs can then be reviewed. Did the activities accomplish what was needed for the expected outcome? Finally, did the short-term outcomes form the foundation for the intermediate and long-term outcomes to occur? The logic model also provides for the impact that environment may have on the desired outcomes. Both quantitative and qualitative measures that examine all stated goals and objectives should be used in the evaluation process. The process is ongoing and provides for constructive self-evaluation and continual work toward accomplishing the goals.

Constructing the Logic Model with an Individual Student

The logic model provides a systematic plan for developing a treatment plan and goals. The following six steps are used to construct the framework.

1. Stating the problem.
2. Identifying short-term, intermediate, and long-term outcomes (results and impacts).
3. Specifying outputs (activities and participation).
4. Identifying resources or inputs (what is invested).
5. Identifying environmental factors.
6. Identifying assumptions.

Step 1: Stating the Problem

Background. Mark, the client, is a 12-year-old, new to the middle school. He is depressed because of the recent death of his grandfather. Mark and his family have recently moved back to live with his father in a different state after being away from his father for 2 years. The mother did not seek a divorce during the separation. The family is again living with the father, whose alcoholism leads to violent outbursts. As a result of the move, the grandfather's death, and the father's drinking, Mark is aggressive at school and is failing all of his classes. Mark's outbursts have caused him to be placed in special education, and he is angry about becoming a special education student. He refuses to do schoolwork and constantly seems angry. He did not pass his classes for the first report card period (6 weeks).

The family consists of the mother, father, Mark, a 9-year-old brother, and a 6-year-old sister. The maternal grandfather recently died, and that is why the family has returned to live with the children's father. The grandfather's death was devastating to their family. The children are grieving over the loss of their grandfather, are upset about being back with the father, and are all doing poorly in school. The school social worker was assigned to work with Mark because he was placed in a special education program for emotionally disturbed students.

The father does not work. The family is supported solely by the mother's income. She is a registered nurse and works extra shifts to help keep the family financially afloat. She is rarely home. The father gets drunk several times a week and tries to hit the mother and whatever children are in his path when he is drinking. Mark is usually successful in protecting his mother and siblings but is afraid that he is going to do serious harm to his father when the father is violent and drunk.

Problem Statement. Mark has emotional outbursts at school and he is failing his classes.

Step 2: Identifying Short-Term, Intermediate, and Long-Term Outcomes

Mark was seen by a school social worker to help him improve his in-school behavior and his grades. The social worker established the following goals for Mark and his family:

1. Learn to manage his anger and express it in ways that do not affect his school performance.
2. Work through his grief over the death of his grandfather.
3. Pass all classes.
4. Make friends and become involved in extracurricular activities at school.
5. Help the family find resources, such as a women's shelter, Alcoholics Anonymous (AA), community mental health services, and employment opportunities for the father.

Short-Term Outcome. Mark is the identified client. Because it was a school setting, the school social worker confined most of the intervention to Mark and to helping him achieve in school. His individual goals were to:

1. Decrease the number of outbursts per week until there were none.
2. Begin doing schoolwork in each class period every day.
3. Turn in completed work at the end of class.
4. Make new friends.

Intermediate Outcome. Help Mark find positive outlets for his anger toward his father, such as athletics. Refer Mark to community mental health services for evaluation of depression and help him express his grief over the loss of his grandfather.

Long-Term Outcome. Eliminate angry outbursts at school until there are none. Pass all classes with a grade of C or better. Join an athletic team or intramural sports to meet new friends and exercise daily, which should cut down on physical aggression and frustration. The school social worker will discuss Mark's problems with the mother and father to clarify the impact of the home situation on the children. Offer resources and help to the family.

Step 3: Specifying Outputs

1. The school social worker will meet with Mark two times per week and include the following in the counseling:
   a. Grief work–work through feelings associated with grandfather's death.
   b. Anger management–including learning to recognize the early onset of anger and the things that trigger it.
   c. Social skills–learn to interact with peers and teachers in a polite and positive way rather than sulking and showing anger.
   d. Problem-solving skills–finding alternative ways to express anger other than at school and work on finding ways to complete schoolwork even when upset.
   e. Seek involvement in extracurricular activities to make new friends and in athletics to help with physical activity.
2. The school social worker will set up a meeting with the parents to let them know how Mark is feeling about the situation at home and

how it is affecting his schoolwork. The social worker will discuss possible referral to a community mental health center for treatment of depression.

3. Mark's special education teacher will:
   a. Help him recognize signs of anger or aggression as they appear. She will help him learn to talk about his frustrations before they become angry outbursts.
   b. Offer individual help with his school tasks so that he can complete his work and pass his classes.

Step 4: Identifying Resources or Inputs

1. School district resources or inputs: The school district's special education placement committee identified the goals that were listed in Step 2 above. The time frame for accomplishing this individualized education plan (IEP) is one academic school year. At the end of that year, the special education committee will meet to review Mark's progress and assess whether there is a continued need for services, such as counseling from the school social worker and individual work with the special education teacher.

2. Mark's input: Spend time in counseling learning new skills, spend time in special education, and redirect his anger and grief into a positive outcome.

3. Parents: Meet with school personnel to help resolve the problem and find out about resources.

4. Community resources: Community mental health services, AA, and employment agency for the father.

Step 5: Identifying Environmental Factors

1. School district with trained personnel in special education and school social work.

2. Community resources: Women's shelter, AA involvement for the father, state workforce to help father find a job, mental health counseling for the family.

3. Family resources: Mother who loves her children, has professional training, and works hard. Mark has a desire to improve his behavior in school, to leave special education, and to become involved in extracurricular activities. Siblings have a positive attitude and want the family to be happy.

Step 6: Identifying Assumptions

1. School district assumption: If the school district provides special education services and school social work services, and helps the student become involved in extracurricular activities, he will be able to eliminate his angry behavior and tantrums at school and will be able to pass his classes.

2. Student assumptions: If Mark invests time with the special education teacher and school social worker, he will be able to improve his behavior and grades. If he becomes involved in extracurricular activities, he will meet new friends.

3. Family assumptions: Placing Mark in special education will help him at school. The school social worker will be able to help Mark and the family.

Outcomes can be clearly stated and measured after all of the steps have been completed. From the beginning of treatment, with the use of the logic model, the client goals and tasks are broken down. Also included is information about the resources available and the level of commitment involved. The success of outcomes and effectiveness of the intervention are easy to measure when they are clearly stated from the beginning of the intervention and when the school social worker utilizes evidence-based practice to choose interventions proven to work with particular disorders. The logic model makes the process of evaluating practice outcomes with individuals a simple task.

PROVIDING SERVICES IN RURAL SCHOOLS

Most of the commentary in this book deals with inner-city and suburban schools. However, schools in rural communities have unique challenges that should be considered. Approximately one-fourth of Americans live in rural settings, including one-third of the nation's poor (Human & Wasem, 1991). Poverty is one of the most severe environmental risk factors associated with higher rates of mental health problems in children (Tuma, 1989). The needs of rural communities are reflected in the local schools. Distance, poverty, lack of resources, and difficulty convincing members of the community to spend funds on social programs often make it difficult to meet the needs of children in the schools. Financial resources have almost always been less available in rural schools than in urban and metropolitan areas. Less populated areas may receive less funding than more densely populated areas. Rural school districts also experience deficits in the retention of quality personnel because of overloaded schedules, noncompetitive salaries, social and cultural factors, and lack of professional development opportunities (Caudill, 1993).

Once youths isolated in rural settings are referred to the social worker, providing mental health and social services poses a special challenge (Maynard-Moody, 1994). Rural communities struggle with the implementation of special programs. Limited resources and cost are two of the major obstacles to the provision of services. Rural school systems face a host of barriers to quality service delivery that urban schools do not. They usually have less tolerance for diversity, more homogeneous populations, more traditional moral values, and an expectation that the community can take care of its own members (Caudill, 1993).

Just as in urban schools, school social workers are more effective in rural settings when they work as part of an interdisciplinary team that includes teachers, counselors, school psychologists, and diagnosticians. A treatment team that utilizes experts in testing, diagnosis, and referral is the most comprehensive way to assist needy children and their families. School teams are more effective if they work on the entire system, not just the individual child. Program evaluations indicate that positive interventions are more effective if they focus on the family and not just the individual child. Family-centered services are intended to help the family maintain the child in the home and prevent out-of-home placement (Sabatino, 2001). School social workers' training and experience in the ecological systems perspective allow them to make a unique contribution to the intervention team. Social workers are in a position to orchestrate and support a unified and comprehensive intervention plan for children (Frey & George-Nichols, 2003).

As already discussed and demonstrated in this chapter, one of the best ways to serve students with emotional problems and their families fully is through interdisciplinary work. The interdisciplinary approach can be especially helpful if the team members understand how to build and sustain rapport with clients, have an understanding of psychotropic medications and mental disorders, and are willing to collect information from collateral sources and coordinate services with community agencies (Bentley & Walsh, 2006). School social workers need to have the skills to build community networks with other mental health service providers. Networking and organizing students, their families, and community professionals are critical aspects of providing thorough treatment plans for students. Three skills are necessary to achieve effective interdisciplinary and interagency work (1) asking questions respectfully to get high-quality information without negative or blaming connotations; (2) setting achievable and measurable goals;

and (3) arriving at a plan with clear achievable and measurable goals that can be understood by both the client and mental health professionals (Aggett & Goldberg, 2005).

A proactive, positive philosophy of practice helps school social workers assist children and families when working with interdisciplinary teams. Social workers need to find out the areas in which children with mental disorders are competent and successful and build on these positives through the use of the strengths perspective. The Phoenix Preferred Care Program in rural Kentucky has adopted the following philosophy for serving the mental health needs of children and adolescents.

- You must show respect before you can confront.
- To us it may be dysfunctional; to someone else it is reality.
- It is easier to add to strength than it is to subtract from weakness.
- Never underestimate the power of resiliency (Nims & Hamm, 2006).

Children with mental disorders have many special needs that can be met through proper treatment methodologies, such as an accurate diagnosis and treatment plan that involves behavior management employed at school and in the home. School social workers should involve an interdisciplinary team of professionals who will provide and monitor medications, link the family to resources, and support the child in school through the services of special education and other programs.

CONCLUSION

The school social worker is able to provide counseling and a link to community mental health professionals. Students with severe mental illness can be successful in school with the proper support of school services, such as special education, the intervention of a school social worker and interdisciplinary team, and referral to community resources. School social workers need to develop programs that link schools to mental health professionals in their communities. They also need to understand how to provide outcome measurements of the effectiveness of their services so that they can apply for funding from external sources. It is a reality that many rural schools and schools in inner-city, low-income neighborhoods lack the resources to provide the support services necessary to combat student mental health problems. School social workers should learn to write grants and use their organizational skills to build community networks that will assist students as well as their families with mental illness.

Discussion Topics

1. What is the most effective method for school social workers to create cooperative relationships with local community mental health providers?
2. How can school social workers provide outreach to children in homeless shelters?
3. Apply the logic model to a case situation with which you are familiar.
4. How would you use the strengths perspective to help a child and his or her family understand a recent DSM-IV-TR diagnosis?

APPENDIX 15.1. Resources Related to Child Mental Health

Mental Health America
800-969-NMHA
www.nmha.org

American Academy of Child and Adolescent Psychiatry
202-966-7300
www.aacap.org

American Psychiatric Association
888-357-7924
www.psych.org

Children and Adults with Attention Deficit/Hyperactivity Disorder
800-233-4050
www.chadd.org

Child and Adolescent Bipolar Foundation
847-256-8525
www.bpkids.org

Federation of Families for Children's Mental Health
703-684-7710
www.ffcmh.org

Depression and Bipolar Support Alliance
800-826-3632
www.ndmda.org

National Institute of Mental Health
866-615-NIMH
www.nimh.nih.gov

U.S. Food and Drug Administration
www.fda.gov

Substance Abuse and Mental Health Services Administration
www.samhsa.gov

Psychological Assessment Resources, Inc.
www.parinc.com

National Alliance on Mental Illness
800-950-NAMI
www.nami.org

Madison Institute of Medicine
608-827-2470
www.miminc.org

Internet Mental Health
www.mentalhealth.com

16

Linking Community, Home, and School

ROSEMARIE HUNTER
ROCIO PAREDES-MORA

My name is Angie. Well, my real name is Angelina Rose, but you can call me Angie. I just turned 11 years old, and I am in the fourth grade. We are getting ready to go out for recess; it is one of my least favorite parts of the day. If I time it just right, I can sneak away from the recess yard and climb over a short wall where no one will see me. Once I am over the wall, I am safe. You see, I don't have any friends at school. When we are in the classroom, it is okay because the teacher is there, and they won't tease me so much. When the recess bell rings, I get a knot in my stomach and hope that today I will make it to the wall before anyone notices. Sometimes I only get part way there and a group of the popular girls see me. I can feel them coming up behind me, a whole group of them.

Rosemarie Hunter, PhD, LCSW, is an Assistant Professor of Social Work, Special Assistant to the President for Campus Community Partnerships, and Director of the University Neighborhood Partners (UNP) at the University of Utah.

Rocio Paredes-Mora, MSW, CSW, has worked at UNP Hartland Community Center, Child and Family Empowerment Services, and the Rape Recovery Center as a therapist and case manager. She is currently working in the Young Parenthood Program of the Psychology Department at the University of Utah as a therapist for Spanish-speaking teenagers and their partners.

Pretty soon, their laughter gets a little louder, and they make sure I can hear that they are talking about me. Sometimes, they surround me so that I can't go anywhere, and they make fun of my old clothes. They talk about how poor and stupid I am, and if I try to run, the circle of girls around me closes in and gets tighter. But today is a GOOD day, I made it to the wall and no one noticed. Don't let them find my hiding place.

The boundaries between community, home, and school have been challenged by school social workers, educators, and parents who believe that the school is a dynamic component of the larger community, a community where families and educators are in reciprocal relationships, each having a unique role and shared responsibility for socializing and educating youth (Constable, 1992). For more than three decades, educational studies have highlighted the importance of family involvement in education as an essential factor for student success. Studies have documented improvements in school readiness, test scores, family empowerment, dropout rates, and student levels of self-esteem and behavior as a result of the integration among family, school, and community relationships (Broussard, 2003).

The traditional role of school social workers includes new challenges as schools and communities collaborate to meet the educational, social, psychological, and developmental needs of youths. Effective collaborative initiatives require that school social workers provide the leadership for system change within inclusive school–community environments. School social workers not only have the necessary knowledge and skills to support school–home–community relationships, but, more important, they have the skills to provide the leadership that will create welcoming school environments where these relationships thrive.

Similarly, school social workers are well positioned to nurture reciprocal relationships. Through their traditional home and community roles, school social workers can get to know families in the environments where they live. School social workers act as a physical link that crosses the traditional boundaries between the school building, the community agencies, and the home environment. Trusting relationships, a focus on strengths, and ongoing communication between home, school, and community partners have resulted in system change. Additionally, these conditions can be tied to improvement in student academic and nonacademic achievements. Furthermore, partnerships lead to the development of a community identity, improved home–school involvement and relationships, enhanced school environments, and better use of school facilities and programs (Peebles-Wilkins, 2004).

This chapter focuses on the difficulties encountered by immigrant families with special needs and the expanding role of school social workers in building community partnerships. School districts, which focus primarily on educational needs, benefit from the services of a school social worker, who is able to reach into the community to families that don't know how to meet their child's needs or are overwhelmed because of financial and cultural barriers. This chapter also provides an example of a community partnership program that is utilizing school social workers to link schools, families, and communities. School social workers must become innovative in delivering services and be aware of the changing population of the schools they serve.

Hi. It's me, Angie. Well, I made it through another day, and I have a lot of homework to do tonight. I don't usually get a chance to do any homework, and I am falling behind in all of my subjects. Most of the time when the teacher is teaching the lesson, I feel like I am in a fog. I sit in the back of the room and it is hard to see the board. I really wish I could learn more about geography. I think I am pretty good at knowing the different countries and continents, but I don't get any time to study. I will walk a little slower now because I am getting closer to home, just a little longer before I have to go in the house. Let Mom already be gone.

NEW REALITIES REQUIRE INNOVATIVE MODELS OF COLLABORATION

At the same time that families are dealing with increased pressures and fewer resources, schools are facing rising expectations about what they can deliver. During the past decade, every state has developed some form of standards-based educational reform. The new emphasis is focused on outcomes rather than inputs. These reforms mark a significant paradigm shift from previous attempts by the federal and state governments to improve education. The direction of standards-based educational reform coincides with broader national movements in higher education that focus on science and technology, outcome-based accountability, and the ability of the United States to compete globally. In short, the educational focus is on productivity (McCarthy, 2001). As a result, educators are faced with new anxieties and may find themselves struggling with understanding their roles in addressing the broader scope of children's welfare. At the same time, school social workers experiencing the shift in educational priorities feel frustrated and abandoned, often feeling that they have been left alone to safeguard the emotional welfare of children (Harker, 2005). National education standards and student testing invoke basic questions about the priorities of the nation and how students are educated (Pearson, Vyas, Sensale, & Kim, 2001).

To support families and communities through this shift, educators and social workers need to understand and appreciate each other's roles and work together to challenge the emerging realities. Often, educators, social workers, families, and students operate from different perspectives. Each group views the world from its own vantage point, with its own set of priorities and its own language to describe and address the group members' needs. Each has a different set of resources and operates from a vastly different power base. Yet each is tied to the others, dependent on and affected by the actions of the others. By coming together in an environment that respects and values the knowledge and contributions of each individual, they can use common goals to create a shared experience. For example, school social workers can ask teachers, families, and students what is most important to them.

Collaboration is rooted in interdependence and shared responsibility. Each stakeholder has a particular role to play and a valuable contribution that is necessary and unique to the partnership (Anderson-Butcher & Ashton, 2004). By using group skills, school social workers facilitate the forming of a group identity where all constituents experience their participation as meaningful.

SUPPORTING FAMILIES AT RISK

I just got home, and I am late, but Mom is still at the house. She yells at me as soon as I walk in. She is busy getting ready for work. She works two jobs most days, and she is almost ready to leave for the night shift at the leather factory. Sometimes, she brings home pretty purses, but they always smell funny. Mostly, my sisters get them because they are older, and I usually get their things once they get something new . . . but I don't mind, I like getting things.

Mom is really angry now; she is running late, trying to finish getting dressed and giving me a list of chores to do tonight. I watch as she is getting dressed, and I think she is pretty; she is putting on red lipstick. I like to look through her jewelry box. She continues to yell at me because I didn't make my bed or do the breakfast dishes before leaving for school, but I don't say anything; I know that will just make it worse. My grandma lives with us and she is sick, so I will need to make sure I make her some dinner and help her get to bed. I am the first one home from school. My brothers and sisters arrive after I do, and they all have evening jobs. I better get busy. I have to change out of my school clothes, do some wash, and get dinner going. Let me find something good to cook for dinner. I'm hungry.

The vast majority of partnerships between home, school, and community are developed to identify and address the needs of children and families who are experiencing difficulties. It is apparent that many students who are struggling in school also have significant risk factors in other areas of their lives that together complicate and impede their ability to learn, often leading to developmental arrest. Just as learning difficulties affect academic success, children struggling with complex life circumstances cannot focus on learning. Social and emotional difficulties spread into all areas of functioning. Additionally, their families often struggle with economic pressures and have few systems supports. These are the same families who are not available to meet with teachers or who will not be at home when social workers come to call. While some educators may view these families as resistant or disinterested, school social workers learn that they are overwhelmed. They are facing all of the challenges associated with living in poverty and, at the same time, trying to understand and negotiate complex systems.

School social workers can promote educational success by intervening in the academic culture and by establishing links between the home, school, and community. In the next section of this chapter, we present one family's experience trying to understand the complexities of the educational and social service systems in order to access special education services for their child with special needs. Their story highlights the helpful role of school social workers in locating appropriate real-life resources and supporting families at risk. The following case example demonstrates the critical need for school social workers to assist immigrant families.

SPECIAL EDUCATION

Daniel's Story

My name is Lucia Martinez, and when I was pregnant for the first time, my husband and I had a lot of expectations. How would our first child look? Would we have a boy or a girl? We were guessing that our baby would be a boy, so we had a lot of dreams for him and wondered, "Will he marry a good woman? Will he get a good education? Will he be able to sustain a family?" But our baby couldn't wait to be among us and before finishing my eighth month of pregnancy, he decided to come under difficult conditions. "Your baby is underweight," the pediatrician told us. "You just have to feed him a lot." As time went by, I knew deep inside myself that there was a problem and that it wasn't just a "weight problem." However, everybody tried to be nice to me, always minimizing my fears and my concerns, which gave me the hope that everything would be fine in the future.

Our son, Daniel, never sat, crawled, or walked on time. At the beginning, he was a few months behind, but later on he would be behind by years. Totally powerless and clueless, we didn't know where to go or how to ask for some type of direction. The pediatrician continued to assure us that it was just a matter of time and constantly reassured me. "Remember, children are different . . . each one is unique." But I still felt that my son was very different from other children.

Our first contact with a mental health counselor happened when Daniel was 2 years old and couldn't walk independently. Surprisingly, Daniel walked that same day after his first session with this professional. This "miraculous" psychologist would be our most supportive resource for several years. After overcoming the anxiety of not seeing him walking, we developed more anxiety because of his speech delay. We thought that it would just be a matter of more sessions with the miraculous psychologist and this problem would be solved too, but unfortunately this never happened, and our son is now 16 years old.

I remember this period of time as one of the most overwhelming of my life. We had so many questions and no answers. Why couldn't he talk? What was the condition he was suffering from? Who could help him, and, moreover, who could help us?! Thus my husband and I experienced many confused emotions, ranging from blaming ourselves to questioning our ability to stand up to this challenge, as we wondered whether it would last all our lives.

School Life: Can They Help?

At school age, Daniel started showing behavioral problems that left the school staff frustrated by not knowing how to handle him. As far as medical assistance is concerned, Daniel was seen by dozens of "experts" who experimented with different drugs, but ultimately nothing helped.

The psychologist suggested that we get him involved in speech and occupational therapy and, after a few sessions with those therapists, they referred our son to a pediatric neurologist. According to the neurologist, in addition to Daniel's autistic tendencies, he also had some abnormal physical features. This made the doctor strongly suspect a particular condition: San Filippo syndrome, a degenerative condition that would allow Daniel to only live up to 16 years. By the time this first diagnosis was submitted, Daniel had been rejected from two different elementary schools because they were unable to manage his violent behavior without compromising other students' safety. Private schools, which accepted only a few children with disabilities, had waiting lists, and even if they could have taken Daniel, their high tuition fees were out of reach for us.

As you might have figured out, this scenario didn't occur inside the United States. Fortunately, in this country children with disabilities have rights, and one of them is access to education. Actually, we are originally from Ecuador, a country in South America, where, in contrast to the United States, people with disabilities can be denied services without real legal consequences. Because of the lack of resources and social support in our home country, my husband and I started reconsidering the invitation from my family–my parents and siblings had lived in New York for several years–and finally we decided to start making plans for the future.

A Life-Changing Decision

The idea of migrating to a different country with a different language, different lifestyle, and different everything made our decision to move very difficult. Many people advised us to stay, since we had good jobs and financial security and a good education for our other child, and I had home assistance in the form of a wonderful full-time nanny. "Besides, are you going to the U.S. to clean bathrooms or work in fast-food restaurants like Jose, my cousin Maria, and other people we know?" they said. But others commented, "You have to sacrifice everything for your son." This last statement was very powerful, since in our Latino culture, children are a central motivating force in family dynamics. Thus, the American dream for us consisted of achieving the best medical and educational assistance for our son, rather than better opportunities for ourselves, as is the case for many people who come to this country. And the Hollywood movies we had seen guaranteed we would have a better life here in the United States.

One additional incident reinforced our decision to come to the States. There was a special education school for children of men enrolled in the army. I had to almost beg the school official to accept Daniel in that school, since my husband was never in the army. The principal finally accepted my son, but 1 month later, one of the teachers physically abused my son by restraining him so strongly that she left finger marks on his back. She was trying to "teach" an assistant how to discipline kids with behavioral problems. This incident was a final determining factor in our decision to migrate.

Moving to the United States: A Stranger in a Strange Land

After going through the painful process of selling all our possessions, we traveled to New York, arriving at JFK airport after 6 hours carrying our two children, Daniel, 10, Bianca, 9, and four suitcases. By the time we arrived at my parents' house it was 4:00 A.M., and everybody fell asleep . . . or at least that's what we thought. However, for Daniel, being in a different world was disorienting. When my sister was ready to leave the house to go to work the next morning, she noticed the back door was wide open. I don't remember a more frightening moment in my entire life than the fear of my child being missing. Everybody started searching for Daniel, but we couldn't find him. He actually was found by the police a mile away, wearing pajamas and no shoes. This incident led to my first contact with the social work field. Child protective services of the state of New York filed a case against my husband and me, but, fortunately, a few weeks later, our case was cleared.

A New School . . . A New Chance for Help

One month later, we decided to move out west. A teacher from our new school district came to observe my son and give me his new school schedule. With my limited English I thanked the teacher for "accepting" my son in the school and commented to my husband about the generosity of this country for wanting to take care of my son during the morning "9:00 to 12:30 session." I was invited to different meetings at which I didn't say much, since in my culture people show respect for authority by not contradicting them. To me, the school staff represented authority and expertise. In my country, parents are contacted by the school only in very specific situations, usually related to problems created by their children. At the same time, I felt scared and frustrated at not fully understanding what was being said. There was an interpreter at those meetings, but even so, things were not clear to me. The words were translated, but I did not understand the American education system. I wish the school system had offered not merely an interpreter but also a cultural broker, someone similar to medical interpreting advocates whose role is to clarify cultural differences for both parties.

My other child, Bianca, went to a different school, closer to where we live, so she did not need transportation. I remember the day when I registered her at school, a school official asked me if Bianca was a legal resident, because otherwise she would "have to call the school district to verify her eligibility for registration." I informed her that my daughter had legal status. It was a long time later when I learned that this is not a question that needed to be asked. Anyway, both of my children were enrolled in school, and everything looked promising.

Did I say "everything"? How could everything look promising? We were struggling and suffering. The migration experience was a total shock! We missed our country, we missed our food, we missed our language, and I missed my children's nanny! Now I had to be dedicated to taking care of my children 24/7 except for the time they were at school. Also, because I did not know how to drive, I was highly dependent on my husband for transportation. In my culture, that is acceptable and even expected. I used to have somebody in my country who did the house work, and so I had to learn with resignation that this was America, and in America you have to clean your own house and cook your own food. It is not my purpose to provide details about all the struggles that we went through in this country as a family. But it is worth mentioning that we have had and continue to have a lot of distress, not about the pain of dealing with Daniel's disability, since we do not consider him a burden, but about the effects that his disability have had on the family. Without respite care, my husband, my daughter, and I have been the only ones on whom we can really count to handle Daniel's severe behavioral problems, and this demanding situation has sometimes been overwhelming.

Knowledge Is Power

We would soon find out that my son's condition was very rare. The health department offered a program that allows children with disabilities and their parents to meet with a multidisciplinary team, including a medical doctor, a psychologist, and a social worker who periodically evaluate the child and the family situation. They helped us discover that Daniel did not suffer from San Filippo syndrome, and it was a relief not having to deal with a degenerative condition. We were also told that it would be hard to get an accurate diagnosis since his condition was a combination of several symptoms and the studies needed to arrive at a diagnosis could be highly costly.

Daniel struggled a lot adjusting to the school system. I can imagine his level of confusion hearing a different language and not being able to communicate verbally in his own native language. He usually misbehaved when riding the bus and at school. His teacher asked me for tips on how to better handle Daniel, and I could not understand how they, being the experts, wanted directions on how to stop his tantrums! Sometimes, the school bus driver asked me to "teach" my son that he needed to stay seated during the ride. I thought those who work with people with disabilities had the skills to deal with these situations and also had a spirit of caring. Again, I was scared, confused, and overwhelmed.

I decided to take college classes to learn English. During my fifth semester, I enrolled in a class titled "Study of Disabilities." This class opened my eyes in a different way. I learned many things, but especially how the system worked! I learned about Public Law 94-142 and the updated Individuals with Disabilities Education Act (IDEA) (Friend, 2005), what an individualized education plan (IEP) was, and about the rights of children with disabilities, and the parents' rights. The first thing I did after I obtained this knowledge was to set up a meeting with the school staff–this time without interpreter–requesting information about Daniel's IEP goals. During that meeting, I asked why my son was at school only until noon. I'll never forget the look on their faces and their confusing explanations. The following week, Daniel attended school on a full-time basis and I saw the school staff implementing different accommodations to make this happen.

When my husband and I moved to an apartment in a different area, Daniel had to move to a different school. Again the transition was difficult, but we found a caring teacher in his new school. We still had the same problem with transportation. The new school bus driver and his assistant were more difficult than the former ones. They wrote incident reports every week and were constantly focused on my son's weaknesses rather than on his strengths. On one occasion, my husband was accused of hiding information that my son had had a bad morning, information that could have helped them to better deal with my son's agitation while riding the bus. On two occasions, the bus driver called us and told us to go and pick up our son where the bus had stopped and take him to school by ourselves. On one of these occasions, I found the bus driver strongly restraining my son, which made Daniel so angry that he injured his own face very badly. This reminded me of his abuse in Ecuador. I consulted with the teacher of my disabilities class about this situation, and she suggested talking with parents' advocates.

To continue my education, I took a technical writing course, and I learned how to use writing as a powerful tool for making changes. Since the transportation issues did not improve much, I sent a letter to the appropriate individuals in transportation services and the school district, and in that letter I included many quotes from their own manual of transportation services. This incident resulted in a general meeting of all the people involved and the creation of a safety plan for Daniel when riding the bus. We stopped receiving incident reports from the bus driver, and when Daniel perceived a less hostile environment, he started enjoying riding the bus, along with a school aide assigned exclusively for him.

During my third year at college, I took Social Work 1010. I fell in love with this class. I wanted to be a social worker and help other people who feel vulnerable as I once felt. Since I had a bachelor's degree from my country, I decided to pursue a master's in social work, and as one of my practicums I decided to study school social work. I had the opportunity to conduct an independent study on how to help Latino children succeed in school. This study included what the school, parents, and school counselors could do to help Latino children–especially newcomers–to succeed at school. Definitely, one of the parts of my practicum that I enjoyed most when I did school social work was to teach parents in workshops how the system works in the United States and how acceptable and important it was for them to get actively involved in the school system. I wanted them to know that parents have rights and have a voice.

The Need for School Social Workers

I have loved being a social worker since then and always wondered about the absence of social workers in the schools when I came to this country because they could have given me a better orientation on how to navigate this system and culture without feeling bad for not understanding it. I wish someone could have supported my family with information about how to access the different services for people with disabilities, for immigrants, and for newcomers. As a family, we needed someone who could have referred us to numerous resources that are available in the community, many of which are not widely known; someone who could have taught me how powerful parents can be when they are involved in their children's education, which they have the right and duty to be; someone who could have just listened to our frustrations and could have understood what it means to feel like an alien, invisible, disrespected, and powerless.

I really think that school social workers are very important in their roles as cultural brokers, advocates, connectors, mediators, counselors, and social change agents. I never encountered a school social worker in my first 6 years of being in this country. If the school system wants to improve its level of educational success, it is absolutely necessary to have social workers in every school and every school district, especially in the special education field. They are needed to serve as helpers, advocates, and resource brokers.

It is my personal experience that children with special needs are very sensitive and perceptive about what is happening in their environment. When they are surrounded by a well functioning system that involves school, family, and community, they tend to improve and feel happy. Every human being has special needs. I am very pleased to report that, despite all the difficulties mentioned above, Daniel, at 16, is learning to communicate by using sign language and pictures, he loves his teachers, and his teachers love him. Moreover, he enjoys riding the bus every day.

* * *

By assisting families in understanding and negotiating the school structure and system and by supporting teachers and administrators to convey openness and encouragement toward families, school social workers can bridge the gaps (Bowen & Bowen, 1998). When positioned in schools, social workers act as family advocates, system change agents, and brokers of resources and services.

HIGHER EDUCATION AS A SCHOOL, HOME, AND COMMUNITY PARTNER

Relationships between universities and the communities in which they reside are essential in order to generate knowledge and provide service. These relationships extend beyond local agendas and seek to define the role of higher education in addressing societal problems. There is an expectation that institutions of learning, in particular, higher education, will create citizens, prepare the workforce, and pursue knowledge that informs best practices and social policies (Jay, 2000). The next section describes an example of a university–community partnership program that links higher education with K–12 schools and the community at large to come together as partners and create solutions to a multitude of social and economic problems.

In order to understand the relationship between the K–12 school system and higher education as a community partner, we must examine the current condition of education as a whole. While one of the goals of K–12 schools is to prepare students to enter institutions of higher education, these same institutions are uniquely situated between secondary education and professional employment. This pivotal position requires higher education to respond to and prepare for the changes that occur at both ends. As primary and secondary educational systems in the United States establish new priorities, universities must adjust appropriately to align themselves with the needs and expectations of incoming students. Similarly, as the economic, social, and political climates change, higher education must prepare graduates who are ready to enter the workforce and contribute to the needs of society (Broadfoot, 2000).

As communities strive to meet the needs of their members in an environment where there is increased competition and shrinking resources, university engagement and community partnership models have reemerged as successful methods toward this end. Although the university and the community have always shared common concerns, the community has frequently characterized the university as an ivory tower with individually focused faculties that utilize traditional research methods and are generally out of touch with the real world. Community members perceive the university faculty as uninterested and too busy, restricted by an inflexible system. There is a lack of trust on both sides. Communities with the potential for involvement in collaborative efforts with universities express concerns that university stakeholders might gain control, representing one-sided agendas. At the same time, faculties point to funding, time, and tenure requirements as insurmountable institutional barriers (Maurrasse, 2001).

THE UNIVERSITY NEIGHBORHOOD PARTNERS/ HARTLAND PARTNERSHIP CENTER

Despite a large average family size and the highest fertility rate in the country, Utah is ranked 49th out of 50 states on per capita spending on pubic education. As in other parts of the country, existing after-school programs, along with state funding for public education, are being cut. In addition, the No Child Left Behind policy has focused public funding on school-based academic programs, which greatly increases the need for better integration between schools, family, and community.

As evident in the previous case example, lack of affordable housing has a direct effect on education. A high number of renters, low incomes, and low supply of units mean high mobility, and this impacts neighborhood and family stability, creating serious disruptions of school attendance and educational success for children.

The University Neighborhood Partners (UNP)/Hartland Partnership Center is one of the community-based programs of the University of Utah, in Salt Lake City. Its mission is to "enable campus-community partners to work together in reciprocal learning, action, and benefit" (University Neighborhood Partners, n.d.). UNP's target neighborhoods have 1 private and 13 public elementary schools, 2 public middle schools, 1 private and 3 public high schools, and 1 charter and Head Start school. All of the schools are Title I schools.

The UNP/Hartland Partnership Center is one of UNP's university–community partnerships. The Hartland community is a 300-unit apartment complex in the Glendale neighborhood that is home to over 800 residents from all over the world—Somalia, Sudan, Peru, Cuba, Mexico, Bosnia, Afghanistan, and the United States. Over 75% of the residents are non-native English speakers, reflecting a rich tapestry of cultural, ethnic, and religious diversity.

The center, which opened in September 2004 in a three-bedroom apartment, serves as an education and community center for residents of the Hartland Apartment Complex, where teams of professors, students, community organization members, and Hartland residents work together to address the needs and maximize the talents of each individual. The UNP/Hartland Partnership Center offers numerous programs that promote reciprocal sharing and learning. The programs include English as a second language (ESL) and citizenship classes, financial literacy and home-buyer education, an early childhood/school readiness program, legal education, health education and screenings, employment and life skills classes, youth programs, a Hartland resident instructor, and social work services. The UNP/Hartland Partnership Center embodies the philosophy that active collaboration between university and community groups and residents enhances learning, teaching, and research, benefiting the entire community. It is a model that supports and builds on the strengths of families and provides them with greater access to education.

The UNP/Hartland Partnership Center is also home to over 20 university students from a variety of disciplines. Under faculty supervision, students placed at the center fulfill practicum requirements and gain valuable professional knowledge and skills by interacting with community partners and residents. Seven master's-level social work students placed in internships at the UNP/Hartland Partnership Center link with area schools and social service agencies to meet the needs of residents while developing pathways for community capacity building and access to higher education for K–12 students. By dividing their practicum hours between the school sites and the Hartland Center, students develop an understanding of the school system and can follow the children both at school and in the community where they live. This provides a tremendous amount of support for the educators and school administrators, who are struggling to meet the needs of immigrant and refugee populations. Further, many of the parents do not speak English and are overwhelmed trying to negotiate the system and provide support for their children's education. As we saw in Daniel's case, when language and culture are barriers, all parties involved in the child's education suffer from the resulting misunderstandings and distrust of differences. Understandably, both educators and parents are overwhelmed and frustrated with their lack of power to influence change under these conditions. Social work students are uniquely positioned to integrate into both the school system and the home environment, providing necessary linking, support, and information that all parties greatly need. Students and educators alike are learning that as understanding develops, partnerships follow.

The philosophy of the UNP/Hartland Partnership Center is that all partners have knowledge to share. Guided by a resident committee, the center works with residents to understand cultural differences, particularly those associated with the role of family members, education, and parenting practices. This information is documented and shared with the school systems and other social service agencies. School social workers utilize this information to inform educators and administrators about appropriate cultural approaches and necessary system change. At the same time, this process validates the knowledge base of community residents and the powerful contributions that they bring to the school setting. The success of this model requires ongoing discussions with school administrators concerning the importance of working as partners and including the voices of residents. School social workers are active in bringing the partners together. Their skills in group dynamics, communication, and advocacy are a good fit for forming new coalitions that come together in reciprocal relationships to learn from each other and to enjoy outcomes that are meaningful for all.

Hi. I bet you thought that you were all through with me. Well, I am still here and hanging in there. I continue to have some hard times, and I still don't have many friends. But my mom got a better job, so she only has to work one job instead of two now. She is not nearly as tired and angry as she used to be. I really like my English teacher, Mrs. Allen, and she introduced me to Ms. Molina, the school social worker. She can speak both Spanish and English. She has taught me a few words and phrases in Spanish. It is really fun to know a second language. Ms. Molina came to my house one time and met my mom. I thought my mom would be really angry, but she seemed to like talking to her. Anyway, today I am staying after school to try out for a part in the school play. I am really scared, but Ms. Molina said she would be there too. Well, wish me luck. I am off to be a star!

CONCLUSION

There is a growing need for innovative school social work services. School districts cannot meet the needs of immigrant and special-needs populations without the expertise of trained school social workers who understand the concepts of diversity, social justice, and empowerment through utilizing existing strengths, and who know how to work with oppressed and disadvantaged populations. Immigrant families with special needs children do not understand school laws or how to utilize the system in order to meet their children's needs. As illustrated by Daniel's case, once parents understand the parameters of the special education laws and the school system, they become empowered and are able to work toward meeting their own child's needs.

Innovative programs such as the UNP/Hartland Partnership Center utilize school social workers and their knowledge of diversity as well as their interpersonal skills to provide links between schools and communities. School social workers are vital in helping school districts reach out to impoverished and culturally diverse communities in order to meet the educational needs of all children.

School social workers have the skills to link schools, families, and communities and build positive interactions. Educators and parents need to understand the unique role a social worker can play in building community support and linking families to the schools. Collaboration and interdisciplinary work are at the heart of school social work. School social workers are in a unique position to develop ongoing community support for schools and provide families with linkages to community and school resources.

Discussion Topics

1. Immigrant populations need to be connected to schools. How would you involve immigrant parents with the school?
2. School social workers need to develop cultural competence to link schools and communities. What is the most effective way to develop cultural competence?
3. How can school social workers provide outreach to immigrant families with special-needs children?
4. How could a school social worker aid a student like Daniel?

References

Aggett, P., & Goldberg, D. (2005). Pervasive alienation: On seeing the invisible, meeting the inaccessible and engaging "lost to contact" clients with major mental illness. *Journal of Interprofessional Care, 19*(2), 83–92.

Akos, P., & Levitt, D. H. (2002). Promoting healthy body image in middle school. *Professional School Counseling, 6*(2), 138–44.

Akutsu, P. D. (1997). Mental health care delivery to Asian Americans: Review of the literature. In E. Lee (Ed.), . *Working with Asian Americans: A guide for clinicians* (pp. 464–476). New York: Guilford Press.

Alexander, J. C., & Harman, R. L. (1988). In the field: One counselor's intervention in the aftermath of a middle school student's suicide: A case study. *Journal of Counseling and Development, 66,* 283–285.

Allen, D. G., & Tracy, E. M. (2004). Revitalizing the role of home visiting by school social workers. *Children and Schools, 26*(4), 197–208.

American Psychiatric Association. (2000). *Diagnostic and statistical manual of mental disorders* (4th ed., text rev.). Washington, DC: Author.

Anderson-Butcher, D., & Ashton, D. (2004). Innovative models of collaboration to serve children, youth, families and communities. *Children and Schools, 26*(1), 39–53.

Angaran, S., & Beckwith, K. (1999). Elementary school peer mediation. *Education Digest, 65*(1), 23–25.

Archibald, A., Graber, J., & Brooks-Gunn, J. (1999). Associations among parent-adolescent relationships, pubertal growth, and body image in young adolescent girls: A short-term longitudinal study. *Journal of Research in Adolescence, 9,* 395–415.

Aspy, D. N., & Roebuck, F. N. (1977). *Kids don't learn from people they don't like.* Amherst, MA: Human Resource Development Press.

Atkins-Burnett, S. (2004). Children with disabilities. In P. Allen-Meares (Ed.), *Social work services in schools* (4th ed., pp. 183–214). Boston: Allyn & Bacon.

Baker, M. L., Sigmon, J. N., & Nugent, M. E. (2001). *Truancy reduction: Keeping students in schools.* Washington, DC: Office of Juvenile Justice and Delinquency Prevention.

Banchy, N. (1977). Due process: Implications for social workers in the schools. *School Social Work Journal, 1,* 26–34.

Barkley, R. A. (n.d.). About ADHD: A fact sheet by Dr. Barkley. Retrieved February 11, 2007, from *www.russellbarkley.org/adhd-facts.htm*

Barton, M. L., & Robins, D. (2000). Regulatory disorders. In C. H. Zeanah, Jr. (Ed.), *Handbook of infant mental health* (2nd ed., pp. 311–325). New York. Guilford Press.

Benard, B. (1993). Fostering resiliency in kids. *Educational Leadership, 51*(3), 44–48.

Benson, P., Leffert, N., Scales, P., & Blyth, D. (1998). Beyond the "village" rhetoric: Creating healthy communities for children and youth. *Applied Developmental Science, 2*(1), 138–159.

Bentley, K. J., & Walsh, J. (2006). *The social worker and psychotropic medication: Toward effective collaboration with mental health clients, families and providers* (3rd ed.). Belmont, CA: Thomson-Brooks/Cole.

Bentovim, A. (1986). Bereaved children. *British Medical Journal, 292*(6534), 1482.

Bernstein, G. A., Layne, A. E., Egan, E. A., & Tennison, D. M. (2005). School-based interventions for anxious children. *Journal of the American Academy of Child and Adolescent Psychiatry, 44*(11), 1118–1112.

Besharov, D. J. (1996). Children of crack: A status report. *Public Welfare, 54*(1), 32–39.

Birtchnell, J. (1980). Women whose mothers died in childhood: An outcome study. *Psychological Medicine,* 10(4), 699–713.

Blades, J. (1985). *Mediate your divorce.* Englewood Cliffs, NJ: Prentice-Hall.

Blessing, S. (n.d.). *Bullying Prevention: Speak Up! Speak Out! Against Bullying.* Richardson, TX: Region 10 Education Service Center.

Blyth, D., Simmons, R., & Carlton-Ford, S. (1983). The adjustment of early adolescents to school transitions. *Journal of Early Adolescence, 3*(1–2), 105–120.

Booth, A., & Dunn, J. F. (Eds.). (1996). *Family–school links: How do they affect educational outcomes?* Mahwah, NJ: Erlbaum.

Boothe, D. (2000). How to support a multiethnic school community. *Principal Leadership, 1*(4), 81–82.

Boulter, L. (2004). Family–school connection and school violence prevention. *The Negro Educational Review, 55*(1), 27–40.

Bowen, N. K., & Bowen, G. L. (1998). The effects of home microsystem risk factors and school microsystem protective factors on student academic performance and affective investment in schooling. *Social Work in Education, 20*(4), 219–231.

Bowlby, J. (1963). Pathological mourning and childhood mourning. *Journal of the American Psychoanalytic Association, 11*(3), 500–541.

Bowlby, J. (1980). *Attachment and loss: Vol. 3. Loss: Sadness and depression.* New York: Basic Books.

Boyle, S. W., Hull, G. H., Mather, J. H., Smith, L. L., & Farley, O. W. (2006). *Direct practice in social work.* Boston: Allyn & Bacon.

Boys Town. (1989). *Working with aggressive youth.* Boys Town, NE: Boys Town Press.

Brent, D. A., Perper, J. A., Moritz, G., Allman, C., Schweers, J., Roth, C., et al. (1993). Psychiatric sequelae to the loss of an adolescent peer to suicide. *Journal of the American Academy of Child and Adolescent Psychiatry, 32*(3), 509–517.

Broadfoot, P. (2000). Comparative education for the 21st century: Retrospect and prospect. *Comparative Education, 36*(3), 357–371.

Brodkin, A. M. (2004, January/February). My Grandpa died–how to help children handle grief. *Scholastic Early Childhood Today, 18*(4), 18–19.

Bronstein, L. R. (2003). A model for interdisciplinary collaboration. *Social Work, 48*(3), 297–307.

Broussard, C. A. (2003). Facilitating home-school partnerships for multiethnic families: School social workers collaborating for success. *Children and Schools, 25*(4), 211–222.

Brown, F. H. (1989). The impact of death and serious illness on the family cycle. In B.

Carter & M. McGoldrick (Eds.), *The changing family life cycle: A framework for family therapy* (2nd ed., pp. 457–482). Boston: Allyn & Bacon.

Bumpass, L. L., & Raley, R. K. (1995). Redefining single-parent families: Cohabitation and changing family reality. *Demography, 32*(1), 97–109.

Califano, J. W. (1999). The least among us: Children of substance-abusing parents. *America, 180*(14), 10–12.

Caple, F. S., Salcido, R. M., & di Cecco, J. (1995). Engaging effectively with culturally diverse families and children. *Social Work in Education, 17*(3), 159–170.

Caudill, M. H. (1993). School social work services in rural Appalachian systems: Identifying and closing the gaps. *Social Work in Education, 15*(3), 179–186.

Chandler, K. A., Chapman, C. D., Rand, M. R., & Taylor, B. M. (1998). *Students' reports of school crime: 1989 and 1995* (NCES 98-241/NCJ-169607). Washington, DC: U.S. Departments of Education and Justice.

Chen, M., & Rybak, C. J. (2004). *Group leadership skills: Interpersonal process in group counseling and therapy.* Belmont, CA: Brooks/Cole.

Chen, W., Cato, B., & Rainford, N. (1998–1999). Using a logic model to plan and evaluate a community intervention program: A case study. *International Quarterly of Community Health Education, 18*(4), 449–458.

Chinman, M. J., Rosenheck, R., & Lam, J. A. (1999). The development of relationships between people who are homeless and have a mental disability and their case managers. *Psychiatric Rehabilitation Journal, 23*(1), 47–56.

Christ, G. H., Siegel, K., & Christ, A. E. (2002). Adolescent grief: "It never really hit me . . . until it actually happened." *Journal of the American Medical Association, 288*(10), 1269–1278.

Colvin, G. (1992). *Managing acting-out behavior: A staff development program to prevent and manage acting-out behavior.* Longmont, CO: Sopris West.

Combs, M. L., & Slaby, D. A. (1977). Social skills training with children. In B. B. Lahey & A. E. Kazdin (Eds.), *Advances in clinical child psychology* (pp. 161–201). New York: Plenum Press.

Congress, E. P. (1994). The use of culturagrams to assess and empower culturally diverse families. *Families in Society, 75*(9), 531–540.

Constable, R. (1992). The new school reform and the school social worker. *Social Work in Education, 14*(2), 106–113.

Constable, R., Kuzmickaite, D., Harrison, W. D., & Volkmann, L. (1999). The emergent role of the school social worker in Indiana. *School Social Work Journal, 24*(1), 1–14.

Constable, R., McDonald, S., & Flynn, J. P. (2002). *School social work: Practice, policy, and research perspectives* (5th ed.). Chicago: Lyceum Books.

Corey, M. S., & Corey, G. (2006). *Groups: Process and practice* (7th ed.). Pacific Grove, CA: Brooks/Cole.

Corley, M.D. (2005). Sexplanations II: Helping addicted parents talk with their children about health sexuality, sexual addiction, and sexual abuse. *Sexual Addiction and Compulsivity, 12,* 245–258.

Courtney, M. E., & Barth, R. P. (1996). Pathways of older adolescents out of foster care: Implications for independent living services. *Social Work, 41*(1), 75–83.

Courtney, M. E., Terao, S., & Bost, N. (2004). *Midwest evaluation of the adult functioning of former foster youth: Conditions of youth preparing to leave state care.* Chicago: Chapin Hall Center for Children and the University of Chicago.

Couvillon, M. (2000). *Preventing power struggles* (Richardson, TX: Region 10 Education Service Center.

Cowger, C. (1997). Assessing client strengths: Assessment for client empowerment In D. Saleebey (Ed.), *The strengths perspective in social work practice* (2nd ed., pp. 106–123). Boston: Allyn & Bacon.

Crick, N. R., & Nelson, D. A. (2002). Relational and physical victimization within friendships: Nobody told me there'd be friends like these. *Journal of Abnormal Child Psychology, 30,* 599–607.

Cunningham, M. (2006). Avoiding vicarious traumatization: Social support, spirituality, and self-care. In N. B. Webb (Ed.), *Mass trauma and violence: Helping families and children cope* (pp. 327–346). New York: Guilford Press.

Czarnopys, B. B. (2002, Summer). Exploring the razor's edge: Understanding adolescent self-harm. *Paradigm,* 12–13, 22.

Dale, O., Smith, R., Norlin, J. M., & Chess, W. A. (2006). *Human behavior and the social environment: Social systems theory* (5th ed.). Boston: Allyn & Bacon.

Daunic, A. P., Smith S. W., Robinson, T. R., Miller, M. D., & Landry, K. L. (2000). Implementing schoolwide conflict resolution and peer mediation programs: Experiences in three middle schools. *Intervention in School and Clinic, 36*(2), 94–100.

Davies, D. (2004). *Child development: A practitioner's guide* (2nd ed.). New York: Guilford Press.

Davis, N. J. (1999). *Youth crisis: Growing up in the high-risk society.* Westport, CT: Praeger.

DeFur, S. (2000). Designing individualized education program (IEP) transition plans (ERIC Digest #E598). Retrieved from *www.ericdigests.org/2001-4/iep.html*

DeMontflores, C., & Schultz, S. J. (1978). Coming out: Similarities and differences for lesbians and gay men. *Journal of Social Issues, 34*(3), 59–72.

den Heyer, M. (2002). Modeling learning programs. *Development in Practice, 12*(3/4), 525–530.

DeVol, P. E. (2004). Using the hidden rules of class to create sustainable communities. Available at *www.ahaprocess.com/files/DeVol_UsingtheHiddenRulesofClass.pdf*

Donahue, A. B. (2000). Riding the mental health pendulum. *Social Work, 45*(5), 427–439.

Dowd, T., & Tierney, J. (1995). *Teaching social skills to youth.* Boys Town, NE: Boys Town Press.

Dowd, T., & Tierney, J. (2005). *Teaching social skills to youth* (2nd ed.). Boys Town, NE: Boys Town Press.

Dowdell, E. B. (1995). Caregiver burden: Grandparents raising their high-risk grandchildren. *Journal of Psychosocial Nursing and Mental Health Services, 33*(3), 27–30.

Doweiko, H. D. (2002). *Concepts of chemical dependency* (5th ed.). Pacific Grove, CA: Brooks/Cole.

Dunn, E. J. (1992). Testimony before the Special Committee on Aging in U.S. Senate, *Grandparents as parents: Raising a second generation* (Serial no. 102-24, pp. 55–73). Washington DC: U.S. Government Printing Office.

Dupper, D. R. (2003). *School social work: Skills and interventions for effective practice.* Hoboken, NJ: Wiley.

Dyregrov, A., Bie Wikander, A. M., & Vigerust, S. (1999). Sudden death of a classmate and friend: Adolescents' perception of support from their school. *School Psychology International, 20*(2), 191–208.

Eastman, E., Archer, R. P., & Ball, J. D. (1990). Psychosocial and life stress characteristics of navy families: Family environment scale and life experiences scale findings. *Military Psychology, 2*(2), 113–127.

Eggert, L. (1994). *Anger management for youth: Stemming aggression and violence.* Bloomington, IN: National Education Service.

Elkind, D. (1967). Egocentrism in adolescence. *Child Development, 38*(4), 1025–1034.

Ender, G. (Ed.). (2002). *Military brats and other global nomads.* Westport, CT: Praeger.

Epstein, J. L., & Lee, S. (1995). National patterns of school and family connections in the middle grades. In B. A. Ryan, T. Adams, R. Gullotta, G. Weissberg, & R. Hampton (Eds.), *The family-school connection: Vol. 2. Theory, research, and practice* (pp. 108–154). Thousand Oaks, CA: Sage.

Evans, W. N. (1998). Assessment and diagnosis of the substance use disorders (SUDs). *Journal of Counseling & Development, 76*(3), 325–333.

Fang, L., & Chen, T. (2004). Community outreach and education to deal with cultural resistance to mental health services. In N. B. Webb (Ed.), *Mass trauma and violence: Helping families and children cope* (pp. 234–258). New York: Guilford Press.

Fast, J. (1999). Where were you fifth period?: Five strategies for high school group formation in the 1990s. *Social Work in Education, 21*(2), 99–105.

Father Flanagan's Boys' Home. (1998). *Administrative training.* Boys Town, NE: Boys Town Press.

Favazza, A. R. (1996). *Bodies under siege: Self-mutilation and body modification in culture and psychiatry* (2nd ed.). Baltimore: Johns Hopkins University Press.

Fay, J. (2006). "Teaseproof" your kids. *Love and Logic Journal, 15*(3), 31–32.

Fitzgibbon, M. L. (2004). Commentary on "Psychiatric aspects of child and adolescent obesity: A review of the past 10 years." *Journal of the American Academy of Child and Adolescent Psychiatry, 43*(2), 151–153.

Fong, R., & Wu, D. Y. (1998). Socialization issues for Chinese American children and families. In E. Freeman, C. Franklin, R. Fong, G. Shaffer, & E. Timberlake (Eds.), *Multisystem skills and interventions in school social work practice* (pp. 141–153). Washington, DC: NASW Press.

Fox, L., Vaughn, B. J., Wyatte, M., & Dunlap, G. (2002). We can't expect other people to understand: Family perspectives on problem behavior. *Exceptional Children, 68*(4), 437–450.

Freiberg, H. J., & Stein, T. A. (1999). Measuring, improving and sustaining healthy learning environments. In H. J. Freiberg (Ed.), *School climate: Measuring, improving and sustaining healthy learning environments* (pp. 11–29). London: Falmer Press.

Frey, A., & George-Nichols, N. (2003). Intervention practices for students with emotional and behavioral disorders: Using research to inform school social work practice. *Children & Schools, 25*(2), 97–104.

Friend, M. (2005). *Special education contemporary perspectives for school professionals.* Boston: Allyn and Bacon.

Furman, E. (1983). Children's patterns in mourning the death of a loved one. In H. Wass & C. A. Corr (Eds.), *Childhood and death* (pp. 185–203). Washington, DC: Hemisphere Press.

Furstenberg, F. F., Jr., Kennedy, S., McLoyd, V. C., Rumbaut, R. G., & Settersten, R. A., Jr. (2004). Growing up is harder to do. *Contexts, 3*(3), 33–41.

Garcia, C. (2004). Assessing foster care from the inside. Retrieved July 14, 2007, from *www.connectforkids.org/node/549*

Germain, C. B. (2002). An ecological perspective on social work in the schools. In R. Constable, S. McDonald, & J. P. Flynn (Eds.), *School social work practice, policy and research perspectives* (5th ed., pp. 25–35). Chicago: Lyceum Books.

Ginsberg, L. (1999). *Social work almanac* (2nd ed.). Washington, DC: NASW Press.

Gomez, C. R., & Baird, S. (2005). Identifying early indicators for autism in self-regulation difficulties. *Focus on Autism and Other Developmental Disabilities, 20*(2), 106–116.

Gosschalk, P. O. (2004). Behavioral treatment of acute onset school refusal in a 5-year-old girl with separation anxiety disorder. *Education and Treatment of Children, 27*(2), 150–160.

Gottman, J. (1997). *Raising an emotionally intelligent child: The heart of parenting.* New York: Fireside Books.

Green, B. L., Wilson, J. P., & Lindy, J. (1985). Conceptualizing posttraumatic stress disorder: A psychosocial framework. In C. R. Figley (Ed.), *Trauma and its wake: Vol. 1.*

The study and treatment of posttraumatic stress disorder (Vol. 1, pp. 53–69). New York: Brunner/Mazel.

Green, F. G., & Nelson, M. (1999). *Bullying stops when respect begins.* Bryant, AR: Keys to Safer Schools.

Grekin, E. R., Brennan, P. A., & Hammen, C. (2005). Parental alcohol use disorders and child delinquency: The mediating effects of executive functioning and chronic family stress. *Journal of Studies on Alcohol, 66*(1), 14–22.

Gresham, F. M. (2002). Responsiveness to intervention: An alternative approach to the identification of learning disabilities. In R. Bradley, L. Danielson, & D. Hallahan (Eds.), *Identification of learning disabilities: Research to practice* (pp. 467-519). Mahwah, NJ: Erlbaum.

Gresham, F. M., & Elliott, S. N. (1990). *Social skills rating system.* Circle Pines, MN: American Guidance Service.

Groves, B. M. (2002). *Children who see too much: Lessons from the Child Witness to Violence Project.* Boston: Beacon Press.

Haddad, J. (1980). Recent legislation invites innovative approaches to social work in schools. In B. Deshler (Ed.), *School Social Work and the Law: Papers from the National Invitational Workshop on School Social Work and the Law, May 29–31* (pp. 35–51). Washington, DC: NASW Press.

Hao, L., & Bonstead-Bruns, M. (1998). Parent–child differences in educational expectations and academic achievement of immigrant and native students. *Sociology of Education, 71*(3), 175–198.

Hardaway, T. (2004). Treatment of psychological trauma in children of military families. In N. B. Webb (Ed.), *Mass trauma and violence: Helping families and children cope* (pp. 259–282). New York: Guilford Press.

Hardy, L. (2003). Helping students de-stress. *Education Digest, 68*(9), 5–9.

Harker, L. (2005, March). School day dreams. *Community Care, 1566,* 16.

Hartman, A. (1978). Diagrammatic assessment of family relationships. *Social Casework, 59,* 465–476.

Hawkins, R., Tan, S.-Y., & Turk, A. (1999). Secular versus Christian inpatient cognitive-behavioral therapy programs: Impact on depression and spiritual well-being. *Journal of Psychology and Theology, 27*(4), 309–318.

Hazler, R., Miller, D., Carney, J., & Green, S. (2001). Adult recognition of school bullying situations. *Educational Research, 43*(2), 133–146.

Heath, S., & McLaughlin, M. (1994). The best of both worlds: Connecting schools and community youth organizations for all-day . . . *Educational Administration Quarterly, 30*(3), 278–301.

Henze, R. C. (2000). A required curriculum for respect. *Principal Leadership, 1*(4), 14–19.

Hepworth, D. H., Rooney, H. R., & Larsen, J. A. (2002). *Direct social work practice* (6th ed.). Pacific Grove, CA: Brooks/Cole.

Heward, W. L. (2003). *Exceptional children: An introduction to special education.* Upper Saddle River, NJ: Pearson.

Hicks-Coolick, A., Burnside-Eaton, P., & Peters, A. (2003). Homeless children: Needs and services. *Child and Youth Care Forum, 32*(4), 197–210.

Huang, L. N. (1989). Southeast Asian refugee children and adolescents. In J. T. Gibbs & L. N. Huang (Eds.), *Children of color: Psychological interventions with minority youth* (pp. 278–321). San Francisco: Jossey-Bass.

Human, J., & Wasem, C. (1991). Rural mental health in America. *American Psychologist, 46*(3), 232–239.

Hurt, R. D., Offord, K. P., Croghan, I. T., Gomez-Dahl, L., Kottke, T. E., Morse, R. M., et al. (1996). Mortality following inpatient addictions treatment. *Journal of the American Medical Association, 275,* 1097–1103.

Hussong, A. M., Zucker, R. A., Wong, M. M., Fitzgerald, H. E., Puttler, L. I. (2005). Social competence in children of alcoholic parents over time. *Developmental Psychology, 41*(5), 747–759.

Jaffe, P., Wolfe, D. A., & Wilson, S. (1990). *Children of battered women.* Newbury Park, CA: Sage.

James, B. (1989). *Treating traumatized children: New insights and creative interventions.* New York: Free Press.

Jay, G. (2000). The community in the classroom. *Academe, 86*(4), 33–37.

Johnson, E. I., & Waldfogel, J. (2002). *Children of incarcerated parents: Cumulative risk and children's living arrangements* (JCPR Working Paper 306). Chicago, IL: Joint Center for Poverty Research, Northwestern University and University of Chicago. Available at *www.jcpr.org/wp/wpprofile.cfm?id=364*

Jones, D. R. (2005, February 24–March 2). The urban agenda: 47% of high school students drop out. *The New York Amsterdam News, 96*(9), 5.

Jonson-Reid, M., Kontak, D., Citerman, B., Essma, A., & Fezzi, N. (2004). School social work case characteristics, services, and dispositions: Year one results. *Children and Schools, 26*(1), 5–22.

Jouriles, E. N., & Norwood, W. D. (1995). Physical aggression toward boys and girls in families characterized by the battering of women. *Journal of Family Psychology, 9*(1), 69–78.

Kao, G. (1995). Asian Americans as model minorities? A look at their academic performance. *American Journal of Education, 103*(2), 121–159.

Kao, G., & Tienda, M. (1995). Optimism and achievement: The educational performance of immigrant youth. *Social Science Quarterly, 76*(1), 1–19.

Kazdin, A. E. (1993). Adolescent mental health: Prevention and treatment programs. *American Psychologist, 48*(2), 127–141.

Kelen, J. A., & Kelen, L. G. (2002). *Faces and voices of refugee youth.* Salt Lake City, UT: Center for Documentary Arts.

Kelley, M. L., & Fals-Stewart, W. (2004). Psychiatric disorders of children living with drug-abusing, alcohol-abusing, and non-substance-abusing fathers. *Journal of the American Academy of Child and Adolescent Psychiatry, 43*(5), 621–628.

Kelley, S. J., Yorker, B. C., & Whitley, D. (1997). To grandmother's house we go . . . and stay: Children raised in intergenerational families. *Journal of Gerontological Nursing, 23*(9), 12–20.

Klein, E. C. (2004). Forging partnerships to meet family needs. *School Administrator, 61*(7), 40–41.

Krovetz, M. L. (1999). Fostering resiliency. *Thrust for Educational Leadership, 28*(5), 4.

Kudlac, K. (1991). Including God in the conversation: The influence of religious beliefs on the problem-organized system. *Family Therapy, 18*(3), 277–285.

Lambert, M. (Ed.). (2004). *Bergin and Garfield's handbook of psychotherapy and behavior change* (5th ed.). New York: Wiley.

Lange, C. M., & Lehr, C. A. (1999). At-risk students attending second chance programs: Measuring performance in desired outcome domains. *Journal of Education for Students Placed at Risk, 4*(2), 173–192.

Lareau, A. (2003). *Unequal childhoods: Class, race, and family life.* Berkeley, CA: University of California Press.

Leslie, L. K., Landsverk, J., Ezzet-Lofstrom, R., Tschann, J. M., Slymen, D. J., & Garland, A. F. (2000). Children in foster care: Factors influencing outpatient mental health service use. *Child Abuse and Neglect, 24*(4), 465–476

Lewellen, A., Openshaw, L., & Harr, C. (2005, February). *Use of a logic model in social work practice.* Paper presented at the 52nd annual program meeting of the Council on Social Work Education, Chicago, IL.

Lewis, D. C. (1997). The role of the generalist in the care of the substance-abusing client. *Medical Clinics of North America, 81*(4), 831–843.

Lynn, C. J., McKay, M. M., & Atkins, M. S. (2003). School social work: Meeting the mental health needs of students through collaboration with teachers. *Children and Schools, 25*(4), 197–209.

Lyon, J. B., & Vandenberg, B. R. (1989). Father death, family relationships, and subsequent psychological functioning in women. *Journal of Clinical Child Psychology, 18*(4), 327–335.

Lyons, J. S., Libman-Mintzer, L. N., Kisiel, C. L., & Shallcross, H. (1998). Understanding the mental health needs of children and adolescents in residential treatment. *Professional Psychology: Research and Practice, 29*(6), 582–587.

Lysyuk, G. L. (1998). The development of productive goal setting with 2- to 4-year-old children. *International Journal of Behavioral Development, 22*(4), 799–812.

MacArthur Research Network on Transitions to Adulthood. (2005). Adolescence and the transition to adulthood: Rethinking public policy for a new century (conference summary). Retrieved May 5, 2007, from *www.transad.pop.upenn.edu/downloads/Conference_Summary_Final.pdf*

Macy, R. D., Behar, L., Paulson, R., Delman, J., Schmid, L., & Smith, S. F. (2004). Community-based, acute posttraumatic stress management: A description and evaluation of a psychosocial-intervention continuum. *Harvard Review of Psychiatry, 12*(4), 217–228.

Malekoff, A. (2002). *Group work with adolescents: Principles and practice* (2nd ed.). New York: Guilford Press.

Maluccio, A. N. (2006). The nature and scope of the problem. In N. B. Webb (Ed.), *Working with traumatized youth in child welfare* (pp. 3–12). New York: Guilford Press.

Manlove, J. (2004, August). School engagement reduces the risk of teen childbearing. Retrieved July 11, 2007, from *http://www.wested.org/ppfy/engagement.htm*

Mapp, I., & Koch, D. (2004). Creation of a group mural to promote healing following a mass trauma. In N. B. Webb (Ed.), *Mass trauma and violence: Helping families and children cope* (pp. 100–119). New York: Guilford Press.

Marcus, R. R. (1991). The attachments of children in foster care. *Genetic, Social, and General Psychology Monographs, 117*(4), 367–394.

Maurrasse, D. J. (2001). *Beyond the campus: How colleges and universities form partnerships with their communities.* New York: Routledge.

Maynard-Moody, C. (1994). Wraparound services for at-risk youths in rural schools. *Social Work in Education, 16*(3), 187–191.

Mazza, J. J., & Reynolds, W. M. (1999). Exposure to violence in young inner-city adolescents: Relationships with suicidal ideation, depression, and PTSD symptomatology. *Journal of Abnormal Child Psychology, 27*(3), 203–213.

McCarthy, R., IV. (2001). Universities and community-based economic development: The case of Crescent City Farmers Market. *Blueprint for Social Justice, 54*(10), 3–11.

McLanahan, S. (1997). Parent absence or poverty?: Which matters more? In G. J. Duncan & J. Brooks-Gunn (Eds.), *The consequences of growing up poor* (pp. 35–48). New York: Sage.

McNeil, J. N., Silliman, B., & Swihart, J. J. (1991). Helping adolescents cope with the death of a peer: A high school case study. *Journal of Adolescent Research, 6*(1), 132–145.

Menacker, J., Weldon, W., & Hurwitz, E. (1990). Community influences on school crime and violence. *Urban Education, 25*(1), 68–80.

Meyer, L. (2000). Home–school collaboration. In A. Ford, R. Schnoor, L. Meyer, L. Davern, J. Black, & P. Dempsey, *The Syracuse community-referenced curriculum guide for students with moderate and severe disabilities* (pp. 17–28). Baltimore: Brookes.

Milgram, N., & Toubiana, Y. H. (1996). Children's selective coping after a bus disaster: Confronting behavior and perceived support. *Journal of Traumatic Stress, 9*(4), 687–702.

Miller, J. (2001). Gender strategies for girls in gangs. In B. R. E. Wright & R. B. McNeal, Jr. (Eds.), *Boundaries: Readings in deviance, crime and criminal justice* (pp. 455–479). Boston: Pearson.

Miller, J., & McMahon, W. M. (2005, August–November). An overview of autism. In *The life of a mental health professional: Professional education series brochure.* Utah Chapter, National Association of Social Workers.

Miller, N. S. (1999). Mortality risks in alcoholism and effects of abstinence and addiction treatment. *Psychiatric Clinics of North America, 22*(2), 371–383.

Minkler, M., & Roe, K. (1993). *Grandparents as caregivers: Raising children of the crack cocaine epidemic.* Newbury Park, CA: Sage.

Mitchell, J., & Everly, G. (1998). *Critical incident stress management: The basic course workbook* (2nd ed.). Ellicot City, MD: International Critical Incident Stress Foundation.

Montano-Harmon, M. R. (1991). Discourse features of written Mexican Spanish: Current research in contrastive rhetoric and its implications. *Hispania, 74*(2), 417–425.

Morin, S. M., & Welsh, L. A. (1996). Adolescents' perceptions and experiences of death and grieving. *Adolescence, 31*(123), 585–595.

Moroz, K. J., & Segal, E. A. (1990). Homeless children: Intervention strategies for school social workers, *Social Work in Education, 12*(2), 134–143.

Morrissey, K. M., & Werner-Wilson, R. J. (2005). The relationship between out-of-school activities and positive youth development: An investigation of the influences of communities and family. *Adolescence, 40*(157), 67–85.

Murray, J. B. (1989). Psychologists and children of alcoholic parents. *Psychological Reports, 64*, 859–879.

Nader, K. (1996). Children's exposure to violence and disaster. In C. A. Corr & D. M. Corr (Eds.), *Handbook of childhood death and bereavement* (pp. 201–222). New York: Springer.

Nader, K. (2001). Treating children after violence in schools and communities. In N. B. Webb (Ed.), *Helping bereaved children: A handbook for practitioners* (2nd ed., pp. 214–246). New York: Guilford Press.

Naierman, N. (1997). Reaching out to grieving students. *Educational Leadership, 55*, 62–65.

National Association of Social Workers (NASW). (2002). *NASW standards for school social work services.* Washington, DC: Author.

National Education Association. (2000). *Hands-on assistance–tools for educators: NEA crisis communications guide and toolkit.* Retrieved January 29, 2007, from *www.nea.org/crisis/images/crisisguide-b4.pdf*

National Healthy Marriage Resource Center. (n.d.). Frequently asked questions about: Divorce. Retrieved June 11, 2007, from *www.healthymarriageinfo.org/aboutmarriage/?d={C990A322-56FD-417D-9395-35120F6C0E81}*

New study uncovers hidden dropout crisis. (2003, June 5). *Black Issues in Higher Education, 20*(8), 10.

Nims, D. R., & Hamm, M. (2006, July). *Phoenix preferred care: Mental health services to children and adolescents in rural Kentucky.* Paper presented at the 31st National Institute on Social Work and Human Services in Rural Areas, Bowling Green, KY.

Oaklander, V. (1988). *Windows to our children: A Gestalt therapy approach to children and adolescents.* Highland, NY: Gestalt Journal Press.

O'Donnell, J. (2000). School social work. In S. Torres & R. Patton (Eds.), *Teaching school social work: Model course outlines and resources* (pp. 21–27). Alexandria, VA: Council on Social Work Education.

O'Hare, T. (2005). *Evidence-based practices for social workers: An interdisciplinary approach.* Chicago: Lyceum Books.

Oliver, R., Hoover, J. H., & Hazler, R. (1994). The perceived roles of bullying in small-town midwestern schools. *Journal of Counseling and Development, 72*(4), 416–419.

Olmedo, R., & Hoffman, R. S. (2000). Withdrawal syndromes. *Emergency Medical Clinics of North America, 18*, 273–288.

O'Neill, R., Horner, R., Albin, R., Sprague, J., Storey, A., & Newton, J. (1997). *Functional assessment and program development for problem behavior: a practical handbook* (2nd ed.). Pacific Grove, CA: Brooks/Cole.

Openshaw, L., & Halvorson, H. (2005). Concurrence of intimate partner violence and child abuse. In L. H. Ginsberg (Ed.), *Social work in rural communities* (4th ed., pp. 207–234). Alexandria, VA: CSWE Press.

Osher, D. M., Sandler, S., & Nelson, C. L. (2001). The best approach to safety is to fix schools and support children and staff. In R. J. Skiba & G. G. Noam (Eds.), *Zero tolerance: Can suspension and expulsion keep schools safe? New directions for youth development* (pp. 127–154). San Francisco: Jossey-Bass.

Osofsky, J. D. (Ed.). (1997). *Children in a violent society*. New York: Guilford Press.

Out in the World. (2005, April). In *Up Front* [online newsletter]. Retrieved May 7, 2007, from *www.asbj.com/2005/04/0405asbjupfront.pdf*

Owens, R. E., Jr. (2003). "Becoming" lesbian, gay and bi-sexual. In B. R. E. Wright & R. B. McNeal, Jr. (Eds.), *Boundaries: Readings in deviance, crime and criminal justice* (pp. 519–555). Boston: Pearson.

Parham, G. T. (1979). Individualized education programs: The New Jersey model. *Social Work in Education, 1*(4), 35–43.

Patterson, G. R. (1982). *A social learning approach: Vol. 3. Coercive family process.* Eugene, OR: Castalia.

Payne, R. K. (1995). *Poverty: A framework for understanding and working with students and adults from poverty*. Baytown, TX: RFT.

Pearson, D. P., Vyas, S., Sensale, L. M., & Kim, Y. (2001). Making our way through the assessment and accountability maze. *Clearing House, 74*(4), 175–184.

Pecora, P. J., Williams, J., Kessler, R. C., Downs, A. C., O'Brien, K., Hiripi, E., et al. (2003). *Assessing the effects of foster care: Early results from the Casey National Alumni Study*. Seattle, WA: Casey Family Programs.

Peebles-Wilkins, W. (2004, July). The full-service community school model. *Children and Schools, 26*(3), 131–133.

Peleg-Oren, N. (2002). Drugs—not here!: Model of group intervention as preventative therapeutic tool for children of drug addicts. *Journal of Drug Education, 32*(3), 245–259.

Perlman, H. (1957). *Social casework: A problem-solving process.* Chicago: University of Chicago Press.

Perry, B., & Rosenfelt, J. L. (1999). The child's loss: Death, grief, and mourning: How caregivers can help children exposed to traumatic death. *Parent and Caregiver Education Series of the Child Trauma Academy, 3*(1), 1–12. Retrieved August 21, 2007 from *www.childtrauma.org/ctamaterials/Loss2.asp*

Perry, B. (2002a). *The brain: Effects of child trauma* [Video]. (Available from Magna Systems, Inc., 330 Telser Road, Lake Zurich, IL 60047)

Perry, B. (2002b). Helping traumatized children: A brief overview for caregivers. In *Parent and Caregiver Education Series of the Child Trauma Academy, 1*(3).

Perry, B. (2002c). *Identifying and responding to trauma in children up to five years of age* [Video]. (Available from Magna Systems, Inc., 330 Telser Road, Lake Zurich, IL 60047)

Perry, B. (2002d). *Trauma and healing* [Video]. (Available from Magna Systems, Inc., 330 Telser Road, Lake Zurich, IL 60047)

Perry, B. (2002e). *What is childhood trauma?* [Video]. (Available from Magna Systems, Inc., 330 Telser Road, Lake Zurich, IL 60047)

Pesce, R. C., & Wilczynski, J. D. (2005). Gang prevention. *Principal Leadership, 6*(3), 11–15.

Pilowsky, D. (1995). Psychopathology among children placed in family foster care. *Psychiatric Services, 46*(9), 906–910.

Plyler v. Doe, 457 U.S. 202 (1982).

Podell, C. (1989). Adolescent mourning: The sudden death of a peer. *Clinical Social Work Journal, 17*(1), 64–78.

Poland, S. (2002). Practical suggestions for crisis debriefing in schools. *National Association of School Psychologists Communiqué, 30*(7), 5.

Poland, S., & McCormick, J. (1999). *Coping with crisis: Lessons learned, a resource for schools, parents, and communities.* Longmont, CO: Sopris West.

Pollard, D. S. (1989). Reducing the impact of racism on students. *Educational Leadership, 47*(2), 73–75.

Pong, S., Hoa, L., & Gardner, E. (2005). The roles of parenting styles and social capital in the school performance of immigrant Asian and Hispanic adolescents. *Social Science Quarterly, 86*(4), 928–950.

Pope, H., Hudson, J., Yurgelun-Todd, D., & Hudson, M. (1984). Prevalence of anorexia nervosa and bulimia in three student populations. *International Journal of Eating Disorders, 3*(3), 45–51.

Poulin, J. (Ed.). (2000). *Collaborative social work: Strengths-based generalist practice.* Itasca, IL: F.E. Peacock.

Prater, C. D., Miller, K. E., & Zylstra, R. G. (1999). Outpatient detoxification of the addicted or alcoholic patient. *American Family Physician, 60*(4), 1175–1183.

Pratt, D., Ford, J., Burke, R., & Hensley, M. (2005). *Tools for teaching social skills in schools.* Boys Town, NE: Boys Town Press.

Pritchard, C. (1996). New patterns of suicide by age and gender in the United Kingdom and the Western World 1974–1992: An indicator of social change? *Social Psychiatry and Psychiatric Epidemiology, 31*(3–4), 227–234.

Radin, N. (1992). A peer feedback approach to assessing school social workers as team members. *Social Work in Education, 14*(1), 57–62.

Rehabilitation Act of 1973, 29 U.S.C. § 794, Section 504.

Roberts, M. C., Jacobs, A. K., Puddy, R. W., Nyre, J. E., & Vernberg, E. M. (2004). Treating children with serious emotional disturbances in schools and community: Mental health program. *Professional Psychology: Research and Practice, 34*(5), 519–526.

Roberts, R. E., Alegria, M., Roberts, C. R., & Chen, I. G. (2005). Mental health problems of adolescents as reported by their caregivers: A comparison of European, African, and Latino Americans. *Journal of Behavioral Health Services & Research, 32*(1), 1–13.

Roe, K., & Minkler, M. (1999). Grandparents raising grandchildren: Challenges and responses. *Generations, 22*(4), 25–32.

Rogers, A., & Henkin, N. (2000). School-based interventions for children in kinship care. In B. Hayslip, Jr., & R. Goldberg-Glen (Eds.), *Grandparents raising grandchildren: Theoretical, empirical, and clinical perspectives* (pp. 221–238). New York: Springer.

Ruble, L. A. (2001). Analysis of social interactions as goal-directed behaviors in children with autism. *Journal of Autism and Developmental Disorders, 31*(5), 471–482.

Rutter, M. (1987). Psychosocial resilience and protective mechanisms. *American Journal of Orthopsychiatry, 57*(3), 316–331.

Rutter, M., & Quinton, D. (1977). Psychiatric disorder: Ecological factors and concepts of causation. In H. McGurk (Ed.), *Ecological factors in human development* (pp. 173–187). New York: North-Holland.

Ryan, B. A. (2003). Do you suspect child abuse? *RN, 66*(9), 73–77.

Sabatino, C. A. (2001). Family-centered sections of the IFSP and school social work participation. *Children and Schools, 23*(4), 241–250.

Saleebey, D. (Ed.). (1997). *The strengths perspective in social work practice* (2nd ed.). New York: Longman.

Sameroff, A. J., Bartko, W. T., Baldwin, A., Baldwin, C., & Seifer, R. (1998). Family and social influences on the development of child competence. In M. Lewis & C. Feiring (Eds.), *Families, risk, and competence* (pp. 161–185). Mahwah, NJ: Erlbaum.

Schlozman, S. C. (2003). The pain of losing a parent. *Educational Leadership, 60*(8), 91–92.

Schwab-Stone, M., Chen, C., Greenberger, E., Silver, D., Lichtman, J., & Voyce, C. (1999). No safe haven II: The effects of violence exposure on urban youth. *Journal of the American Academy of Child and Adolescent Psychiatry, 38*(4), 359–367.

Shaw, P. A. (2004). Death and divorce: Teaching dilemmas or teachable moments? *Kappa Delta Pi Record, 40*(4), 165–169.

Sieger, K., Rojas-Vilches, A., McKinney, C., & Renk, K. (2004). The effects and treatment of community violence in children and adolescents: What should be done? *Trauma, Violence, Abuse, 5*(3), 243–259.

Simmons, R. G. (1987). Social transition and adolescent development. In C. E. Irwin (Ed.), *Adolescent social behavior and health* (pp. 33–61). San Francisco: Jossey-Bass.

Simmons, R. G., & Blyth, D. A. (1987). *Moving into adolescence: The impact of pubertal change and school context.* New York: Aldine.

Simpson, R. L., & Zionts, P. (2000). *Autism: Information and resources for professionals and parents* (2nd ed.). Austin, TX: PRO-ED.

Slater, P. E., (1958). Contrasting correlates of group size. *Sociometry, 21*(2), 129–139.

Smith, S. W., Daunic, A. P., Miller, M. D., & Robinson, T. R. (2002). Conflict resolution and peer mediation in middle schools: Extending the process and outcome knowledge base. *Journal of Social Psychology, 142*(5), 567–586.

Snelgrove, T. (1998). *Managing acute traumatic stress: Trauma intervener's resource manual* (11th ed.). West Vancouver, BC, Canada: Easton-Snelgrove.

Snyder, H., & Sickmund, M. (1999). *Juvenile offenders and victims: 1999 national report.* Washington, DC: National Center for Juvenile Justice and Delinquency Prevention.

Soricelli, B. A., & Utech, C. L. (1985). Mourning the death of a child: The family and group process. *Social Work, 30*(5), 429–434.

Spence, S. H. (2003). Social skills training with children and young people: Theory, evidence and practice. *Child and Adolescent Mental Health, 8*(2), 84–96.

Stallard, P., Velleman, R., Salter, E., Howse, I., Yule, W., & Taylor, G. (2006). A randomized controlled trial to determine the effectiveness of an early psychological intervention with children involved in road traffic accidents. *Journal of Child Psychology and Psychiatry, 47*(2), 127–134.

Stevahn, L., Johnson, D. W., Johnson, R. T., & Schultz, R. (2002). Effects of conflict resolution training integrated into a high school social studies curriculum. *Journal of Social Psychology, 142*(3), 305–331.

Stevenson, R. G. (2002). Sudden death in schools. In N. B. Webb (Ed.), *Helping bereaved children: A handbook for practitioners* (2nd ed., pp. 194–213). New York: Guilford Press.

Stewart, R. (2001). Adolescent self-care: Reviewing the risks. *Families in Society, 82*(2), 119–126.

Stout, E. J., & Frame, M. W. (2004). Body image disorder in adolescent males: Strategies for school counselors. *Professional School Counseling, 8*(2), 176–181.

Stovall, K. C., & Dozier, M. (2000). The development of attachment in new relationships: Single subject analyses for ten foster infants. *Development and Psychopathology, 12*(2), 133–156.

Substance Abuse and Mental Health Services Administration. (2003). Help for Children of addicted parents. *SAMHSA News, XI*(2). Retrieved May 7, 2007 from *www.samhsa.gov/samhsa_news/VolumeXI_2/article5.htm*

Sue, D., Sue, D., & Sue, S. (1994). *Understanding abnormal behavior* (4th ed.). Boston: Houghton Mifflin.

Tallmer, M., Formanek, R., & Tallmer, J. (1974). Factors influencing children's concept of death. *Journal of Clinical Child Psychology, 3*(2), 17–19.

Teasley, M. L. (2004). Absenteeism and truancy: Risk, protection, and best practice implications for school social workers. *Children and Schools, 26*(2), 117–128.

Theberge, S. K., & Karan, O. C. (2004). Six factors inhibiting the use of peer mediation in a junior high school. *Professional School Counseling, 7*(4), 283–290.

Teens court danger with risky behavior. (2005, December 9). Retrieved January 27, 2007, from *abcnews.go.com/2020/story?id=1387316*

Torchia, M. M. (2003). Reaching out to children of addicted parents. *Brown University Child and Adolescent Behavior Letter, 19*(8), 3–6.

Toseland, R. W., & Rivas, F. R. (2001). *An introduction to group work practice* (4th ed.). Boston: Allyn & Bacon.

Tracy, E. M. (1994). Maternal substance abuse: Protecting the child, preserving the family. *Social Work, 39*(5), 534–540.

Travers, P. (2002). *The counselor's helpdesk.* Pacific Grove, CA: Brooks/Cole.

Tuma, J. M. (1989). Mental health services for children: The state of the art. *American Psychologist, 44*(2), 188–199.

Turner, F. J. (1974). Psychological therapy. In F. J. Turner (Ed.), *Social work treatment: Interlocking theoretical approaches.* New York: Free Press.

Tyre, P. (2006, January 30). The trouble with boys. *Newsweek, 44,* 52.

Ufema, J. (2005). Insights on death and dying. *Nursing, 35*(5), 24–25.

Underwood, D. J., & Kopels, S. (2004). Complaints filed against schools by parents of children with AD/HD: Implications for school social work practice. *Children & Schools, 26*(4), 221–233.

United Nations High Commissioner for Refugees. (1994). *Refugee children: Guidelines on protection and care.* UNHCR Refworld©. Available at *http://www.unhcr.org/cgi-bin/texis/vtx/refworld/rwmain?docid=3ae6b3470*

United Way of America. (1996). *Measuring program outcomes: A practical approach.* Alexandria, VA: Author.

University Neighborhood Partners. (n.d.). What we do. Retrieved January 22, 2006, from *www.partners.utah.edu/about/whatWeDo.htm*

U.S. Census Bureau. (2006). *U.S. Military Personnel on Active Duty in Selected Foreign Countries: 1995 to 2005.* Available at *www.census.gov/compendia/statab/tables/07s0501.xls*

U.S. Department of Education. (1994). *Strong families, strong schools: Building community partnerships for learning.* Washington, DC: Author.

U.S. Department of Education. (2002). *Twenty-third annual report to Congress on the implementation of the Individuals with Disabilities Act.* Washington, DC: U.S. Government Printing Office.

U.S. Department of Health and Human Services. (1999). National Clearinghouse on Child Abuse and Neglect Information: Reports from the states to the national child abuse and neglect data system. Retrieved July 8, 2001, from *www.acf.dhhs.gov/programs/cb/publications/cm99/index.htm*

U.S. Department of Health and Human Services. (2006). Quick stats: General information on alcohol use and health. Retrieved January 30, 2007, from *www.cdc.gov/alcohol/quickstats/general_info.htm*

U.S. Department of Health and Human Services. (2001). *Youth violence: A report of the surgeon general.* Rockville, MD: U.S. Department of Health and Human Services.

van der Kolk, B. A., Perry, J. C., & Herman, J. L. (1991). Childhood origins of self-destructive behavior. *American Journal of Psychiatry, 148*(12), 1665–1671.

Vygotsky, L. S., & Kozulin, A. (Eds.). (1986). *Thought and language* (rev. ed.). Cambridge, MA: The MIT Press.

Walker, H. (1995) *The acting-out child: Coping with classroom disruption* (2nd ed.). Longmont, CO: Sopris West.

Walker, H. M., Colvin, G., & Ramsey, E. (1995). *Antisocial behavior in schools: Strategies and best practices*. Pacific Grove, CA: Brooks/Cole.

Walrath, C. M., Petras, H., Mandell, D. S., Stephens, R. L., Holden, E. W., & Leaf, P. J. (2004). Gender differences in patterns of risk factors among children receiving mental health services: Latent class analyses. *Journal of Behavioral Health Services and Research, 31*(3), 297–311.

Walrath, C., Ybarra, M., Holden, E. W., Liao, Q., Santiago, R., & Leaf, P. (2003). Children with reported histories of sexual abuse: Utilizing multiple perspectives to understand clinical and psychosocial profiles. *Child Abuse & Neglect, 27*(5), 509–524.

Walsh-Bowers, R. T. (1992). A creative drama prevention program for easing early adolescents' adjustment to school transitions. *Journal of Primary Prevention, 13,* 131–147.

Walsh-Bowers, R., & Basso, R. (1999). Improving early adolescents' peer relations through classroom creative drama: An integrated approach. *Social Work in Education, 21*(1), 23–33.

Webb, N. B. (Ed.). (1998). *Play therapy with children in crisis: Individual, group, and family treatment* (2nd ed.). New York: Guilford Press.

Webb, N. B. (Ed.). (2002). *Helping bereaved children: A handbook for practitioners* (2nd ed.). New York: Guilford Press.

Webb, N. B. (2003). *Social work practice with children* (2nd ed.). New York: Guilford Press.

Webb, N. B. (Ed.). (2004). *Mass trauma and violence: Helping families and children cope*. New York: Guilford Press.

Wehlage, G. G., Lipman, P., & Smith, G. (1989). *Empowering communities for school reform: The Annie E. Casey Foundation's New Futures Initiative*. Madison, WI: Center for Education Research.

Weiner, M. (1980). ABCs of the realities of legalities: The impact of law on school social workers. In B. Deshler (Ed.), School social work and the law: Papers from the National Invitational Workshop on School Social Work and the Law, May 29–31, 1980 (pp. 42–45). Washington, DC: NASW Pew.

Wentzel, K. R. (2003). Motivating students to behave in socially competent ways. *Theory Into Practice, 42*(4), 319–326.

Wertsch, M. E. (1991). *Military brats: Legacies of childhood inside the fortress.* Bayside, NY: Aletheia.

Whitaker, J. K. (1980). Models of group development: Implications for social group work practice. In A. S. Alissi (Ed.), *Perspectives on social group work practice* (pp. 133–153). New York: Free Press.

Whitehouse, B. (2000). Alcohol and the family. *Parenting, 14*(5), 154–162.

Williams, M. B. (2004). How schools respond to traumatic events: Debriefing interventions and beyond. In N. B. Webb (Ed.), *Mass trauma and violence: Helping families and children cope* (pp. 120–141). New York: Guilford Press.

Willwerth, J. (1991). Should we take away their kids? *Time, 137*(19), 62.

Wilson, J. J., Nunes, E. V., Greenwald, S., & Weissman, M. S. (2004). Verbal deficits and disruptive behavior disorders among children of opiate-dependent parents. *American Journal on Addictions, 13*(2), 202–222.

Wilson, P. M., & Wilson, J. R. (1992). Environmental influences on adolescent educational aspirations: A logistic transform model. *Youth & Society, 24*(1), 52–70.

Winnicott, D. W. (1971a). *Playing and Reality*. New York: Basic Books.

Winnicott, D. W. (1971b). *Therapeutic consultations in child therapy*. New York: Basic Books.

Woititz, J. G. (1983). *Adult children of alcoholics*. Pompano Beach, FL: Health Communications.

Wong, M. (2000, April). Critical incident stress debriefing. *School Safety Update,* 5–6.

Wooten, H. R., Jr. (1994). Cutting losses for student-athletes in transition: An integrative transition model. *Journal of Employment Counseling, 31*(1), 2–9.

Worden, J. W. (2002). *Grief counseling and grief therapy: A handbook for the mental health practitioner* (3rd ed.). New York: Springer.

Wu, S. (2001). Parenting in Chinese American Families. In N. B. Webb (Ed.), *Culturally diverse parent–child and family relationships: A guide for social workers and other practitioners* (pp. 235–260). New York: Columbia University Press.

Youakim v. Miller, 440 U.S. 125 (1979).

Zachry, E. (2005). Getting my education: Teen mothers' experiences in school before and after motherhood. *Teachers College Record, 107*(12), 2566–2598.

Zastrow, C. (2001). *Social work with groups: Using the class as a group leadership laboratory* (5th ed.). Pacific Grove, CA: Brooks/Cole.

Zastrow, C. (2006). *Social work with groups: A comprehensive workbook* (6th ed.). Belmont, CA: Brooks/Cole.

Zinner, E. S. (1987). In the field: Responding to suicide in schools: A case study in loss intervention and group survivorship. *Journal of Counseling and Development, 65*(9), 499–501.

Index

Page numbers followed by an *f* or *n* indicate figures or notes.